Keeping Your Child Safe: A Manual for Parents

Paul Gilligan

Gill & Macmillan

Gill & Macmillan Ltd
Hume Avenue
Park West
Dublin 12
with associated companies throughout the world
www.gillmacmillan.ie

© Paul Gilligan 2008
978 07171 42873

Index compiled by Helen Litton
Print origination in Ireland by O'K Graphic Design, Dublin
Printed and bound by ColourBooks Ltd, Dublin

The paper used in this book is made from the wood pulp of
managed forests. For every tree felled, at least one tree is planted,
thereby renewing natural resources.

A CIP catalogue record for this book is available from the British
Library.

1 3 5 4 2

Keeping Your Child Safe

*To all victims of child abuse, whose courage and resilience is
an inspiration to us all*

Contents

Foreword

As Director of Services of the ISPCC I am conscious of the worry and anxiety many parents feel about their children's safety. This concern is very natural and reflects a desire for our children to have the wonderful childhoods they deserve. On the other side of the coin, however, the responsibility attached to being a parent can often loom large, in particular for first-time parents.

In my daily work I am constantly reminded of the real dangers that exist for children and, for those children unfortunate enough to experience abuse, the impact such experiences can have on them. I am also aware of how often it is a simple lack of knowledge about keeping children safe that can hinder parents' ability to protect their children.

Keeping Your Child Safe provides reassuring advice, support and information for all parents, presented in a down to earth fashion.

This book is aimed directly at parents and will be a resource that they can use throughout their children's development. Paul Gilligan recognises the important role that parents have in meeting their children's needs, in protecting their children from all forms of abuse and being the main source of support for their children. *Keeping Your Child Safe* not only explains the child protection risks facing children and their families today but also gives clear advice on how parents can safeguard their children from abuse. This book empowers parents; it builds parents' confidence in meeting their children's needs and in keeping their children safe.

Not only is this book a useful guide for dealing with children's needs, development and the everyday occurrences in family life; it also assists parents in developing plans, choosing child care, and adopting discipline techniques that develop the parent–child relationship while increasing children's self-esteem.

The chapter on mental health issues illustrates the author's skill in dealing with difficult topics. He guides the parent through a number of steps: understanding mental health difficulties; dealing with the issues; practical tips; prevention; developing emotional intelligence in children and examining belief systems. This progression is written exceptionally well and demystifies the area of mental health. The author again empowers the reader to recognise their own expertise, their ability to meet their children's needs and to acknowledge that parents need support, too.

The book offers information, advice and support to all parents in a way that is not lectured or forced, but supportive in nature, outlining all the options available. The use of case studies throughout the book highlights the main topics exceptionally well and I am certain that any parent who takes the time to read this book will find that it was time very well spent.

I would like to congratulate the author for providing parents with such important information and advice on the area of child protection, which will no doubt assist parents in all their parenting challenges. I am sure that it will also help to secure a child-centred approach to meeting children's needs in society and keeping children safe.

Caroline O' Sullivan
Director of Services
Irish Society for the Prevention
of Cruelty to Children

Foreword

Most practitioners in childcare have had to find considerable extra space on the bookshelf in the last number of years to accommodate the growing number of books that have been written on every aspect of child protection. In the last decade, the knowledge that has grown in all fields of child abuse should give us comfort in relation to the safety of children in Ireland today. However, *Keeping Your Child Safe* exposes a key area that up until now has been virtually neglected in Ireland regarding the protection of children. With the publication of this book, Paul Gilligan has addressed the need for parents in Ireland to be informed and empowered, enabling them to become active participants in the protection of their children. This book illustrates how parents can become involved in their child's safety in all settings and situations and in particular when their children are not directly in their care.

Parents and guardians must be central to all child protection systems. Children typically become visible to professionals in the childcare system only after a suspicion of abuse has been detected. Child abuse in most cases is preventable, and this book illustrates clear and practical ways in which parents can help protect their child from abuse and harm.

The dramatic rise in the number of abused children reported to the statutory authorities over the past twenty years has heightened parents' concern about the problem of child abuse in Ireland. Media proliferation in modern society has also added to the increased awareness of the incidence of child abuse, and has taken us into the lives of families that are experiencing trauma caused by child abuse at a very personal level. Due to the greater level of awareness regarding child abuse and the deficit in good child protection and prevention information available to parents, there is an increasing risk that children will become 'overprotected'. When decisions made regarding the protection of children are based on fear and lack of information they can be poor decisions that can adversely affect the child's growth and development. For this reason it is essential that a book such as *Keeping Your Child Safe* is available to parents to provide good, balanced information on the subject of child abuse, which will support them in making informed and rational decisions regarding their child's safe passage through childhood.

The chapter headings in this book speak for themselves and are organised in a way that makes the information accessible and easy to follow. Due to the straightforward layout and clear chapter topics the reader may decide to use this book as a reference book and consult each chapter if and when it becomes a particular issue that is current in their child's life. If using the book in this way helps keep one child safe, then the book has achieved its goal. However, the book will offer much more to parents who read it in full, the complete value of the book lying not only in its safety advice but in its underlying values and principles of parenting and childhood.

Keeping Your Child Safe is written in a simple and clear way that sets out the risk areas for children and practical ways in which parents can establish safeguards that will allow their children to be safe, active participants in their families and communities. This book also helps parents to examine their beliefs, styles and motivations vis-à-vis the parenting of their children. By exploring these issues parents will not only help keep their child safe but may also deepen the communication and positive relationship that they have with their child.

Áine Lynch
CEO
National Parents Council Primary

Author's Preface

Keeping our children safe from those who wish to hurt them is a serious concern for all parents. Over the last five years, awareness and knowledge of child abuse and child protection has grown significantly, both within Ireland and across Europe. Each day, parents are confronted by media reports of children being sexually abused, abducted or murdered.

Although awareness has been heightened, there are few supports for parents to help them understand more about the dynamics of abuse. There are many books and resources written on the issue of child protection aimed at professionals, but there are few aimed at parents.

Most parents are confused about child abuse. What exactly is child abuse? Why does a person, particularly a parent, abuse a child? Are particular types of children more vulnerable to abuse than others? In particular, parents want to know how they can best ensure their child does not experience abuse. Are there things they can do to keep their child safe? Are they doing enough to protect their child?

Having been involved in the area of child protection for fourteen years, I have worked with many children and adults who have experienced child abuse. These people's experiences not only help us to learn more about how to prevent child abuse, but help us understand the resilience and courage of those who experience such abuse. Their decisions to disclose the abuse they experienced makes it easier for others to come forward and also allows us to discuss a topic that has previously remained 'taboo' and hidden.

Keeping Your Child Safe is a book about child protection, for parents. It aims to provide a practical resource for parents, pointing out the potential risks existing for children, but also pointing out practical ways parents can protect their children against abuse.

The book has ten chapters, each addressing a different aspect of children's lives, such as:
- identifying the types of risk associated with each of these aspects;
- the reasons these risks can arise;

- how parents can best assess organisations, individuals or situations;
- how parents should deal with difficulties if they arise; and
- the best ways for parents to prevent any difficulties from arising.

The first chapter of the book, 'Understanding Parenting', outlines some of the important information parents need to know about parenting, while Chapter 2 provides an understanding of child abuse, why it occurs, how it can impact on children and how it can best be dealt with.

Chapter 3 discusses child abuse within the family and outlines the best ways to keep a family healthy, Chapter 4 deals with safety in alternative care settings, such as crèches and nurseries, and Chapter 5 deals with safety in school.

Chapter 6 outlines ways of keeping children safe when they are with babysitters, when they are on holidays and when they are participating in leisure and sports activities. Chapter 7 deals with the safe use of technology, such as mobile phones and the Internet, and Chapter 8 deals with the issue of self-abuse by children, including drug and alcohol misuse, premature sexualisation and self-harm.

Chapter 9 deals with mental health risks for children, including anxiety and depression. Chapter 10 discusses parent welfare.

This book aims to provide child-protection information to parents that will:

- empower them and help them make better choices for their children;
- help them feel more confident that their children are safe; and
- help them feel more confident about their parenting in general.

This book will have most relevance to parents of children under the age of thirteen, but will also be a useful resource to parents with older children.

Acknowledgments

My thanks and gratitude are due to a number of people.

In the first instance, to all of the children and families I have worked with over the years, from whom I have learned so much. To all the staff and volunteers with whom I have worked, particularly those in the ISPCC, who work tirelessly to help and support children.

In particular, I am indebted to Graham Smith of WordSmith for his ongoing guidance and support throughout the process of writing this book; to Kieran Woods, Principal Psychologist; Fiona Lane, Research Consultant; Clodagh Hopkins, Solicitor; and Marie Corbett, Children's Rights Alliance, for all their help.

The team at Gill & Macmillan has assisted me greatly, particularly Fergal Tobin, Sarah Liddy, Emma Farrell and Liz Raleigh.

This book would never have been possible without the invaluable support of my wife Lorraine, and my daughters Katie and Aisling.

Chapter 1
Understanding Parenting

To understand how best to keep children safe and, in particular, how best to keep our own child safe, we must first acquire an understanding of parenting and what it means to be a parent.

While there are many different ways to define parenting, it is probably best defined as the rearing of a child, or children, through care, love and guidance. Parenting comprises all the tasks involved in raising a child to become an independent adult. Parenting begins even before the child is born or adopted and may last until the death of the parent or child. Parenting is a core part of the relationships within a family.

In the Ireland of the new millennium, the exact nature of what it means to be a parent is becoming more difficult to define. How we define parenting is influenced not only by our own views of what it is to be a parent, but by a number of other factors, such as our parenting partner's views, family factors, societal factors, cultural factors and parenting traditions (i.e. accepted parenting views and practices passed to us from previous generations). As a result of all of these factors, our understanding of parenting can sometimes become confused.

Is parenting primarily about spending quality time with our children? Is it primarily about discipline? Is it primarily about keeping our children safe? Is it primarily about providing financially for our children? Where do our responsibilities as parents end and the crèche's, childminder's, school's, sports club's begin? Are there essential things we need to know and practise for us to be good parents? Are there sure ways we can protect our children and ensure they thrive?

In many ways, parents in modern Ireland feel less certain and less confident of their parenting abilities and skills than parents of previous generations. Within social circles, communities and the media there seems to be much more discussion about children and parenting than ever before. If we are not hearing about horrific cases of child abuse or children's alcohol and drug usage spiralling out of control, we are hearing about more children becoming involved in sexual behaviour and anti-social behaviour at younger and younger ages.

It seems that it is getting harder and harder to spend time actually parenting. The number of pressures and commitments each of us has in our lives often makes it next to impossible to do all of the good parenting things we know we ought to be doing. However, there are some core parenting principles that, if we can remember and implement them, will not only help us parent our children well and keep them safe, but will also enable us to keep a healthy perspective on parenting.

LOVING CHILDREN COMES NATURALLY
It is part of every person's natural make-up to want to love, nurture and protect children. While emotional, environmental, social and personal obstacles can often contrive to prevent us from fully achieving this aspiration, we all have a natural desire and ability to do what is best for our children. For this reason, one of the most important things a parent can do is to allow the love of their child to guide their parenting. There are four things we can try to help us to do this:

1. Value our child for who he/she is
Many of us feel that our job as parents is to mould our child so that he/she grows up to be what we consider a successful adult. From the moment our children are born, we are inclined to fill them with information, advice and guidance, sometimes trying to influence every aspect of their lives. What we sometimes forget is that all children have their own built-in wisdom, abilities, curiosity and sense of what is important to them.

Our job as parents is to help our children grow to understand their true selves, to discover who they are and to fulfil themselves in their own unique way. We do this best by creating a loving, safe environment in which we give our child the space to grow while allowing us to discover and learn about our child.

Parenting children is a process of discovery. When we acknowledge and value our children as the very special people they are, their full intelligence, abilities and potential become available to them. This kind of child will not become aggressive, distracted and filled with insecurities and fears. When a child's basic nature is not interfered with, the child will function best. In other words, we must try to take our lead from our child and not impose our expectations, ideas or fears upon them.

2. Avoid conformity and comparisons

Conformity and comparisons have become a common practice in parenting. Many parents spend a great deal of time comparing their child's development, abilities and achievements with other children's progress, forgetting that there are many ways, and many different timetables, for developing. Comparing our child's development with that of other children tells us absolutely nothing about who our child is or how he/she will do in his/her life. Continuous comparisons and pressure on our child to conform to how other children are developing will impact negatively on our child's self-esteem. We need all kinds of different children to make a healthy society; being different doesn't mean being better or worse.

3. Allow our child to express who he/she is

Due to our desire to conform to society's expectations and norms, we sometimes try to repress our child. Driven by a need to conform to those norms, we control and censure what we allow our child to do, to say and sometimes even to think, worrying that certain actions, statements or thoughts will be perceived as bad or strange.

As a result, a child can sometimes begin to believe that certain parts of his/her character or personality are bad and unacceptable. This in turn causes them to hide these parts of themselves, sometimes leading to emotional difficulties. We need to help our child to find a way to communicate and express whatever he/she is thinking and feeling. We need to allow children to express themselves through their behaviour

– as long as this behaviour does not hurt or cause unnecessary distress to others.

We need to give our children the choice to express themselves via whatever medium they are most comfortable with, no matter what others expect or think. This can be through words, song, art, playing, dancing, planting flowers, sport, etc. We need to make sure we find a way to let our children know that we truly hear what it is they need to say and that we accept who they are. Then, their self-worth will grow.

4. Look for and see the best in all our child does

The sad reality for many children is that praise and acknowledgment are given rarely. Driven by pressure, stress and high expectations, parents sometimes parent within a context of criticism and complaint. If we are one of these parents, we need to become aware of this behaviour and then turn it around.

Instead of finding fault, criticising, punishing and negating a child in the thousands of ways many people can do, we need to try to look specifically for and see the best in our child and all that he/she does. We also need to acknowledge this goodness to the child. For example, we should try to ensure that every day we let our child know that we are pleased with or proud of them for something specific.

Even when he/she makes mistakes, we must work to help our child realise that though he/she may have messed up, the totality of who they are is wonderful. Throughout their lives, our children will be subjected to enough criticism and negativity from others: they do not need it from us.

When our parenting is guided by love, we raise healthy, expressive, creative children who are easily in touch with who they truly are. These children are naturally curious about life, experiencing each day as an adventure, going to sleep at night feeling happy. These are children to whom sharing comes naturally, who can laugh when things are funny and cry when things are sad, who are not terrified of the consequences of their behaviour or focused unnecessarily on the reactions of adults. These children go on to become strong and stable, able to weather all kinds of conflicting demands and pressures.

Some parents, for many reasons, forget or experience difficulties getting in touch with the natural love they have for their child. They sometimes start to think that they cannot, or never have, loved this child. It is important to remember that love for our child is natural, it is always within us. It may be that life circumstances or other difficulties are blocking us from seeing it, but it is there and if we give it a chance and allow it to guide our parenting, it will ultimately benefit our child and us.

GOOD PARENTING IS GOOD FUN

One of the myths of modern-day living is the perception that if it is to be done right, parenting must be stressful and intense. Parenting, in itself, is neither demanding nor stressful – it is the myriad other demands on a parent's time and energies that cause the difficulties. Parents should be able to enjoy their children; those who do not are missing out on something very special.

Key to ensuring we enjoy parenting is understanding what makes parenting special for us, and to focus on these things. Simple things we can do include:

- **Saying I love you:** Telling our child we love him/her as often as possible makes a big difference, no matter what age he/she is. Even on difficult days, or after a disagreement when we might not feel particularly loving, it is very important to express this love. A simple 'I love you' goes a long way towards developing and then strengthening a strong parent–child relationship. Creating a special name for our child that is positive and special, or a codeword that we can use between each other, provides a simple way to reinforce and express our love. It can even be used when our child wants to tell us that he/she is uncomfortable or does not want to do something (such as a sleepover that is not going well) without causing undue embarrassment to the child.
- **Making bedtime special:** For younger children, reading a favourite bedtime book or telling stories often makes bedtime special. Older children need something special, too. Once children start reading, getting them to read a page, chapter or short book to us can be special. Even with teenagers, we need to remember that they still enjoy the ritual of being told goodnight in a special way by a parent – even if they don't act like it!
- **Letting our child help us**: Parents sometimes miss out on opportunities to build closer relationships with their children by not allowing them to help with various tasks and household jobs.

Washing the car, choosing which shoes look better with our dress, doing the dishes or tidying the house are all things that can be done together. Including our child in such activities lets him/her know that we like spending time with him/her and that we value his/her opinion.

- **Playing with our child:** Playing with our child is very important. Playing anything – dolls, balls, make believe, board games, singing songs, whatever is fun and interesting – will help us to communicate with our child. Younger children will usually have fun playing anything, as long as it involves us! It doesn't matter what we play once we are enjoying each other! We need to let our child see our silly, fun side. Even with older children, we can play more structured games, like cards, chess and computer games. What must be remembered is that we are never too old to play, and neither is our child.

- **Eating meals together:** Eating together sets the stage for conversation and sharing. Turning off the TV and spending time over a meal helps us to build communication time with our child. When schedules permit, we should really try and eat, talk and enjoy each other's company. Meals can become a quality time that sustains the family throughout life.

- **Having special times together:** Having special times with our child individually is important. Some parents have special nights with their children. Whether it is going for a walk, a special trip to a playground or a night at the cinema, it is important to spend special time with each of our children individually. Although it is more of a challenge the more children there are in a family, it is achievable if we think creatively.

- **Giving our child space and choice:** We may not like our child's clothes or the way he/she keeps their bedroom, but it is important for us to respect our child's choices. Children reach out for independence at a young age, and parents can help to foster that individualism and those decision-making skills by being supportive – and even looking the other way on occasion.

- **Making our child a priority in our life:** Our child needs to know that we believe he/she is a priority in our life. Children can observe excessive stress and notice when they feel we are not paying them attention. Sometimes, part of being a parent is not worrying about the small things, but enjoying our children. Our child will grow up fast, so every day is special. We need to take advantage of our precious time together while we have it.

- **Teaching beliefs:** Teaching our child about beliefs is important. Just as a child needs to develop physically and emotionally, he/she also needs to develop spiritually. Preaching our beliefs in a dogmatic way will not help. Helping our child understand and learn about what we believe in and allowing our child the space to explore and develop his/her own beliefs is important. Allowing time for our child to ask questions and answering them honestly is also important.

Essential to enjoying ourselves is being fair to ourselves. We need to recognise and accept our own limitations and to be wary of becoming a 'parenting perfectionist'. Enjoying parenting is about remembering that it is meant to be enjoyed. Simply being with our child will be enjoyable for us and for our child.

LISTENING TO OUR CHILD IS CRUCIAL

One of the best parenting tools and most effective ways of keeping children safe is to listen to them, to find out how they are feeling and hear what they want to say. While this is quite a simple principle, it is surprising how many parents ignore it. At times, listening to our child can be difficult. It can be hard to hear exactly what they are saying because they express themselves differently from adults. Sometimes, we dismiss what they are saying as silly and just assume they do not fully understand. Sometimes we do not have the time to listen to them, and sometimes they say things we do not want to hear.

We may, at times, be unable to do what our child wants or may disagree with their view, but we must be prepared to really hear them. Time and time again, we hear of examples of parents discovering their child is being mistreated or abused and realising that their child has been trying to tell them about this for a long time.

Listening to our children means paying attention to what they say and encouraging them to share their thoughts and feelings with us. It also means paying attention to their actions and behaviour because, as we know from understanding how a child develops, children can't always put their feelings into words. Children who are listened to are usually balanced and self-confident individuals.

How we listen will change as our child grows older. We can communicate with our baby long before he/she starts to talk by smiling, stroking, cuddling and talking to him/her and making eye contact. From the very first day after he/she is born, our baby will be listening to us and in a few weeks will be communicating with us by smiles and those first cooing sounds. Even dealing with crying is about listening because crying is a very important part of a baby's language. Crying is meant to be a sound parents find difficult to ignore; it is Nature's way of ensuring that our baby's needs will be met.

Communicating with babies involves simple things, such as:

- rocking our baby in a pram or cradle;
- walking up and down with him/her;
- singing or talking gently to him/her;
- carrying our baby close to us;
- cuddling our baby.

Children learn to talk by listening to adults speaking directly to them. By the time our child is three or four years old and has mastered quite a lot of language, he/she will want to practise it as much as possible and will use it to learn about the rest of his/her world. This may mean endless talking and lots of questions. We need to try to listen to this talk and answer as many of the questions as we can. If we encourage our child to talk to us when he/she is young, he/she will learn that we want to listen. They will know that we care about them and will be much more likely to talk to us as they get older.

We also need to give our child plenty of encouragement. When our child is learning to talk, he/she will probably use funny words of their own and get words mixed up. Trying things out and making mistakes are important parts of learning. In the early stages, we should not correct our child too much, and give him/her lots of praise for getting things right. We should try to:

- **Answer all our child's questions:** Children can sometimes wear parents out with endless questions. We might find it easier to cope with this if we remember it is helping our child to learn. Our child will probably be happy with very simple answers to questions, but we should always try to answer their questions nonetheless.

- **Spending time reading with our child:** Just being with our child inevitably helps us to listen. Reading, walking or spending time relaxing together gives us time to communicate. Reading is particularly useful because it improves our child's listening and language skills and gives us a starting point to talk about our child's thoughts and feelings.
- **Setting aside some special listening time:** If we're busy, it can be hard to make time to listen to our child. We might find it easier to set aside a special part of the day, such as just before our child goes to bed. We need to be flexible about this, though. Small children sometimes just can't wait to talk about something that is important to them.

UNDERSTANDING OUR CHILD'S ABILITIES IS IMPORTANT

For parents, one of the most important things to understand about a child is how their thinking, emotions and social ability might be evolving as they get older. Our child is an ever-changing person, with rapidly developing physical, emotional and social abilities and needs. To have a chance of understanding or being in tune with our child's needs, we must invest time and effort in our child. To this end, spending time with our child is the best way to ensure that we stay attuned to their ever-changing individual personality.

Psychologists believe that children pass through several stages, or take specific steps, on their road to becoming adults. For most children, there are four or five such stages of growth where they learn certain things: infancy (birth to age two), early childhood (ages three to eight years), later childhood (ages nine to twelve years) and adolescence (ages thirteen to eighteen). Persons eighteen and over are considered adults by our society.

While as parents we cannot be expected to know all about the way a child is likely to develop during these various ages, it is important for us to have some knowledge about this. If we have too high an expectation about what our child can do at certain ages, we may be inclined to give him/her too much independence and not enough support. Likewise, if our expectations are too low, we may be inclined to smother or disempower our child. It is extremely important for us to remember that an individual child will develop at his/her own individual pace.

Thinking and language: There is a great deal of psychological research and theory dedicated to how a child's thinking and language might develop. A detailed description of these theories is beyond the scope of this book, but what is important for parents to know is that until a child reaches the age of eighteen, their thinking and language abilities cannot be expected to be as developed as those of adults. We need to continually remind ourselves of this, particularly when it comes to communicating with and setting expectations for our child.

It is easy for a parent to understand and accept that a baby has very limited language and is only beginning to develop thinking ability. Most parents understand that communication with a baby occurs mainly through the baby's senses. In other words, a baby needs to see, hear, touch, smell or taste something to realise it exists. For babies, language is often just sound and has no meaning. In these terms, therefore, a baby does not have the ability to be bold and does not have the thinking ability to be deliberately troublesome. The baby is completely dependent on his/her parents to meet his/her needs.

As children grow up, their thinking and language ability changes, but it is still important for parents to remember that there are many things they cannot expect their children to understand or communicate in an adult way. For example, up to the age of seven, rules of a game are not developed for a child, so children's games will usually have to be supervised by adults to ensure they can progress. The ability to think abstractly only really begins to develop between the ages of eleven and fifteen.

Keeping firmly in mind our child's language and thinking limitations helps us to remember that they are still children and that they need to be treated like children until they have had the opportunity to develop fully.

Emotion and personality: Equally important as thinking and language is our child's emotional and personality development. Again, there are a number of different theories about how emotion and personality develop and psychologists do not necessarily agree on which theories are the most accurate. What is important for parents to remember, however, is that a child's ability to understand and deal with emotions is not the same as an adult's and that it takes time to develop fully. Similarly, it is important to remember that our child will have his/her own unique personality, which we have to work to understand.

It is important that parents realise the key role they have to play in the development of their child's emotional capabilities. For a child to be an emotionally healthy adult, he/she needs to develop a strong sense of trust and self-value as a young child. He/she also needs to develope a sense of self-confidence to allow him/her to take chances, a sense of an ability to achieve and a sense of positive self-image. What is important to remember is that our child is developing these emotional capabilities throughout his/her childhood.

Our child will have his/her own unique temperament, which needs to be allowed to develop. Temperament is best explained as a set of congenital traits that organise our child's approach to the world, and also influence how our child learns about the world around him/her. These traits are never 'good' or 'bad.' Rather, how they are received determines whether the child perceives them as being a bad thing or good thing. If parents can understand the temperament of their child, they can avoid blaming themselves for issues that are normal for their child's temperament. For example, some children are noisier than others, some are more affectionate than others, some have more regular sleep patterns than others.

When we understand how our child responds to certain situations, we can learn to anticipate issues that might present difficulties for them. We can prepare our child for the situation or, in other cases, we may avoid a potentially difficult situation altogether. Parents can tailor their parenting strategies to the particular temperamental characteristics of their child. We feel more effective as parents when we come to understand and appreciate our child's unique personality more fully.

Whether parents take the time to inform themselves about a child's capabilities or not, most parents, if they watch their child carefully, will know what their child is capable of. What is key to parenting is that we understand that children need to be supported and protected until their thinking, their emotions and their social abilities are developed enough to enable them to be able to protect themselves.

HONEST COMMUNICATION HELPS PARENTING

Honest communication is a very important part of parenting. One of the most effective ways of promoting our child's healthy development is to communicate with him/her and all those who care for him/her in an honest and open way. It is crucial that from the earliest age our child understands how he/she can expect to be communicated with by adults, and how adults expect him/her to communicate with them. It is important that those looking after our child fully understand our expectations and that we understand theirs.

In particular, it is important that the communication between ourselves and our parenting partner is honest and constructive. In parenting, it is very important to create an environment in which there is honest and constructive communication with all those who have a stake in our child's life and, in particular, with our child.

What is honest communication? It involves doing everything possible to understand and to be understood. It involves being committed to being truthful in a constructive manner. The practical principles of honest communication are:

- listening with genuine attentiveness, with understanding, with respect;
- asking questions and reflecting back what we understand we are hearing;
- seeing through negative statements in order to understand what another person is actually saying;
- taking responsibility for our own feelings and wishes, e.g. using the 'I' word;
- where possible, telling the truth.

Honest communication involves expressing love and acknowledging successes, achievements and happiness when we feel these things. It also involves being prepared to deal with the difficult issues and being prepared to confront problems.

It is important to be mindful of two important principles in relation to being honest. The first is to be sure to speak truth constructively. At times, honesty will be painful, so we need to say what needs to be said with tenderness and compassion. It is necessary to always take into consideration the feelings of the one with whom we are speaking, i.e. to empathise with them and their situation. We must ask ourselves: how would we feel if we were the ones being told what we are about to tell this person?

The second principle of honesty is to determine if what we are going to say absolutely needs to be said. Some things can go without being said, and it will not hurt anyone. This is not the same as the idea that 'What they don't know can't hurt them.' There are definitely issues that hurt others whether they know about them or not. But there are some things that just do not need to be said at all. In essence, our communication must be honest, and we must work to understand others and to be understood by others. It is imperative that we actively work at understanding what others in our family are trying to communicate to us, and that we do everything we can to be understood.

There are obstacles to honest communication that will arise from time to time, and these need to be anticipated and avoided. The main obstacles to good communication are disrespecting one other, failing to listen, being too dogmatic, saying one thing but indicating another through our actions, jumping to conclusions and making assumptions. One of the single biggest obstacles to communication is secrecy, which is effectively a person refusing to communicate in any constructive way. It usually indicates that a person does not want a constructive communication, or is concerned that if his/her true feelings became clear, the relationship would break down.

Honest communication does not come easy: it involves working continually to strengthen and enhance our relationships and to remove any blocks that threaten that process.

CHILDREN ARE ACTIVE PARTICIPANTS IN THE PARENTING PROCESS

Children, no matter what their age, are people with rights, views, beliefs and feelings that need to be integrated into the parenting process. Ignoring our child's individualism and personality results in a passive parenting relationship that becomes focused on either protection or control. When we learn to accept and treat our child as a young citizen with his/her own unique personality, we not only make a success of our parenting, but we also enhance the rich experience that is the parenting process.

Involving children as active participants in the parenting process should be guided by the following principles:

Getting the balance right: To involve children fully in the family and in decision-making, we need to remember that there is an inevitable imbalance in power and status between parents and children. This power imbalance is necessary for some components of parenting, such as protection, but can make it difficult to involve children as equals. We counter this imbalance by ensuring that our children are able to freely express their views and opinions, that they are listened to seriously and that their views and opinions are taken into account.

Our children need to be clear about the purpose of their participation and involvement, i.e. what it involves and what impact it may have. We need to give our children the relevant information, in an age-appropriate manner, regarding their involvement. We need to allow them to consider their involvement and give their personal informed consent to it.

For example, one of the most common ways that we involve children in a family is by asking them to choose with whom they wish to spend time. This decision can be particularly difficult if parenting partners are not living together, but it can also cause difficulties even when parenting partners are living together and have a good relationship. Children being asked who they would like to accompany – for instance, their mother shopping or their father to wash the car – can be distressed by such a choice if it is not presented in a balanced way.

If parents invest emotion in the decision, whether directly or implied – 'you never come with me, do you not enjoy being with me?', etc. – then the child is being asked to participate in a decision that is inappropriate. If a child is given a straightforward choice based on what he or she wishes to do and understands fully what each event entails, that is real and meaningful participation.

Ensuring that children's participation is relevant and voluntary: Our children should be given the choice whether to participate or not. It is also important that children are allowed to participate on their own terms and for lengths of time chosen by them. Children should be involved in ways, at levels and at a pace appropriate to their capabilities and interests.

For example, when parents who find it difficult to spend time with children do find the time to do so, they often expect their child to participate fully. But a child may not want to discuss the family holiday, no matter how excited we are about it. He/she may have no interest in who wins an election, no matter how important it is to us. What is relevant to us may not be relevant to our child. Therefore, we need to involve them in the components of family life in which they have an interest.

Creating a child-friendly environment: We need to create an environment that is child-friendly. The involvement of young children in family decisions is usually best done through play; older children, on the other hand, may find informal chats the most stimulating. Finding the best way to engage children is a key step, otherwise we can easily turn them off being involved at all. If a parent sits a small child down at a table for a serious conversation, it is usually interpreted by the child as either boring or that he/she is in trouble. Finding the right way to involve our child takes time and energy, but is worth it in the end.

Keeping participation safe: We need to ensure that a child's participation in the family is safe for the child. One mistake parents can make is that they misinterpret participation to mean treating a child like an adult. They involve a child in all family discussions, allow him/her to choose to do things they should not be doing and give the child impossible choices. In order to be effective, a child's participation in the family should be at an age-appropriate level and should not present any emotional or physical risk to the child. Allowing a young child to try their hand at the lawnmower or discussing with a child the family's financial difficulties in detail is not safe.

Working for democracy and non-discrimination: We need to try to ensure that the participation of our children in our family is democratic and non-discriminatory. This is easiest if we have one child, but becomes more difficult when we have more than one. Where possible, it is necessary to ensure all of our children participate equally in the family and in the parenting process. Children's personalities differ, therefore we may need to use different means to engage different children.

Children themselves will quickly make it clear if they are not being involved. We need to be sensitive to our children feeling left out or feeling less involved in decision-making than their brother or sister. For example, we sometimes make the mistake of telling one child something and thinking we have told all of our children. Sometimes, one child becomes the unofficial spokesperson for all of the others. We need to strive to create a family democracy based on age-appropriate participation.

Providing follow-up and feedback: To ensure that children's participation is real, we need to ensure there is follow-up and evaluation. This means committing, from the beginning of the process, to provide feedback to our children and, where appropriate, to evaluate together the quality and impact of their participation. This sounds very formal, but in effect it means simply following through on the discussions or decisions we make in partnership with our children.

For example, if we discuss where we would like to go on holidays, we need to feed back to each child the final decisions we make, why we are making these decisions and why, if it is the case, their first choice has not been picked. Involving children does not necessarily mean that we will agree with everything they want or say. The point is that our children feel their views have been heard and given fair consideration.

TEACHING POSITIVE DISCIPLINE CREATES EMOTIONALLY HEALTHY CHILDREN

Children need to learn about right and wrong. They need to learn how to control their own behaviour, to respect others, to give and take and to make the right choices when confronted with moral and ethical decisions. Teaching our child self-discipline is a core function of parenting.

Discipline is a crucial component of good parenting because a well-disciplined child will be a more secure and a more confident child. Teaching discipline takes time, patience and self-discipline.

The best way to teach a child discipline is through:

- modelling good behaviour;
- talking about the decisions our child faces on a daily basis and listening to how our child is resolving these issues;
- influencing our child to think about the rights and wrongs of situations and to make the right choices;
- giving support and guidance to our child to help them to control their behaviour.

When it comes to disciplining children, some parents believe that punishment is an important tool. Perhaps they themselves were taught discipline through punishment and felt it did them no harm.

Perhaps they find their child's behaviour extremely difficult to handle, or perhaps they feel under pressure from family, friends or other parents to use punishment-based disciplinary techniques. Whatever the reason, it is not the right route to take: simply put, punishment-based discipline does not work and creates difficulties in the parent–child relationship.

Children do need to understand and learn that behaviour has consequences, and that difficult, disruptive or violent behaviour will have negative consequences. This is a different matter from a parent imposing a consequence on a child simply to hurt, upset or punish the child. For example, a young child who cycles his/her bike onto the road should have the bike taken from them until he/she understands how to use the bike safely. This may cause upset to the child, but it is being done because the child does not have the maturity to understand the safe use of the bike. The reason why the bike is being taken from the child needs to be explained to the child carefully so that he/she does not feel he/she is bad or bold, but understands that we are taking this decision in order to give him/her a chance to learn about safety.

Slapping or punishing a child teaches a child nothing, makes the child feel bad and makes parents feel guilty. Even when disciplining our child, we need to value and respect him/her at all times. A core part of enhancing our child's welfare is disciplining our child appropriately. By disciplining our child, we teach him/her about right and wrong, which enables them to contribute to society in a constructive way and to be more secure and happier in themselves. Slapping and punishment have no constructive part to play in this process.

PARENTS AND CHILDREN DESERVE SPECIAL TREATMENT

The healthiness of any society can be measured by the way it views and treats its most vulnerable citizens: children. Children are the most valuable asset of any society and need to be nurtured and given every opportunity to fulfil their potential as citizens.

Those who choose to have and rear children are contributing to society in a very constructive and committed way by giving the most personal and valued of all contributions: human life. As a society, we need to recognise how this contribution enhances the whole community and provide the necessary supports to sustain it.

Ideally, communities and employers would acknowledge the importance of parents and children and act to ensure they receive the special treatment they deserve, but this is not always the case. For example, one recent Irish report indicates that time families spend together is decreasing as a consequence of commuting and participation of both parents in the workforce, despite the introduction of a number of family-friendly measures over the last number of years. As a result, parents need to demand special treatment, and sometimes this involves fighting against the hidden, and not so hidden, pressures to prioritise other things.

Demanding special treatment to protect the parent–child relationship will not only help us to be better parents, but will also protect our society by helping us to raise productive, balanced people who will in time be able to love and protect their own children.

TO BE ABLE TO LOOK AFTER OUR CHILD'S WELFARE, WE NEED TO LOOK AFTER OURSELF

Parents who are too tired, too stressed and too busy will have children who are over-active, undisciplined and demanding. Parenting is a mutually dependent relationship between parent and child, with both parties' physical, psychological and social health dependent on the other's. Prioritising parenting and family life means building and maintaining the necessary level of physical, emotional and social well-being to enable us to engage actively and in a positive manner with our child.

Protecting our personal welfare benefits not only our child, with whom we can engage positively, but also ourselves because it helps us to grow as people. When we are engaged in helping our child to grow and develop, we are simultaneously growing ourselves. The way we treat another human being reflects back upon us. By staying psychologically and emotionally healthy, we loosen the ties with which we can bind our children to negative forces.

Parenting stress and anxiety forces us into power struggles with our children, which has a detrimental effect on the parent–child relationship. When we free ourselves from these unhealthy emotions, it reduces power struggles and allows love and respect to flourish.

WHAT DO WE KNOW ABOUT PARENTING?

While most parents feel that parenting has changed and is continuing to change, it is hard to get an exact measure of these changes.

The Irish government has recently begun to gather and publish information that provides some objective yardsticks by which to measure parenting and children's welfare. The first comprehensive report, *The State of the Nation's Children*, was published in 2006 and it is likely that many more such documents will be published by future governments, which will allow us to chart these changes more effectively in the future. For now, *The State of the Nation's Children* report gives us a statement of the key indicators of children's well-being. It covers many different aspects of children's lives, such as their health, behavioural and educational outcomes, relationships and the services available to and accessed by children. (Much of the information contained in this report is referenced throughout this book.)

Alongside children's welfare, the report gives some indication of the nature of parent–child relationships in modern society. It examines five components of the parent–child relationship:

- relationship with mothers;
- relationship with fathers;
- talking to parents;
- parental involvement in school;
- eating a main meal together.

It also draws on international data to show how parents and children in Ireland rank on these measures as compared to children and parents in other countries.

The report indicates the following:

- 77.6 per cent of children aged ten to seventeen years report that they find it easy to talk with their mothers when something is really bothering them. The international average is 82.7 per cent; Ireland ranks twenty-seventh among thirty-five who countries;
- 56.2 per cent of children aged ten to seventeen years report that they find it easy to talk with their fathers when something is really bothering them. The international average is 64.2 per cent; Ireland ranks twenty-fourth among thirty-five who countries;
- 61.6 per cent of children aged fifteen years report that their parents spend time just talking with them several times a week. The

international average is 59.6 per cent; Ireland ranks eleventh among twenty-seven OECD countries;

- 47.9 per cent of children aged fifteen years report that their parents discuss with them how well they are doing at school several times a week. The international average is 52.3 per cent; Ireland ranks fourteenth among twenty-seven OECD countries;
- 77.1 per cent of children aged fifteen years report that their parents eat dinner with them around a table several times a week. The international average is 78.9 per cent; Ireland is ranked sixteenth among twenty-seven OECD countries.

While there are many other aspects of parenting and parent–child relationships that could be assessed, what appears clear from these statistics is that on some of the most important indicators, parent–child relationships among Irish children and parents are weak in comparison to their counterparts in other countries. Perhaps this has always been the case, or perhaps the nature of parenting is changing in Ireland, with the result that these relationships are weakening. If this is the case, it has implications for the future welfare of our children.

The State of the Nation's Children report acknowledges that relationships between parents and children are of great importance to the life of a child. This is reflected in the large body of research that indicates that parenting styles, family communication and parent–child relations have a big impact on children in terms of their life skills, psycho-social adjustment, mental health and behaviour. This gives us many reasons for striving to protect and strengthen the role of parents and their understanding of that role.

KEEPING CHILD SAFETY IN PERSPECTIVE

While a key component of parenting is keeping our child safe, it is important to keep child safety in a sensible perspective. Many experts in the field of childcare are becoming increasingly worried that parents are tending to be too protective of their children, as a result of which they are depriving them of normal childhood experiences. There are concerns that children are no longer being given the freedom to play on streets or in playgrounds, that they no longer walk or cycle to school and that many parents are now reluctant to leave their children with anybody other than family members. It is important that we do not allow worries about child safety to dominate our parenting because over-protecting our children can be as damaging to them as under-protecting them.

While appropriate vigilance and care are necessary , it is also worth remembering that if we work to be good parents and work to have a good relationship with our children, by doing so we will create a safe environment for them. Keeping our child safe is essentially about building a strong relationship with our child so that we are more likely to identify potential risks before they arise, quickly recognise risks or difficulties if they do arise and be available to support our child if they need us.

180.211

Mary's story: Communication

Mary was four years old when her twenty-nine-year-old uncle started sexually abusing her. Mary's family spent most of their holidays with her uncle and saw him at every family occasion. Mary's uncle sexually abused her until she was sixteen.

Mary became a very depressed, angry adult, who suffered from deep feelings of insecurity, shame and distrust. When aged thirty-four, Mary's life changed when she had a baby girl. She resolved to love and protect her and although she still became depressed and angry at times, she made a point of showing her love for her baby consistently. The one thing she got satisfaction and joy from was playing with her daughter.

Through seeing how happy her daughter was, she realised how wrong her uncle's abuse of her was. In addition, she began to worry that this uncle might be abusing other children. At the age of thirty-six, Mary decided to report the abuse she had experienced to the child protection authorities.

When asked why she had never told anybody about the abuse, she said that at first she did not understand what was happening and that as she began to realise what her uncle was doing, she did not know how to tell anybody.

She said that what made her most angry was that when she was a child, she did everything she could to avoid being left on her own with her uncle – pretending she was sick; dragging a friend or her brother along with her; crying and telling her parents she did not want to go with her uncle because she wanted to be with them. No matter what she did, her parents insisted that she go with her uncle because they liked him and got on very well with him. As an adult, Mary felt that her parents should have known what she was trying to say to them when she was a child.

Mary resolved that she would never make the same mistake with her own daughter.

Chapter 2
Understanding Child Abuse

For most of us, child abuse is something we do not want to contemplate. The idea that a person would knowingly and intentionally hurt a child is beyond our comprehension. What we know about child abuse we have most likely learned from the media, which tends to report the most horrific, most distressing cases. As a result, most of us do not have any real insight into why abuse occurs or what type of person abuses a child. The horrific nature of the information we do hear usually forces us to withdraw from wanting to find out any more. Like serious illnesses, we often prefer not to seek too much information, not to delve too deeply, hoping that we will never need to know the facts. For many of us, this is a reasonable reaction because child abuse will never touch our lives.

So why concern ourselves? It is true that most children do not experience child abuse. A small, but significant, number of children do experience it. Some are the victims of serious abuse, which causes them immense physical, psychological and social damage. Many more experience abusive situations which adversely affect their psychological and social well-being. We want to try to ensure that our child is not one of those who experiences abuse of any kind. The best way for us to do this is to arm ourselves with solid, accurate information and to develop the best parenting skills we can.

So, first, we need to understand the dynamics of abuse. Most child abuse is preventable. Some children are abused because they are simply in the wrong place at the wrong time and there is very little parents can do to prevent this. Incidents of children being abducted by passing motorists or attacked in the toilets of fast-food restaurants are terrible, random events that ultimately are the responsibility of the child protection and Garda authorities to prevent. It is important to remember that these situations are the exception.

Most child abuse does not involve one-off, random incidents; it involves evolving patterns of interaction with a child that become increasingly dysfunctional. It is behaviour that is both planned and engaged in with the knowledge that it will hurt or cause damage to the child. It takes the form of interactions that begin with treating a child with disinterest, disrespect and animosity and end with hurting and damaging a child.

These interactions differ depending on the type of abuse intended. Physical and emotional abuse involve building a relationship with a child that is based on fear, hurt and intimidation; sexual abuse usually involves first gaining and then exploiting a child's trust; neglect involves continually ignoring and failing to care appropriately for a child's basic needs. Every kind of abuse involves either exploiting a child's feelings of low self-worth and self-esteem or lowering their self-worth and self-esteem in order to create a situation where they can be exploited and manipulated.

Understanding child abuse in this context helps us to understand why it is usually preventable. If we are committed to respecting and empowering our children, to building their self-esteem and their self-worth and working to identify dysfunctional interactions before they become ingrained, then we can help prevent our children from becoming the victims of abuse.

Of course, understanding child abuse in this context presents us with some very personal challenges. If most child abuse involves evolving patterns of dysfunctional interaction with a child, exploitation of a child's psychological vulnerability or a gradual disempowering of a child, then most serious abuse must be carried out by people who know the child. If most child abuse begins with disrespect and animosity, do we ourselves sometimes create an environment that has the potential to become abusive for our children?

The most difficult aspect of learning about child abuse is that it forces us to confront our own attitudes and parenting practices and to assess our children's relationships with those who are closest to them.

This is a very difficult thing to do and requires a great deal of personal strength, courage and commitment.

Learning about child abuse can also be frightening, leading us to feel insecure about our own parenting and wary of those with whom our child is interacting. Nonetheless, being prepared to endure and resolve these feelings is important. Part of good parenting means being prepared to question ourselves and being prepared to be reasonably vigilant about the people with whom our child interacts. Through insightful and vigilant parenting, it is possible to ensure that we do not place our child in dangerous situations and, more importantly, that we arm our child with the necessary psychological and social skills to protect him/herself.

Sometimes, as we gather knowledge and develop understanding, we become more anxious, more insecure and more distrusting. To prevent this from happening, we need to remember to keep what we learn about child abuse in perspective. None of us is a perfect parent, so it is important that we do not become overly despondent or critical about our relationships with our children. Most of us want to do what is best for our children and will very quickly realise if difficulties are arising in our interactions with them. Similarly, we need to be careful that we do not start to become suspicious of everybody who shows an interest in our children. We want people to care for and show interest because children benefit from this. Most people who care for and work with our children are safe and would not dream of hurting them. Most of these people are vigilant of their own and other people's behaviour around and with children, and they will act quickly to resolve any difficulties that arise.

Ultimately, arming ourselves with the facts about child abuse not only helps us prevent abuse, but should also empower us and reinforce for us just how good we are with our children, and how good are the majority of those people who interact with our children.

WHAT IS CHILD ABUSE?

Child abuse is, quite simply, the mistreatment of a child. It can take many forms and can be carried out by adults or by other young people. Children can also abuse themselves by engaging in behaviour that they know will damage and hurt them – this phenomenon is dealt with in more detail in Chapter 8.

There are four main types of child abuse:

1. Physical abuse: Knowingly causing, or not preventing, physical injury to a child

Physical abuse is any form of non-accidental injury or any injury that results from wilful or neglectful failure to protect a child.

Examples of physical abuse include:

- shaking;
- use of excessive force in handling;
- deliberate poisoning, suffocation;
- allowing or creating a substantial risk of significant harm to a child;
- beatings or severe corporal punishment.

2. Sexual abuse: Involving a child in sexual activity they do not fully understand and to which they cannot give informed consent

Sexual abuse occurs when a child is used by another person for his or her gratification or sexual arousal, or for that of others.

It includes things such as:

- exposure of the sexual organs or any sexual act intentionally performed in the presence of the child;
- intentional touching or molesting of the body of a child, for the purpose of sexual arousal or gratification;
- masturbation in the presence of the child or the involvement of the child in an act of masturbation;
- sexual intercourse with the child, whether oral, vaginal or anal;
- inciting, encouraging, propositioning, requiring or permitting a child to solicit for, or to engage in, prostitution or other sexual acts;
- involving a child in the exhibition, modelling or posing for the purpose of sexual arousal, gratification or sexual act, including its recording (on film, videotape or other media) or the manipulation, for those purposes, of the image by computer or other means;
- showing sexually explicit material to children, which is often a feature of the 'grooming' process by perpetrators of abuse.

3. Emotional abuse: Persistently manipulating a child's feelings or rejecting the child

Emotional abuse is normally to be found in the *relationship* between a carer and a child rather than in a specific event or pattern of events. It involves things such as:

- persistent criticism, sarcasm, hostility or blame directed at a child;
- conditional parenting of a child, in which the level of care shown to a child is made contingent upon his/her behaviour or actions;
- emotional unavailability by the child's parent/carer;
- unresponsiveness and inconsistent or inappropriate expectations of the child;
- premature imposition of responsibility on the child;
- unrealistic or inappropriate expectations of the child's capacity to understand something or to behave and control him/herself in a certain way;
- under- or over-protectiveness of the child;
- failure to show interest in or provide age-appropriate opportunities for the child's intellectual and emotional development;
- use of unreasonable or overly harsh disciplinary measures;
- exposure to domestic violence.

4. Neglect: Not looking after a child properly, resulting in the child suffering significant harm or impaired development

Neglect includes things such as being deprived of food, clothing, warmth, hygiene, intellectual stimulation, supervision and safety, attachment to and affection from adults, or medical care. This form of abuse generally becomes apparent in different ways *over a period of time*, rather than at one specific point.

Abuse of a child by another child is called bullying or peer abuse. In addition, children can sometimes abuse themselves through drug and alcohol misuse, self-harm or premature early sexualisation.

HOW COMMON IS CHILD ABUSE?

Ascertaining how many children experience child abuse is very difficult because child abuse often goes undetected and unreported. One method is to measure the number of child abuse cases coming to the attention of the child protection authorities. However, it is generally recognised that these cases represent only a small number of the actual occurrences of child abuse.

Another possible method is to ask children in the general population if they are being abused through surveys, etc. This method poses ethical problems, however, and most children would find it difficult to report abuse in this context. Another way of estimating how many children are abused is to ask adults about abuse in their childhood, but, again, there are also many flaws and difficulties with this approach.

Despite these obstacles, there are a number of patterns emerging from research that give us some insight into the extent of child abuse. One comprehensive study was conducted in Ireland in 2002 by a research team from the Royal College of Surgeons in association with the Dublin Rape Crisis Centre, and it produced the report *Sexual Abuse and Violence in Ireland* (SAVI).

The SAVI report found that:

- one in five women (20 per cent) reported experiencing contact sexual abuse in childhood, with a further one in ten (10 per cent) reporting non-contact sexual abuse. In over a quarter of cases of contact abuse (i.e. 5.6 per cent of all girls), the abuse involved penetrative sex – either vaginal, anal or oral sex;

- one in six men (16 per cent) reported experiencing contact sexual abuse in childhood, with a further one in fourteen (7 per cent) reporting non-contact sexual abuse. In one of every six cases of contact abuse (i.e. 2.7 per cent of all boys), the abuse involved penetrative sex – either anal or oral sex.

The *State of the Nation's Children* report indicates that in Ireland in 2004:

- 6,188 children were assessed by the former Health Boards for child welfare concerns, representing a rate of sixty-one children per 10,000 under eighteen years. Of these assessments, 34 per cent concerned neglect, 20 per cent concerned physical abuse, 28 per cent concerned sexual abuse and 18 per cent concerned emotional abuse;

- 1,425 substantiated cases of abuse were notified to the Child Protection Notification System. This represents a rate of fourteen children per 10,000 under eighteen years. Of these, 42 per cent concerned neglect, 19 per cent concerned physical abuse, 15 per cent concerned sexual abuse and 24 per cent concerned emotional abuse.

The report indicates that since 2000 there has been an inconsistent decrease in the number of assessments for child welfare and child protection concerns, and an inconsistent decrease in the number of substantiated notifications. These statistics might indicate that the number of cases of child abuse is decreasing, or they might indicate that fewer cases of abuse are being disclosed to the child protection authorities.

In 2006, the ISPCC/Childline service received 16,801 calls relating to abuse and violence.

Child Maltreatment, a report produced by the US Department of Health and Human Services, based on statistics gathered from the fifty US states, District of Columbia and US territories, indicates that in 2005:

- an estimated 899,000 children were determined to be victims of abuse or neglect;
- since 2001, the rate and number of children who received an investigation have been increasing. For 2001, the rate was 43.2 children per 1,000 children, resulting in an estimated 3,136,000 children who received an investigation; for 2005, the rate was 48.3, resulting in an estimated 3,598,000 children receiving an investigation;
- of the substantiated cases of child abuse, 62.8 percent of child victims experienced neglect, 16.6 percent were physically abused, 9.3 percent were sexually abused and 7.1 percent were emotionally or psychologically maltreated. Rates of victimisation by maltreatment type have fluctuated only slightly during the past several years;
- in 2005, a nationally estimated 1,460 children died of abuse or neglect, i.e. a rate of 1.96 children per 100,000 in the national population. More than three-quarters of these children (76.6 per cent) were younger than four years old.

While statistics vary from country to country and from year to year, it is reasonable to surmise that too many children experience child abuse every year, in every country.

HOW WOULD I KNOW IF MY CHILD WAS BEING ABUSED?

Recognising child abuse is never straightforward. In some cases, a child's behaviour or a physical injury may indicate clearly that the child has been abused. In most cases, however, the signs of abuse are not so obvious. The following guidelines can help us:

- **Trust our instincts:** It normally never enters our heads to consider that our child might be mistreated or abused. Therefore, if we start to suspect something is not right, it is important to explore these thoughts. If we start to suspect something, we should try to identify what it is that is causing us to worry. Even if our suspicions are vague, we should check them out and discuss them with somebody we trust.

- **Children will express unhappiness and distress in different ways:** How each child expresses his/her distress will vary because each of us has our own individual ways of expressing emotion. In general, however, young children tend to express their emotions through their behaviour, and will express unhappiness and distress through difficult behaviour. Older children tend to express their difficulties verbally or through self-destructive behaviour.

- **Sadness and troublesome behaviour tell us that something is not right:** It is important to remember that no child wants to be sad or distressed, so when they are, there is always a reason. Children want to impress their parents, carers and teachers, so when they are being troublesome there is always an underpinning reason. Parents will know best if something is not right with their child, and should always seek to get to the bottom of what is bothering him/her.

ARE THERE SIGNS AND SYMPTOMS OF ABUSE?

Signs indicating that a child is being abused will vary depending on the age of the child and the type of abuse the child is experiencing. While there are some common signs that suggest a child is possibly being abused, it is important to remember that these signs are not, in themselves, evidence of abuse. It becomes a cause for concern when there are a number of these signs occurring simultaneously, the associated behaviour is out of character for the child and there is no apparent explanation for that behaviour.

General signs of abuse

When a child is being sexually, physically or emotionally abused or neglected, there can be developmental signs, such as the child's language and speech being impaired; physical signs, such as the child being bruised or cut; emotional signs, such as the child being tearful or withdrawn; and social signs, such as the child not having any friends. Abuse of any kind will impact on and be visible in many aspects of the child's welfare.

The following table gives the most common signs and symptoms of abuse exhibited by children of different ages.

0–4 years	5–12 years	13–18 years
• Repeated minor physical injuries.	• Deterioration in schoolwork.	• An air of detachment or 'don't care' attitude.
• Being dirty, smelly, poorly clothed or underfed.	• Unusually bold behaviour.	• Has few school friends, depression.
• Being sick all the time with no explanation.	• Overly compliant behaviour, watchful attitude.	• Does not trust adults, particularly those who are close.
• Aggressive behaviour or temper tantrums.	• Sexually explicit behaviour or conversation.	• Eating problems, including over-eating and loss of appetite.
• Inappropriate sex play or open masturbation.	• Frequently absent from school, does not join in school activities.	• Disturbed sleeping, reverting to younger behaviour, withdrawal.
• Bed-wetting.	• Tummy pains with no medical reasons.	• Running away from home, suicide attempts, self-harm.

It is important to note that some older children will show signs more commonly seen among younger children, while many forms of abuse will not display any physical signs at all.

In addition to these general signs, each form of abuse will have specific signs.

Sexual abuse

The following are the most common signs that a child is being sexually abused.

1. Child tells us that he or she is being sexually mistreated.

2. Child has physical signs, such as:
   - difficulty in walking or sitting;
   - stained or bloody underwear;
   - genital or rectal pain, itching, swelling, redness, or discharge;
   - bruises or other injuries in the genital or rectal area.

3. Child has behavioural and emotional signs, such as:
   - difficulty eating or sleeping;
   - soiling or wetting pants or bed after being potty-trained;
   - acting like a much younger child;
   - excessive crying or sadness;
   - withdrawing from activities and from others;
   - talking about, or acting out, sexual acts beyond normal sex play for age.

Physical abuse

The following are the most common signs that a child is being physically abused.

1. Appearance:
   - bruises or welts on body or face – especially in various states of healing, in unusual patterns or clusters that would reflect the instrument used, or in multiple areas of the body;
   - burns – cigar or cigarette burns, glove- or sock-like burns on extremities, doughnut-shaped burns on buttocks, or any burn that shows the shape of the item used, such as an iron.
   - fractures – spiral fractures of long bones without a history of

twisting force as the cause, multiple fractures in various stages of healing, any fracture in a child under two years of age;
- internal injuries;
- lacerations and abrasions (especially around the mouth, lip, eye or external genitalia);
- human bite marks.

2. Behavioural and emotional signs:
   - agitation, anger and rage;
   - anxiety or fearfulness;
   - apprehensive when other children cry;
   - avoids social contact or seems withdrawn;
   - behaves aggressively;
   - changes in a child's behaviour or in school performance;
   - cries frequently;
   - demonstrates extremes in behaviour;
   - destroys or throws things;
   - depression;
   - drug and alcohol abuse;
   - fights with other children;
   - flashbacks – seems in shock;
   - hard-to-believe stories about how accidents occurred;
   - immature behaviour, such as thumb-sucking or rocking;
   - lack of interest in surroundings;
   - lies frequently;
   - loiters at school or with friends – indicates a reluctance or fear to go home;
   - nightmares;
   - passive or withdrawn behaviour;
   - poor self-image;
   - reports injury by parents;
   - sadness or other symptoms of depression;
   - school problems or failure;
   - seems afraid of a parent or other adults;
   - self-destructive or self-abusive behaviour, suicidal thoughts;
   - startles easily;
   - stealing;
   - tired often;
   - trouble sleeping;

- wary of physical contact with adults;
- high-risk behaviours (e.g. speeding, dare-devil sports).

Emotional abuse

The following are the most common signs that a child is being emotionally abused:

- finding it hard to make or keep friends;
- avoiding being places where he or she is expected to be loving;
- avoiding doing things with other children;
- tending to be pushy and hostile;
- having a hard time learning, being overly active;
- having problems, such as bed-wetting or soiling;
- acting falsely grown-up;
- having to care for adults or others far beyond what should be expected for the child's age;
- becoming gloomy and depressed, unable to enjoy him/ herself;
- doing things that work against him/herself;
- becoming self-destructive, injuring him/herself or attempting suicide;
- being insecure and anxious;
- low self-esteem.

Neglect

The following are the most common signs that a child is being neglected:

- hunger, inadequate growth or low weight from poor nutrition, or unmanaged obesity;
- developmental delays;
- lack of attention to personal cleanliness – the child may be very dirty, smelly or unkempt;
- inappropriate or lack of clothing for the season;
- delay or failure to get needed healthcare;
- not following healthcare recommendations;
- pattern of tardiness or missing school;
- lack of shelter, heat, water, bedding or clothing;
- insufficient sleeping arrangements;
- unsanitary conditions and housekeeping problems;
- structural and fire hazards;

- substance abuse – a child who is poorly supervised by parents may have access to drugs or alcohol and develop related behavioral problems;
- poor social skills – neglected children may not have appropriate role models to learn responsible behaviour from and may also lack opportunities to interact with peers;
- poor school performance, tardiness or absenteeism – neglected children may not have enough supervision to help them prepare for and get to school regularly.

HOW COULD ABUSE AFFECT MY CHILD?

The effects of abuse on children vary depending on the severity of the abuse, who the abuser is/was, how the child was silenced and how people reacted to the abuse when it was discovered. The effect on a child can change over time as the child matures. The table on page 31 illustrates the more obvious ways in which child abuse can affect a child.

Underpinning these outward manifestations are a number of psychological factors, the most significant of which is the impact that abuse has on a child's self-image and self-esteem. Child abuse makes a child feel dirty, shameful and inferior to others. It affects the child's ability to trust and often makes the child feel that he/she has no control over his/her own life. By virtue of the secret nature of many forms of child abuse, it also has an effect on the relationship a child has with his/her parents, siblings and friends. If these problems are not resolved, the child becomes depressed, anxious and angry and begins to behave in a withdrawn or aggressive manner.

WHO ABUSES CHILDREN?

What do we know about those who abuse children? Research from Ireland suggests that the majority of those who sexually abuse children are men and that they are usually known to or are close to their victims. The term 'perpetrator' is the term usually used to refer to the person considered to have abused or neglected a child.

The savi report indicates that:
- most perpetrators of child sexual abuse (89 per cent) were men acting alone; 7 per cent of children were abused by a female perpetrator. In 4 per cent of cases, more than one abuser was involved in the same incident(s);

- one-quarter (24 per cent) of perpetrators against girls were family
  members, one half (52 per cent) were non-family but known to the
  abused girl, and one-quarter (24 per cent) were strangers;
- fewer family members were involved in child sexual abuse of boys:
  one in seven perpetrators (14 per cent) was a family member, with
  two-thirds (66 per cent) non-family but known to the abused boy;
  one in five (20 per cent) was a stranger;
- in one out of every four cases, the perpetrator was another child
  or adolescent (seventeen years old or younger);
- in four-fifths of cases, the perpetrator was known to the abused
  person; strangers were in the minority.

The SAVI report makes it clear that, apart from the broad conclusion
that perpetrators of childhood sexual abuse are most likely to be
known to the child and to be male, there are few other clues to
identify likely abusers. These findings are consistent with the statistics
emerging from other countries.

International data suggests that the majority of those who
physically abuse, emotionally abuse or neglect children are the
children's parents. Statistics produced by the Canadian Public Health
Agency (2003) on those who physically abuse children tell us that:

- perpetrators are split evenly between mothers and fathers, with
  female parents being perpetrators in 53 per cent of cases (50 per
  cent biological mothers and 3 per cent stepmothers), and male
  parents in 50 per cent of cases (38 per cent biological fathers and
  12 per cent stepfathers). This finding is somewhat biased by the
  fact that 30 per cent of physical abuse victims were living in lone
  female-parent families. The alleged roles of mothers and fathers in
  two-parent families are somewhat different, with fathers being
  perpetrators of 67 per cent of physical abuse and mothers of 51 per
  cent;
- in 4 per cent of cases where physical abuse was the primary
  concern, other relatives were considered perpetrators;
- the boyfriends and girlfriends of parents were the non-familial
  figures reported most frequently as the perpetrators.

In the case of neglect, the Canadian statistics tell us that biological
mothers are more likely to be perpetrators (83 per cent) than

biological fathers (36 per cent). Again, though, this finding needs to be viewed in context, as 42 per cent of cases of neglect involved lone female-parent families. Fathers/stepfathers were considered to be perpetrators in 45 per cent of cases of substantiated neglect.

In the case of emotional abuse, mothers and fathers were also the main perpetrators, with the Canadian figures showing that biological fathers/stepfathers were perpetrators in 56 per cent of cases, mothers/stepmothers in 66 per cent of cases.

The statistics recorded for cases of exposure to domestic violence, which is treated as a distinct category of child abuse in Canada, indicate that biological fathers/stepfathers were considered to be responsible in 88 per cent of substantiated cases. Mothers/step-mothers were considered to have failed to protect their children from exposure to domestic violence in 28 per cent of these cases. It is important to note that the core focus of child welfare investigations in these cases was the question of the parents' ability to protect a child from exposure, rather than the identification of the perpetrator of the violence.

Examining the personality characteristics of those who abuse children tells us that there is no one, single personality characteristic or group of characteristics that identify such a person. Instead, various research studies have identified particular characteristics that arise more frequently in people who abuse children. Many studies have found that men who abuse tend to be immature and suffer from feelings of inadequacy, have low self-esteem, poor social skills and poor impulse control. Some tend to be hostile, aggressive, manipulative and lacking in empathy, while others suffer from cognitive distortions (disturbed thinking) or show psychopathic (abnormally violent/anti-social) tendencies.

In terms of women who sexually abuse children, studies describe them as being 'loners', socially isolated, alienated, likely to have had abusive childhoods and likely to have emotional problems. Of course, it is important to remember that just because a person demonstrates one or all of these characteristics, this does not mean he/she has the potential to abuse a child.

As a means of preventing child abuse, seeking to identify particular characteristics has not been a particularly helpful approach and is one that has many difficulties. As such studies concentrate on those who have already abused children, it is quite likely that some of the characteristics identified could have resulted from the person engaging in abusive behaviour. For example, a person who sexually abuses a child is likely to develop low self-esteem because of the attendant feelings of guilt and shame. In addition, it is very difficult to identify a causal link between one, or a combination of, characteristics and abusive behaviour. The most that can be surmised from the research is that what causes a person to exploit or hurt a child is a complex combination of characteristics that interact with a variety of social and psychological factors.

Some research has taken a different approach and sought to identify the social factors associated with child abuse. This research method is also fraught with difficulty, however. Many of the social factors identified as possible causes of abuse could result from the abuse itself. For example, some research has identified marital difficulties as a cause of child sexual abuse, but in fact it is more likely that when child sexual abuse occurs within a family, it will cause marital difficulties. Social factors alone cannot give us any insight into why a person might abuse a child and such an isolated approach will serve only to create false impressions and confuse us. The reality is that child abuse spans all spheres of society and those who abuse children come from a a broad spectrum of social backgrounds.

In the end, all that the research can really tell us about those who abuse children is that they are most likely to know and to be close to the child they choose to abuse and that the abuse occurs for a number of complex reasons.

More recently, the search for an understanding of why someone might abuse a child has focused on attitudes to and treatment of children. Those working in the area of child abuse are starting to ask the question: 'What factors can make a person susceptible, under certain circumstances, to abusing a child?' One of the most distinctive features emerging from this work is a consideration of a person's overall mindset with regard to children. If a person feels it is acceptable to treat a child with disrespect, sarcasm or disregard, then this person could, under certain circumstances, begin to abuse children. Identifying why a person might develop such negative attitudes towards children and how this might be prevented is now emerging as an important component in the prevention of child abuse. Other factors that are emerging as crucial in prevention are parenting and the care environment. If this environment is healthy, then a person is less likely to abuse a child, no matter what personal circumstances or difficulties arise. Understanding the way in which such environments are created and maintained is crucial to preventing child abuse.

WHY DO CHILDREN NOT TELL?

It is generally known and accepted that most children who are abused do not tell anybody; the research conducted in Ireland clearly confirms this. While each child will have his/her own individual reasons for not telling, some useful insights can be gained from talking to adults who were abused as children and who did not disclose the abuse until later. What these adults tell us is that, in general, it is very difficult for a child to talk about child abuse and that telling others about it is even more difficult. They identify some very important obstacles that prevent children from telling.

Primary among these obstacles is the effect of the abuse itself. What many adults who were abused tell us is that abuse causes a child to feel frightened, ashamed and confused. One of the key features of abuse is the fact that it makes the child feel responsible for what is happening. The abuser often leads the child to believe that he/she is responsible for what is happening in the case of sexual abuse, that they have initiated and sought the sexual interactions; in the case of physical and emotional abuse, that they are bold, bad people who deserve what they were getting. In many instances these feelings are induced and exploited deliberately by the abuser, while in others the only way a child can make sense of what is occurring is to blame him/herself.

Related to this is the child's inability to realise or understand that what is happening to them is wrong. Many adults who were abused as children tell us that when they were being abused, they did not fully understand what was happening to them and did not realise that it was wrong. This is particularly true of younger children who, while distressed about how they are being treated, often believe that all children are being treated like this and that it is a normal part of childhood. Sometimes the abuse can cause a child to become depressed or hopeless and they begin to believe that nothing can be done to stop what is happening.

Adults who were abused as children tell us that perhaps one of the biggest obstacles to telling about child abuse is the fact that most children do not know who to tell. This is not surprising given that most children are abused by a person they know well and trust. Often the child feels that he/she will not be believed, particularly if the person abusing them is a close relative or a trusted person in their lives.

For older children, one of the biggest obstacles to reporting abuse is the feelings of shame and disgust they feel about themselves. Many of these children become angry with themselves for having allowed the abuse to have occurred and then feel too ashamed to tell anybody else. Like any bad secret, the secrecy itself adds to the difficulty in telling. Undisclosed abuse becomes harder and harder to disclose.

Sometimes, children do try to tell about abuse, but adults do not hear what they are saying. Children often do not have the language to explain what has happened and adults often do not ask, or do not ask the right questions. This is made more difficult by the fact that most adults do not want to contemplate child abuse – they do not want to consider that somebody they know, trust or love might be abusing their child. Child abuse is both difficult to ask about and to hear about.

It is the case that abuse of a child is rarely ended by a child telling an adult about the situation. In the vast majority of situations, it comes to an end only when the child refuses to participate, when the child stands up to the abuser or when somebody accidentally discovers what is happening.

Perhaps one of the most damaging aspects of child abuse is the impact it has on the child's ability to trust others. This will affect all of the child's relationships, including his/her relationships with his/her parents. Aside from the abusive nature of the behaviour itself, one of its most damaging effects is that it leads the child to believe that there is nobody he/she can trust enough to tell and that there is nobody who can help him/her.

The children who are most likely to report abuse are those children who understand what is happening, have the self-worth and self-esteem necessary to feel they are not to blame and have somebody in their lives whom they trust and believe will protect them. The adults who are best placed to hear or ask about child abuse are those who have knowledge and awareness.

WHAT DO I DO IF I DISCOVER MY CHILD IS BEING ABUSED?
Finding out that our child is being, or has been, abused is one of the

most traumatic experiences a parent will ever face. The initial reaction is usually a mixture of shock, anger, guilt and sometimes disbelief. These distressing feelings can often result in a parent denying that the abuse has happened, feeling uncomfortable and embarrassed about the abuse, becoming overly protective of the child or deciding not to seek help. Sometimes it can cause a rift between parents who respond differently. While these feelings and reactions are natural and understandable under the circumstances, they can make responding to the child's needs difficult.

The most important thing for parents to remember if we discover that our child is being abused is that we should try not to show our emotion, shock or horror because our child needs to feel that we are able to support them and that we can cope. The best way for us to respond is to try and remember that, first and foremost, our child needs reassurance. It is crucial that we:

- listen carefully, stay calm and assure our child that he/she is not to blame;
- take what our child says seriously, but don't make judgmental statements;
- praise our child for speaking about the abuse, but face up to the fact that something has to be done;
- remember that most children do not want to upset the people they love, so may only reveal a little at a time to test the reaction;
- do not lose patience with our child and give them the space and time to tell their story.

As soon as possible, the appropriate services must be involved and informed about the situation. This is essential to ensure that we and our child get the necessary help and also to ensure the abuser is prevented from abusing our child again or from abusing other children.

WHAT WILL HAPPEN IF I TELL THE AUTHORITIES?
If the time comes to involve the child protection authorities, it is important that we know what to expect. No matter how angry, upset or concerned we are about our child, involving social workers and the Garda Síochána in our lives is always very frightening.

One of the most common reactions of parents when they discover that their child is being abused is to start questioning themselves: 'Why did I not realise what was happening? I should never have left her alone with him. People will think I am a terrible parent. People will think I knew and did nothing.' All of these are normal reactions. One of our greatest fears is that if we involve the child protection authorities, they might blame us for what has happened and remove our child from our care. Many of us have heard stories about social workers taking children from parents for little or no reason or making serious mistakes about families. There is usually also an underlying fear that involving the authorities will mean the abuse will become public and our lives will be destroyed.

So what happens when the child protection authorities are informed? First, the authorities are obliged to follow certain procedures that require them, in the first instance, to conduct an assessment. This will normally comprise a series of interviews and physical examinations. In the case of a sexual abuse allegation or report, a child may be brought to a specialist 'Validation Unit' where the details of the allegations are explored. During this process, a child may be asked to undergo a physical examination. Similarly, in response to allegations of physical abuse, emotional abuse or neglect, a child may be examined by a GP or by a paediatrician in a hospital. The key component of such assessments is not the physical exam, however, but the interviews conducted with the child, with you the parent and separately with the person accused of the abuse.

The child will not be removed from his/her home unless he/she is deemed to be at immediate and substantial risk and cannot be protected adequately from that risk. In most situations, the authorities will advise that the child be kept away from the suspected abuser until the abuse has been investigated; if the alleged abuser is living within the child's home, that person will be removed from the house or asked to leave. Investigating and assessing the allegations takes some time, so the authorities will seek to ensure that the child is safe while the investigation is ongoing.

When an allegation of child abuse is reported to the authorities, there are effectively two different investigations conducted: a child protection investigation – usually conducted by social workers and other child welfare professionals, psychologists, psychiatrists, etc. – and a criminal investigation, which is conducted by the Garda Síochána. While the child welfare professionals and the Garda

Síochána will most likely work together, the purposes of their investigations are quite different. The child welfare professionals will want to ensure that the child is protected, that the family and the child are provided with the necessary supports to cope with what has happened and that a management plan is put in place for the offender. The Garda Síochána, on the other hand, will focus on assessing whether there is evidence that a crime has been committed and whether there is enough evidence to bring a prosecution. It can sometimes happen that the child welfare authorities conclude that there are child protection concerns, while the Garda Síochána do not have enough evidence to prosecute.

In most situations the initial assessments, physical examinations and interviews will take place quickly, but the complete investigations can take a substantial amount of time. At some stage during the investigation, the child welfare authorities will hold a meeting of all the professionals involved. This is called a case conference and you and your child will be invited to attend. The purpose of the case conference is to decide how best to proceed in order to support and protect your child. One key worker, usually a social worker, will be allocated to you and his/her role will be to keep you informed about what is happening and to give you support and advice. You will only be provided with child protection advice and support but, if you need it, you, your child and family will also be provided with counselling and therapeutic support. Of course, like any other system, the type of support and help you receive often depends on the quality of the particular social worker assigned to you and the available resources. It is important that you are aware of what is available and thereby ensure that you and your child receive the best possible support and advice; this may involve persistence and assertiveness.

For a variety of reasons, many cases of child abuse do not result in prosecutions or criminal proceedings. Even when there is enough evidence to prosecute a case, there are usually substantial delays in bringing cases to court. It is important that you and your child do not become preoccupied with the criminal proceeding, but stay focused on the welfare and support issues. If the case is brought to court, your child may have to give evidence and it will be important that he/she receives appropriate support to help him/her through this process. You must at all times remember that it is the role of the authorities to help and support you and your child.

WILL ABUSE DESTROY MY CHILD'S LIFE?

Child abuse can, and often does, have an impact on a child into adulthood. This effect is dependent on the type of abuse experienced, the way it emerged and how it was dealt with. While some adults who were abused as children experience substantial psychological and emotional difficulties, others are able to find ways to resolve their experiences.

The difficulties experienced as a result of abuse include:

- mental health problems, such as depression and anxiety;
- sexual problems, such as confused sexuality or sexual difficulties;
- relationship problems, such as inability to trust and lack of assertiveness;
- self-esteem problems, such as low self-confidence and low self-worth;
- parenting problems, such as over-protectiveness or apathy.

Being abused as a child should not destroy a person's life. If the child or adult receives the appropriate help, he/she should be able to overcome any problems caused by the abuse. The earlier a child gets help, the less likely it is that he/she will experience long-term difficulties. Nonetheless, it is *never* too late for a child, or indeed an adult, to get help.

DISPELLING MYTHS ABOUT CHILD ABUSE

In order to fully understand child abuse, it is necessary to dispel the unhelpful myths surrounding the issue.

General myths

1. Many allegations of child abuse are false and malicious

There is an increasing opinion that many false and malicious allegations of child abuse are made against innocent people. This has devastating consequences for those falsely accused, and support groups have been established to highlight the cases of false allegations and to seek justice for those so accused.

So, how many allegations are false or malicious? This is not an easy question to answer: some professionals claim they are extremely rare, others maintain they have become a serious problem. In truth, no one knows how many false allegations are actually made. First of all, there are problems in defining what is meant by 'false or malicious'. Some define 'false allegations' as all those allegations that are not proven or are found to be untrue; others limit the term to refer to deliberate fabrications.

There is no doubt that deliberate fabrications of child abuse do occur and for a variety of reasons, including for financial gain and sometimes where two parents are disputing custody of and access to a child. However, we must also remember that it is very difficult for a child to report abuse, that most children do not report abuse and that child abuse is a very difficult thing to prove. The SAVI report (2002) indicated that while 20 per cent of women and 16 per cent of men experienced child sexual abuse, 47 per cent of them had never told anybody about the abuse. It therefore seems reasonable to surmise that deliberate false allegations of child abuse are relatively infrequent and that deliberate false allegations by children are extremely rare.

2. Child abuse is tolerated in some countries, so what is so wrong with it?

Different countries have different attitudes and different laws governing how children should be treated. In some countries, extreme poverty, social disadvantage or poorly developed legal systems can mean that children are treated in very abusive ways. For example, there are places where child prostitution and child brides are common, and others where children are regularly subjected to horrendous forms of physical abuse, such as severe physical beatings and female genital mutilation. In many countries, children are used as soldiers or as slave labour to shore up the economy. In the modern world children are murdered, mutilated and raped as part of ongoing conflicts and are allowed to die because of disability or because of their gender.

Some children's rights activists argue that Western European values cannot be applied to developing countries because poverty, disease and poor education often necessitate children being treated in ways that would not be accepted in more developed societies. For example, in some Eastern European countries children are forced to have their tonsils removed without anaesthetic because there is a shortage of anaesthetics in their health systems. Others argue that in some African countries child prostitution is the only means by which some families can acquire income, and that without this income the family would starve.

Even within developed societies there are many debates about what constitutes child abuse. As our understanding and insight about child welfare expands, so too does our view of abuse. For example, now that we know that shaking a baby can cause brain damage, we consider this behaviour abusive, but a number of years ago shaking babies would not have been considered abusive.

Despite the differing treatment of children and the debates about what constitutes abuse, there are certain forms of mistreatment of children that developed societies simply cannot construe as anything other than abuse. Various international protocols make it clear that there are certain types of behaviour that cannot be tolerated by any society that is truly committed to nurturing children. The most important protocol, the United Nations Convention on the Rights of the Child, which is signed by every country in the world except Somalia and the USA, makes this absolutely clear.

Accordingly, attempting to justify child abuse by applying the norms of less-developed societies is to ignore the moral, psychological and human rights lessons that have been learned by more developed societies. Child abuse cannot be justified as a norm because it is a norm that defies humanitarian values and sows the seeds for a dysfunctional society.

3. If my child is abused, I am a failure as a parent

When a family discovers that a child has been or is being abused, it is extremely traumatic – not just for the child, but also for the child's parents and siblings. Alongside the upset and concern parents feel for their child, they will often also be feeling guilty and responsible for what has happened. Sometimes they feel that they have let their child down, that they should have done more to protect him/her or that they should have realised what was happening. Sometimes these feelings of guilt and responsibility make it difficult for us to believe what our child is telling us or cause us to blame our child for what has happened.

While these feelings and reactions are normal, they are not helpful. It is very important to remember that responsibility for abuse rests firmly and solely with the abuser. If we take responsibility upon ourselves, blame our child or refuse to believe our child, it not only helps the abuser to abrogate responsibility, but also makes it more difficult for our child, and for us, to overcome the impact of the abuse.

4. Emotional abuse and neglect are not as serious as the other forms of abuse

We hear little about emotional abuse and neglect, so we sometimes think that this type of abuse is less common and less damaging than sexual or physical abuse. In fact, emotional abuse and neglect can be more difficult to identify and more difficult to prevent. As a result, this type of abuse can go undetected for a far longer time, causing significant emotional and physical damage to the child. Chronic neglect can result in serious physical damage and sometimes death; emotional abuse not only causes immense psychological damage but can make children susceptible to other forms of abuse as well. There is still a great deal we need to learn about these forms of abuse.

Myths about sexual abuse

1. Stranger/danger

Most media coverage of child sexual abuse focuses on abuse of children by strangers. We often read in the papers distressing stories about children being abducted by men in vans or being abused by men in public parks. As a society, we have traditionally dealt with child sexual abuse by warning our children about strangers, i.e. 'never take a lift or sweets from a stranger', 'if you see strange men hanging around, never talk to them', etc. In many ways, viewing child sexual abuse as something that is perpetrated by strangers is the only way that we can make sense of it. The idea that a person who knows our child or is in a position of trust might hurt or abuse him/her is extremely difficult for us to confront and accept.

Nevertheless, the facts clearly tell us that most child sexual abuse is committed by people who are known to the victim and who are in positions of trust. This is hard for us to accept, but it is an important fact for us to face up to so that we can protect our children adequately.

2. Only 'perverts' abuse children

Many of us consider child sexual abuse to be something that is carried out by 'perverts' – men in dirty overcoats, sick people, sadistic people. We want to view those who sexually abuse children as 'different' or 'sick' because it is the easiest way for us to handle the idea of sexual abuse of a child. We do not want to accept that an abuser might be 'normal', just like us.

Again, the facts tell us otherwise. We know that those men and women who sexually abuse children come from all walks of life, work in all sorts of different occupations and have a wide variety of lifestyles. Although some may have a sexual preoccupation with children, most do not. This is not to say that what they do to children is not wrong or extremely disturbing. It is only to acknowledge that those who sexually abuse children are not overtly 'different' – they are individuals who, for a variety of reasons, express and attempt to resolve their psychological difficulties by abusing a child.

3. Victims of sexual abuse go on to sexually abuse others
One of the most common myths about child sexual abuse is the idea that people who are abused go on to abuse others. This myth stems from the fact that many people who sexually abuse children were themselves sexually abused as children.

In reality, only a small number of people who are abused go on to abuse others. Some children who are sexually abused do begin to behave in an inappropriately sexualised manner, such as kissing other children or adults, trying to touch them or making inappropriate sexual statements. However, this behaviour, which is usually a mirroring of what the child has experienced, can be dealt with very effectively through support and counselling. Similarly, most adults who were abused as children do not go on to sexually abuse children.

The idea that the abused become abusers can be extremely damaging because it adds to the feelings of shame, guilt, panic and anxiety that parents often feel when they discover that their child has been victimised in this way. Often parents become suspicious and distrusting of their own child, worrying that they might abuse a sibling or a friend. This fear is unfounded: being sexually abused as a child does *not* mean that a person will go on to abuse others.

4. Children can be sexually provocative
Sometimes the people who sexually abuse children try to defend their behaviour by claiming that they were 'led on' by the child, or that the child acted in a sexualised manner. They might also try to justify their behaviour by suggesting that the child had been sexually active with boys or girls of their own age before they had become involved with him/her.

Alongside this, there is a growing view that, in the modern information society, children and young people are becoming more sexualised at younger ages. This idea can be, and has been, utilised as a justification by those who abuse or want to abuse children. In one European country, for example, there is now a small but vocal political movement seeking to have paedophilia acknowledged as an accepted sexual orientation. Hearing these types of ideas can sometimes begin to have an impact on our thinking. Seeing the way children and young people are dressing and acting, we can begin to question whether it is possible that in some cases of sexual abuse the child initiates or encourages the sexual interaction.

This thinking is based on the myth that children understand fully, and can give informed consent to, sexual activity. It is a myth stemming from the many pressures and forces in society that are working to sexualise children inappropriately. The bottom line is: no matter how a child dresses or acts, he/she has neither the psychological nor the social maturity to fully understand sex and sexual behaviour. In addition, a child does not have the necessary maturity or intellectual ability to give informed consent to sexual activity. This is why there are laws to protect children and to prevent them from engaging in sexual activity until a later stage in their lives. What can help us to deal with this particular myth is to remember how we ourselves were as children and how little we knew or understood about sex, even if we pretended or acted otherwise.

Myths about abuse not only confuse our understanding, but also protect those who are a risk to children and mask the true nature of abusive behaviour towards children. Being prepared to challenge ourselves about these myths is important if we are to face up to the reality of child abuse.

Barbara's story: Telling behaviour

Barbara had become extremely tearful and edgy of late, crying over little things and losing her temper with her little brother easily. Then she started refusing to go to the youth club and refusing to go to her best friend Monica's house, saying she was not well. Since starting at the youth club, Barbara had always loved going and had made lots of friends.

She had been best friends with Monica since she was five years old and they both spent lots of time in each other's houses. Both sets of parents were friends and Monica's father helped out at the youth club.

Before her eleventh birthday, Barbara said she did not want a party. When her mother suggested that she would bring her and Monica to the cinema instead, Barbara completely lost her cool, screaming and shouting and locking herself in her bedroom. Her parents attributed her behaviour to her growing up and the onset of puberty.

Then one day, Barbara and her mother met Monica's father while shopping. It was only a brief conversation, but Barbara's mother noticed that her daughter had become very anxious and quiet on meeting him. Her initial suspicions were that Barbara had been in trouble at the youth club and was embarrassed about meeting Monica's father.

When she confronted her about it that evening, Barbara denied that anything was wrong and began crying. But when her mother suggested possible problems in the youth club, Barbara lost her temper and started shouting that Monica's father was a pervert and had tried to 'touch her up' on a number of occasions when she had been in his house.

Naturally shocked, her mother could say nothing and just began to cry. When she asked her what she meant by 'touched her up', Barbara – not wanting to upset her mother any further – said that it was not really a big deal and that he had just touched her a couple of times on her leg and bottom.

The following day, her mother talked to a social worker friend and brought Barbara to the local child guidance clinic, where she subsequently disclosed that Monica's father had sexually molested her on a number of occasions and on one occasion had attempted to have intercourse with her.

Barbara said that the main reason she had not told anybody was that she did not want to upset her best friend and did not want to get into trouble at the youth club.

Chapter 3
Keeping Children Safe within Families

On 1 March 1993, a forty-eight-year-old Co. Kilkenny father of two received a seven-year jail sentence, having pleaded guilty to six charges of rape, incest and assault. What made this case most horrifying was that these offences had been committed against his own daughter over a fifteen-year period, starting from when she was aged eleven. The young girl had had a number of hospital admissions over the fifteen years for the treatment of serious physical injuries and had been in contact with numerous health professionals, including general practitioners, social workers and public health nurses. None of the professionals involved had acted to protect the girl, not even when she gave birth to a baby of her own and her father sought to adopt the baby.

The public outcry regarding this case was so great that the government of the time established an independent inquiry. Ireland woke up to the reality of familial child sexual abuse.

Children need families. This seems like an obvious statement, and few would disagree with it. From our own childhoods and experience of being parents, we know just how important families are. Many of the ideas and feelings we have about ourselves stem from our family: 'I am the eldest and when anybody in the family has a problem they come to me', 'I am the youngest and everybody still treats me like a baby'. In many countries, and in many parts of Ireland, the family name determines how we are viewed: 'He is one of the Castledermot

Maguires', 'She is one of the North Mayo Sullivans'. Our family is a fundamental part of who we are as individuals.

What do we mean by the term 'family'? Providing a definition can be tricky and, at times, controversial. In many countries the legal definition of 'family' is often at odds with the practical definitions people use on a day-to-day basis. Many people see themselves as living in families even if they do not fit the legal definition, while others want to distance themselves from being considered family even if they do fit the legal definition. In some countries, like Ireland, the family has special status within the law: the Irish Constitution recognises and gives special status to a family constituted through heterosexual marriage.

The nature of families has changed significantly in Ireland over the last twenty years. Some couples now live together as a family, but do not get married; others separate or divorce and although not living together, are bound as a family through their children. The term 'family' is often used to refer to the broader family as well, such as grandmothers and cousins, etc. In a society where co-habiting, separation, divorce and same-sex couples are now a common occurrence, families have naturally become more complex. For example, a child whose parents are separated could have a mother, father, stepfather, stepmother, brothers, sisters, stepsisters and stepbrothers, etc., all of whom, or some of whom, the child might consider to be his/her 'family'.

No matter what the legal definition or social construction of a family is, the important thing to remember is that, ultimately, children define who their family is to them. Why is this important? Because once a child defines a person as being family, this not only indicates that the child feels that he/she has a special relationship with this person, but it also invests additional responsibility on this person. By defining particular people as family, the child is indicating that he/she has made a decision to love and trust these people and to see his/her relationship with them as special. This in turn makes exploitation or abuse of this relationship particularly traumatic and damaging for a child.

Children need families because a family plays a crucial part in ensuring a child is happy, safe and well cared for. A family has a significant influence on a child's happiness and welfare, but also on how happy and healthy that child will be as an adult.

THE ROLE OF PARENTS WITHIN FAMILIES

The most important relationship within a family is the relationship between a parent and child because most of a child's physical, emotional and social needs are met by his/her parents. While the nature of a child's relationship with his/her parents will change and develop over time, parents continue to influence and shape their children's psychological and emotional well-being throughout their lives.

In the context of changing and differing parenting structures, parents sometimes need to be reminded of just how important they are to their children. A common reaction of a mother working outside the home is to feel challenged by the closeness of her child's relationship with the childminder; separated fathers often feel threatened by the arrival of a new stepfather. But no matter what the circumstances of the parent–child relationship, parents will always be of critical importance to their child. The child wants to know what you think, what you feel, whether you are proud of them, why you didn't keep contact with them. For children, feeling that their parents love and care for them and continue to do so throughout their lives is essential to their self-image, self-worth and self-esteem. Even if a parent is abusive to a child, the child will still want to have a relationship with that parent. Rather than seeing the abusive parent as not loving them or wanting to hurt them, children will often construe abuse as *their* fault or try to excuse it as behaviour caused by external factors. Children need parents and they need to believe their parents love them.

This means that, as parents, we carry a great deal of responsibility. Unlike any other undertaking in life, having children is a lifelong commitment. Regardless of whether we play an active or distant role in their lives or whether we play a constructive or destructive role, we will always be essential to their identity, their welfare and their happiness.

Most parents love and care for their children and most families are places where children are nurtured and protected. Loving and caring for children comes naturally to us and creating a positive, healthy family environment is something most of us naturally strive to achieve. However, sometimes things go wrong within families, sometimes a parent, or parents, intentionally hurts, abuses or neglects his/her children. When this happens, it not only has a detrimental effect on the child, it is also very difficult to identify and to stop.

What goes on in families or between parents and their child is very difficult to monitor, assess or change. Most parents and families do not see the need for and do not welcome outside interference. Most parents and families find it very difficult to be self-aware enough or brave enough to identify that the family environment has become unhealthy or that a relationship between a parent, or parents, has become abusive. Asking parents or families to assess and analyse themselves, or to assess and analyse their partner's relationships with their children, is difficult and uncomfortable.

Most parents who buy a book like this will already be committed to caring for and protecting their children. But it is important to remember that families are not created unhealthy, they *become* unhealthy; relationships between an adult and a child are not created abusive, they *become* abusive. For example, a sexually abusive relationship between a father and daughter often begins with something as simple as inappropriate secrecy developing between the two, or a father disclosing inappropriate personal emotional information to his daughter. While these features in themselves are not abusive, they are not conducive to creating a positive parenting or family relationship and can easily develop into an abusive relationship. Similarly, a physically abusive relationship often begins with a parent slapping a child.

Another element we must be aware of is that while one parent may be committed to caring for and protecting a child, the other may be developing an abusive relationship with that child. Therefore a fundamental aspect of parenting is being cognisant of the need to continually assess and monitor our relationships with our children and ensuring our family is working together to create a healthy environment. We must be brave enough to self-analyse, to accept challenge from our parenting partner and to challenge our parenting partner in order to ensure parenting remains healthy.

Child abuse occurs as part of a relationship, a relationship that takes time to develop and to become dysfunctional. The best way to prevent child abuse is to identify dysfunctional relationship components early on and to address them before they become problematic. If we strive to create the best relationships for and with our children, the worst types of relationship are unlikely to develop. The benefit of doing this, both for children and for parents, can be immense. Striving to forge the best relationships possible helps to create a more fruitful and more enjoyable life with our children, forming bonds that will be strong enough to last throughout life.

THE FACTS ABOUT ABUSE WITHIN FAMILIES

Sadly, child abuse within families is common and child abuse by parents is all too frequent:

- research indicates that the vast majority of children who experience physical abuse, emotional abuse (including exposure to domestic violence) and neglect do so at the hands of their fathers and mothers (see Chapter 2). This is not surprising given that these forms of abuse are closely associated with the everyday care of children;
- a significant amount of sexual abuse is perpetrated by parents or other family members. In Ireland, the Sexual Abuse and Violence in Ireland study (SAVI 2002) indicated that incest was reported in 8.1 per cent of cases (i.e. by 5.6 per cent of women and 2.5 per cent of men). Incest is defined broadly as contact or penetrative child abuse by any relative, whether blood relative or not: 4.5 per cent of perpetrators identified in this study were fathers, 0.5 per cent were mothers, 6.8 per cent were brothers, 11.6 per cent were uncles and 8.9 per cent were cousins. Statistics from Canada indicate that of those cases of sexual abuse substantiated by the child protection authorities, 9 per cent of the perpetrators were biological fathers, 5 per cent were biological mothers, 13 per cent were stepfathers or common-law partners and 35 per cent were 'other relatives'.

Why do some parents abuse their children? Why do some families become very unhealthy places for children? In Chapter 2 we looked at the types of people who are most likely to abuse children, but it is also useful to look at some of the common characteristics that arise in parents who are most likely to abuse their children. Reading this section might be difficult for us because we may identify some characteristics that we can see in ourselves or in our partner. It is important to remember that the presence of these characteristics does not, in itself, mean that a person will abuse a child. Nonetheless, identifying such characteristics should be helpful to us in ensuring our family does not become an unhealthy place for our children and in addressing what might be causing any unhealthiness that does arise.

Parents who physically abuse, emotionally abuse or neglect their children

Perhaps one of the most striking characteristics of parents who engage in this type of abusive behaviour is that they receive little enjoyment from parenting. Of course, all parents go through times when they feel stressed and 'fed up' and there are many times when parents, if they are to be honest, would admit that they are not necessarily enjoying parenting. It is when these negative feelings become dominant and constant that difficulties can arise.

Parents who begin to feel negative about parenting all the time often become angry with themselves or their child, can start to feel depressed and sometimes lose interest in their child. Despite the everyday stresses and difficulties associated with parenting, parents should generally feel a sense of satisfaction, fulfilment and happiness in their interactions with their child. If they do not, something is wrong.

Parents who are more likely to physically abuse, emotionally abuse or neglect their children tend to be those who are more isolated from their communities. These are people who feel they have few supports or friends and who do not engage in many community activities. They are often afraid to or emotionally unable to ask for help from sources of support within their community. These parents usually keep themselves to themselves, do not like others to come into their home, are reluctant to visit others' homes and do not mix easily.

Most abusive parents have unrealistic expectations of their child. These expectations usually arise from a lack of knowledge, or from a parent's social and emotional difficulties. They often expect their child to behave more grown-up than he/she is, or to be able to understand and deal with complex emotions. Abusive parents often interpret a young child's behaviour as boldness when it is merely appropriate behaviour for the child's age.

The way in which parents deal with crying is a good example because crying is often one of the triggers for parents to physically abuse their child. These parents often interpret the child's crying as 'boldness' or behaviour deliberately calculated to be annoying, rather than as a young child's primary way of communicating. Similarly, parents who emotionally abuse their children often do not understand how important positive emotional reinforcement is for a child's development. They often believe that the child is capable of dealing with consistent threats, humiliation and criticism.

Parents who neglect their children often forget, or simply do not appreciate, how dependent their child is on them to meet his/her basic needs and to keep him/her safe. As a result, they often leave their children to fend for themselves. As abusive parents often have unrealistic expectations about their child's development and abilities, they demand a level of physical, social and emotional maturity that is not appropriate for the child's age.

Many parents who abuse their children view themselves as victims in life generally, and in the parent–child relationship in particular. They feel that they have lost control of their children and of their own lives. Therefore when their children behave in a manner they perceive as disrespectful or overly demanding, they lash out physically or emotionally in an effort to re-establish control, or else they give up on their children and disengage from them.

Parents who sexually abuse their children

It is generally accepted that parents who sexually abuse their children are not necessarily people who have sexual difficulties or a sexual preoccupation with children. In fact, only a very small number are obsessively sexually attracted to children or have sadistic tendencies.

The reality is that most parents who sexually abuse or exploit their children choose to do so in order to express, or attempt to resolve, their own emotional and psychological difficulties. In a similar vein to those parents who physically abuse, emotionally abuse or neglect a child, those who sexually abuse are usually isolated from their communities, have unrealistic expectations of their child and view themselves as victims.

Unlike the other forms of abuse mentioned, however, parents who sexually abuse a child usually feel they have a very good relationship with their child and believe they are in complete control of the child. They often believe the child is the only person who understands them and that the child is, in some way, a willing participant in the abuse. They create a relationship with the child that completely excludes all others, including the other parent, other siblings and the child's friends. Consequently, a parent may often abuse more than one child within his/her family and none of these children will tell each other because of the dominant nature of the relationship the abusing parent has with each of them.

Sometimes the abusing parent threatens the child, but more usually he or she coerces the child. Utilising the love and trust the child feels for him/her, the abusing parent engages the child and then attributes the responsibility and blame for the abuse onto the child.

Alcohol or drug misuse is common among parents who sexually abuse their children and is usually the factor that disinhibits the abuser enough to allow him/her carry out the abusive behaviour. It is important to remember, however, that abuse of alcohol or drugs does not in itself explain why a parent sexually abuses their child. Most people who abuse drugs or alcohol do not sexually abuse children.

As is the case for abuse in general, there is no one, single profile that explains why a parent or other family member might abuse a child within his/her family. When the abuser is a family member, he/she is usually a person we love and care for, which makes his/her behaviour even more difficult to accept and understand, and presents us with conflicting and confused emotions.

Preventing child abuse from occurring within a family will not be achieved by attempting to identify individual characteristics within individual family members: doing this will only create an atmosphere of tension and distrust within a family and will achieve very little. The most effective way to prevent abuse from occurring within our family is to ensure that the family is healthy and the relationships within it are kept healthy. By doing this we substantially reduce the risk of problems arising and relationships becoming dysfunctional. If we focus on keeping our family healthy, we are more likely to identify abuse if it is occurring.

How do we keep our family 'healthy'?

Just as there are many different types of family, there are many different characteristics that make a family 'healthy' – a number of which are common to those families in which children are nurtured and protected.

RESPECT

A key factor in the healthiness of a family is how much respect the members of the family have for each other. This respect is reflected not only in the way we behave towards each other, but also in the way we prioritise each other's needs and wishes.

A healthy family respects the individual rights of all the family members and finds compromise and agreement when making key decisions about the family or individual members. This mutual respect is determined by a number of factors, the most important being each family member's own self-respect. Family members who find it hard to respect themselves will find it almost impossible to respect other family members. This mutual respect begins as soon as a new person enters the family structure as, once established, patterns are extremely difficult to break.

For example, one way that we respect each other is by respecting one another's possessions. Living in the one house can make this difficult, but that just makes it even more important. A child has very little that he/she can call his/her own, therefore even the smallest child will want to try and declare ownership of things, starting with a particular toy or teddy and moving on to other items. This is because children need to know that there are certain things that belong to them and that nobody, including their parents, will take or use these things without their agreement. Of course, siblings do borrow or take things from each other without asking, which often creates friction. Children have a right to be annoyed when others take their things without their consent, and they should be allowed to be annoyed because that is the one way they can demand respect.

Respect also involves consulting members of the family about important things and about their wishes. A good example of this might be how the weekend television-viewing schedule is arranged. A child feels important if he/she is consulted about these things and feels he/she can influence these decisions. While the family may not always agree with what a child wants, if the reasons for not agreeing are explained, a child will feel respected enough to have been included in the decision-making process. All of these may seem like small things, but they can make a real difference to how a child views him/herself and how a child comes to respect him/herself.

GOOD COMMUNICATION
Communication is the energy that fuels the functioning of the family. While people can live together under the same roof, it is the communication between them that defines them as a family. When communication is secretive or destructive, families disintegrate. When communication is open, honest and constructive, families thrive. Children need to understand clearly what is being

communicated to them and need to be confident that their parents and other family members understand what they are trying to communicate to them.

One example of how this might work is to set aside time for children to tell us about their day and for parents to talk about their day to their children. Doing this most days not only helps us understand our children's lives better, but also helps everyone to learn how to communicate with others. Integrating this into normal everyday activities, such as having a meal together or doing a task like the dishes or tidying together, is better than trying to set aside 'special time'.

A child often finds a direct focus on communication difficult to handle and will prefer communication to occur as part of normal, everyday activity. By integrating communication we ensure that it has a better chance of continuing as a daily occurrence, whereas trying to find 'special times' can become increasingly more difficult and therefore unlikely.

Another example is giving children permission to be in bad form and to permit discussion of problems or worries. This can be difficult because we might not often see the significance of a particular event or upset. Nonetheless, listening actively to our children, exploring what they mean, continually clarifying what we mean and continually checking that we are understanding one another are all important components of communication.

Talking to and listening to one another about good and bad things is equally important. Families often find time to communicate about problems or sad things, assuming the good things do not have to be discussed. This is not so. Good communication involves sharing the happiness and the joy as well as the sadness and the difficulties.

STRONG PROBLEM-SOLVING SKILLS

Within families there will always be conflict: it is a natural part of resolving individual needs and wishes. It is how a family resolves conflict that will impact significantly on the welfare of children. Negative patterns of conflict resolution compromise a child's welfare and often place a child at risk. Positive patterns of conflict resolution protect the child and allow him/her to grow and develop maturely.

Families solve problems every day. If children do not want to do their homework because they want to go out to play, the choice is either to tell them to do it, give in to them or explain to them why it has to be done. Sometimes finding ways to solve small problems prepares children and adults alike for the bigger problems: negotiation, compromise, understanding consequences and being reasonable are important components of good problem-solving skills.

In many families bedtime provides a good example of problem-solving. This is where children start to practise their negotiating skills and where parents have to solve the issue of getting their child to bed at a decent hour. If parents can reach agreement with their child about bedtime and do it in a way that acknowledges their wishes but also achieves the outcome of the child getting adequate sleep, then this indicates good problem-solving skills.

Compromise and negotiation are not the same as 'giving in'. We are often prone to see compromise or negotiation as weakness, particularly when it involves a child. However, these skills do serve to empower a child to learn to solve problems constructively and to trust that, together, difficulties can be solved.

ABILITY TO DEAL WITH FEELINGS

How families deal with feelings is often one of the key determinants of how a child is nurtured within the family. 'Emotional intelligence' is the term used to describe the ability to understand and deal with our own feelings and the feelings of those with whom we interact.

A child will prosper within a family:

- with a well-developed emotional intelligence;
- with the ability to understand and express feelings constructively;
- in which love is expressed openly, both physically and verbally;
- in which there is time for fun and play;
- in which people care for each other; and
- in which there are constructive ways to deal with anger, frustration and sadness.

For example, we should not be afraid to show physical emotion to our children, to hug, kiss, tickle, massage or horseplay with them, as long as they are comfortable with it. As children get older, they become less comfortable with some forms of physical emotion and more comfortable with others. Similarly, no matter what their age, our children should feel comfortable to cry or to be appropriately angry in front of us.

Children should be able to tell us they feel down and want to withdraw for a while, or should be comfortable enough with us to be 'hyper' or 'mad' from time to time. We, too, should be comfortable to cry or to be sad in front of our children, or to be very happy. As long as emotion is expressed in a constructive way and for appropriate reasons, we should be comfortable with it. While expressing emotion in a negative way, i.e. temper tantrums, silences, screaming and shouting, etc., creates problems, not expressing emotion can be equally damaging.

Families often develop their own words to express emotion and this is fine as long as the members of the family know and understand what that language is. 'I feel terrible' or 'not in the mood' can mean one thing in one family and quite another in a different family. Sometimes forcing a child to use very emotionally explicit terms inhibits him/her from expressing and resolving his/her feelings. Just as important as learning to express emotion is learning to respond to others' emotions in a healthy way. Children usually learn this by modelling their own responses on their parents' responses.

POSITIVE DISCIPLINE
Teaching your child self-discipline is a core function of parenting and is integral to family functioning. Children need to learn how to distinguish right from wrong in order to learn how to make the right decisions. Discipline is also crucial because a well-disciplined child will be better able to protect him/herself. Many of us are confused about positive discipline, believing it is simply a child 'doing what he/she is told'. Others take a more liberal attitude to discipline, believing a child should be allowed do as he/she wishes.

Discipline is neither of these two, in fact. It is the process of helping a child to learn about right and wrong so that he/she will be able to make the right decisions for themselves, in time. If we get discipline wrong, we make our child vulnerable. If, for example, our child thinks that good discipline is about 'doing what you are told', then he/she becomes vulnerable to people who are in positions of power and trust who might tell them to do the wrong things.

On the other end of the scale, children who are allowed to do as they wish are also open to exploitation by people who can cajole and coerce them with the promise of immediate gratification. A child who learns to think for him/herself about what is right and wrong, who is encouraged to consider right and wrong and to question, challenge and take personal responsibility will be in a far better position to protect him/herself from harm.

For example, we continually find ourselves under pressure to control our children in the supermarket, in the bank or in the restaurant. They do not want to be controlled – they want to explore, or else they do not want to be there in the first place. We often resolve this discipline problem by not bringing our child with us at all, or by bringing him/her then losing our temper, shouting and screaming or even slapping him/her. In such situations, positive discipline involves understanding the situation from our child's perspective, planning the trip, limiting the time, being consistent with the messages we give to the child, providing reinforcement or distraction and ignoring the inconvenience caused to others.

Children are rarely 'bold'. While their behaviour can often be annoying, out of control, dangerous or aggressive, there is usually an explanation for it. Challenging behaviour is usually underpinned by tiredness, boredom, wanting something they cannot have or feeling angry towards us. It is important that we deal with this in a positive way, teaching our child how to control the expression of their negative emotions and to behave in an appropriate manner. If we exclude our child from the awkward activities, lose our temper or slap our child, it achieves nothing.

FAMILY INTROSPECTION AND AWARENESS

A family's ability to honestly examine how it is functioning is crucial to its health. Most families are good at this, doing it through everyday challenge and reinforcement, saying things such as: 'Why am I always the one who has to answer the phone?' or 'You never ask me my opinion'. Within 'healthy' families, challenge and reinforcement balance each other, allowing the family to adapt, to grow and to facilitate and protect all of its members. A family that cannot 'look in' on itself and critically assess what is happening within it can be a difficult place for a child to be.

It is important to remember that even in families where many of the above factors exist, a child can be abused. But working to create a family that is healthy and safe will significantly reduce the risk of your child being abused, and will certainly make it more likely that your child will seek your help if he/she does experience abuse or trauma.

More importantly, perhaps, working to create a healthy family will undoubtedly help to further your child's emotional and psychological development.

What can make a family 'unhealthy'?

All parents and family members have a natural instinct to care for and to protect children. Sometimes, however, various factors can arise that cause family members to hurt or abuse children through physical violence, sexual exploitation, emotional exploitation or neglect. These factors may arise from outside the family and cause stress or difficulties, or they may arise within individuals themselves, such as unresolved psychological problems.

The psychological factors that can lead a person to abuse a child are complex and there is no one psychological profile that fits all. What can be identified, however, are those factors within a family that cause it to become 'unhealthy' and that create the environment in which children become vulnerable to abuse. These factors are as follows.

1. When treating children with disrespect, cynicism or disdain becomes acceptable within the family

Families become extremely unhealthy and dangerous for children when it is permissible for them to be treated badly within the family. A pattern of mistreating a child often goes hand-in-hand with a pattern of treating other family members badly.

Where there is domestic violence or where partners treat each other with cynicism and disdain, a child will inevitably be subjected to the same type of treatment. Within this kind of environment, a child will begin to believe that being treated badly is all he/she can expect. Overt negative behaviour of this nature is usually easy to spot, e.g. siblings calling each other nasty names, hitting or deliberately hurting each other, saying nasty things about family members to friends or to neighbours; all of these are unhealthy signs. But sometimes this behaviour is subtle and ingrained. For example, it may be that only one child within a family becomes subject to this type of treatment, for a variety of reasons.

Once there is permission within a family to treat a child badly, that child becomes vulnerable to being abused, whether by a family member or by somebody outside the family. Where a child is mistreated within a family, he/she is less likely to tell if he/she is being abused.

2. When children are encouraged to become secretive and manipulative

A secret is something that is hidden and guarded against discovery. A family in which there are secrets is an unhealthy place for a child to be. While there are always private things that will not be discussed outside the family and certain things that will not be told to certain people at certain times, a 'culture of secrecy' within a family is dangerous and unhealthy.

Communication within families is constantly changing: as children get older, they tell their parents less; as children get older, their parents tell them more. Parents of teenagers will feel they can discuss more issues with their sons or daughters than they could have when they were younger, while teenagers will feel they can discuss fewer issues with their parents than they were prepared to do when they were younger. This change in communication patterns is natural, but secrecy is not. It breeds collusion and manipulation and fosters an atmosphere in which 'bad' things do not get discussed. Indications of these sorts of problems are dishonesty, cheating or stealing from each other or not sharing important information.

3. When children are criticised and punished continually and are rarely praised

Low self-esteem is one of the key factors that makes a child vulnerable to abuse. A child with low self-esteem will not only have lower expectations of themselves, but will find it difficult to stand up to a person who wishes to hurt them.

A child develops low self-esteem when he/she lives in a family where he/she is continually punished and criticised. If parents do not praise their child, he/she will find it harder to develop self-esteem because a key determinant of a person's self-esteem is positive reinforcement from those closest to them.

Many parents deliberately use punishment and criticism as part of their discipline, believing it achieves results. However, if discipline is viewed in the context of creating responsible social individuals, then negative techniques, such as criticism and punishment, have no part to play in this process. In fact, these techniques can make a child more vulnerable.

Indicators of unhealthy behaviour of this sort are slapping, beating, sarcastic comments, undermining, belittling, labelling and depriving children of food as punishment.

4. When children do not receive positive physical contact

Positive physical contact is vital for children because it helps them to feel loved and valued and to understand the nature of a loving physical relationship. Receiving positive physical contact, particularly from parents, is essential for a child's healthy emotional development. The type of positive physical contact children need varies depending on their age. We know that babies require lots of hugging, kissing, cuddling and tickling, but even teenagers require hugs and physical warmth from their parents.

Children who do not receive sufficient positive physical contact within the family will be more susceptible to inappropriate physical approaches and less capable of identifying such approaches as abusive. Worrying indicators of this sort of behaviour within a family are children not being given physical comfort when they are upset, parents and children not acknowledging greetings and goodbyes through physical gestures and parents not demonstrating positive physical contact with each other.

5. When sexuality and gender relationships are not discussed in a healthy, open, constructive manner

While children can learn about sexuality and gender relationships from a number of places, the best place is within their own family. Open family discussions on these topics allow children to explore and identify healthy sexuality and to develop a healthy attitude towards gender relationships.

It is essential that discussions of this nature are age-appropriate, allowing children to develop at their own pace and level of understanding. Families in which sexuality and gender relationships cannot be discussed or are discussed in a secretive or negative manner are not healthy places for a child.

Where there do exist negative sexual or gender relationships within a family, it makes a child vulnerable: a child can only identify abusive sexual relationships if he/she understands what constitutes a positive sexual relationship. Indicators of possible problems in this regard are sex and sexuality not being discussed or being discussed in overtly suggestive or inappropriately explicit ways, explicit sexual material being made freely available and unmonitored within the family, sexual aggression in the family or gender relationships being discussed in sexual terms only.

It is important to remember, however, that even where one or more of these factors occur in a family, it does not mean that a child is being abused within that family. What these factors serve to do is to create an environment that is conducive to abuse, which can then be easily exploited by an individual who needs or desires to hurt a child.

How can we keep our child safe within the family?

The most effective way for us to protect children within the family is to create the most positive, child-centred environment we can for them. This environment will encourage and enable the child to develop to the best of his/her abilities and will significantly lessen the possibility of child abuse taking place. So, how do we create this environment?

1. Building respect

Within families, we can create a respectful environment for our children by:

- respecting their privacy;
- respecting their possessions;
- talking *to* them and not *at* them;
- seeking their views and opinions;
- giving them real choices;
- helping them to make decisions for themselves;
- acknowledging their right not to be touched, kissed, hugged or subjected to any physical procedure without been consulted and informed;
- expecting the same respect for ourselves.

How we deal with our children's bodily integrity, their right to decide who sees their body and who touches their body is a good indicator of how we respect them. A child's attitude to his/her body and being naked or semi-naked will change as he/she grows older. Babies and young children have no inhibitions about their bodies and will happily run around naked, if permitted. As the child grows older, however, he/she becomes more self-conscious and is not so willing to be seen naked or semi-naked. This development is natural and coincides with the child's growing independence.

Similarly, young children seek physical affection from their parents and suffer emotionally if they do not receive it. But as they grow older, children become more self-conscious about physical emotion from their parents and often avoid it, or at least ensure that it occurs only in non-public places. Again, this is normal development.

For every parent, accepting these changes and new rules is very difficult: the first time a child refuses a goodbye kiss at the school gate or asks a parent to leave the room while he/she undresses is upsetting. However, in a healthy family a child's right to total bodily integrity is always respected. If parents – no matter how close or trusting a relationship they have with their child – do not respect this, it creates an environment where their child's bodily integrity and self-respect could be exploited.

2. Building good communication
We build strong communication with our child by:

- integrating communication with them into our everyday activities;
- using age-appropriate language that he/she understands;
- listening and ensuring we understand what our child is telling us;
- controlling and expressing our emotions appropriately;
- being honest and open;
- allowing our child to challenge us;
- allowing our child to express his/her emotions in appropriate ways.

How we communicate bad news to our child is one good indicator of how good communication is within the family. At some stage, every parent is faced with the daunting task of communicating bad news to their child. Whether it is about a death, a separation, a disappointment or a mistake we have made, it is always a very difficult thing to do. We worry that our child will be severely traumatised, may not understand or might blame us. How we cope with this challenge is a good measure of the type of communication we have built – and wish to build – with our child.

Sometimes we fall at the first hurdle and decide not to tell or to lie. For example, instead of telling our child that Mummy and Daddy have separated, we say, 'Daddy is working away from home for a while.' Sometimes we fudge the message in an attempt to make it more acceptable to the child, for example by telling a child that 'Granny has gone to a happier place' when she has died.

Building good communication means being able to tell and to listen to bad things as well as to good things. It means ensuring our child understands us fully and being brave enough to allow our child to express how he/she feels, even if this hurts us. For example, telling a child that 'Mummy and Daddy have not been getting on lately so they have decided to live in separate houses, that they both still love him/her and will see him/her regularly' may be very upsetting for a child to hear, but it will ultimately reassure the child that he/she is being told truthfully what is happening and that it is not his/her fault.

Building positive communication works two ways: it gives us the means to discuss difficult situations with our child and also gives permission to the child to tell us 'bad' things. If we avoid talking about or listening to such things, our child will not tell us when he/she is feeling uncomfortable or threatened.

3. Learning to problem-solve
We can learn to problem-solve with our child by:

- listening to each other;
- being fair and reasonable;
- being consistent in our decisions;
- being prepared to compromise and negotiate.

How we problem solve with our child can be best illustrated by those difficult situations that arise when other parents are allowing their children to do something we do not want our child to do, for example the dreaded 'sleepover'. How do we react when our child asks permission to go on a sleepover and all the other parents have given permission to their children, but we are not happy to let our child go? We feel that we are not only at loggerheads with our child, but also isolated from the other parents and their ideas of best practice.

The first obstacle to overcome when faced with these situations is to avoid making it into a conflict or a battle of wills. It is important not to become either defensive or to cave in just because other parents have agreed. In the case of the sleepover, it quite often happens that we find that other parents gave their permission because they were told everyone else had already done so. This is the type of situation when we must problem-solve with our child.

To do this, we need to:

- listen to exactly what our child wants. Sometimes, our child may not be sure that he/she really wants to go, but needs us to make the decision rather than having to admit to friends that it is his/her decision;
- ask ourselves if our concerns are fair and reasonable. We might have very good reasons for concern, such as school the next day, poor parental supervision in the house or the fact that our child does not cope well with sleep deprivation. However, our concerns might not be so fair or reasonable: we might not want to be on our own overnight, for example;
- make sure that whatever we decide is consistent with other decisions we have made and the reasons we have made them. Did we agree to a sleepover in the same circumstances before because we were going out and it suited us, etc.?;
- find a compromise, if we can: 'I don't want you sleeping over, but you can stay as late as you want and I will pick you up.'

Failing to resolve situations like this appropriately creates a family environment that is incapable of dealing with problems. This will discourage a child from coming to us with difficult or important problems, believing we will either dig our heels in and be unreasonable or give in and be intimidated by others too easily.

4. Building good emotional intelligence

We can develop good emotional intelligence within families by:

- being open about our feelings;
- showing physical emotion;
- finding a common emotional language;
- finding a healthy way to react to each other's emotions;
- challenging emotions or expressions of emotions that are unreasonable;
- working to help each other understand the source of our emotions.

A good illustration of emotional intelligence is provided when parents have a row. In families, it is inevitable that disagreements will occur from time to time and parents will row. This is not a problem. For children, seeing their parents disagree and resolving disagreements fulfils an important function: it helps them to understand and learn about emotions, how emotions can and should be expressed and how conflicting viewpoints and emotions can be resolved.

What children learn from these situations depends on how disagreements are resolved. If they are handled in an emotionally mature manner, then children will learn a great deal that will be helpful to them in their own lives. If difficulties or rows are resolved through negative emotional interactions, such as sarcasm, insults or aggression, children will learn nothing more than to express and resolve emotion in a dysfunctional manner. For a child, developing emotional intelligence is an important component of learning personal safety skills because it enables the child to identify dysfunctional emotional interactions quickly and cope more effectively with them.

5. Establishing positive discipline
We can establish positive discipline in families by:

- trying to understand people's, particularly our child's, behaviour;
- predicting and planning for difficulties;
- using praise and reinforcement;
- not expecting too much self-control too early;
- ignoring pressure from others;
- controlling our frustration and annoyance.

We can see everyday examples of positive or negative discipline in our local supermarket. Being in a supermarket with a young child usually presents a range of challenges. For our child, a supermarket is a paradise, laden with 'goodies' of all sorts that are freely available. For us, the supermarket is usually 'a hassle'. Our aim is to get in and get out as quickly and as cost-efficiently as possible. As a result of these conflicting viewpoints, the confrontation at the sweets, crisps, minerals or magazine displays is inevitable. The challenge is how we prepare for this eventuality and how we handle it when it occurs.

If our child is young, then we are expecting too much self-control from them if we think they will not want 'goodies'. At their age, it is normal to want to touch and have these treats. Therefore, being able to say 'No' effectively and dealing with the difficult behaviour that ensues is important.

The first step is realising that confrontation is going to occur and planning how to handle it. The next step is to discuss the scenario beforehand with our child and set some parameters for their behaviour: 'If you are good in the supermarket, I will buy you a treat when we are leaving.' It can also be useful to be armed with distractions!

Even if all of these measures fail, the key to positive discipline in the supermarket, or any other public place, is to:

- adhere to what we have agreed in advance. Say to the child: 'Remember what we agreed? Mummy will get you an ice cream when we are leaving';
- never getting angry or losing our temper;
- ignoring pressure from others, whether subtle or obvious, and holding firmly to our strategy. For example, our child starts to scream and kick and everybody in the supermarket is looking. We must not panic or become embarrassed. We need to repeat our agreement, indicating by our body language and actions that, no matter what happens, we are not giving in;
- reinforcing our child every step of the way through praise and reinforcement: 'You are very good for putting that back when I told you to', 'Thank you for getting me the cheese when I asked you', etc.

Establishing positive discipline is an important component of protecting our child because a child who is undisciplined becomes vulnerable to exploitation by others.

6. Developing good family awareness
Introspection and awareness are best developed within families by:

- talking openly within the family about the family, its good and bad points;
- reinforcing the healthy aspects of the family;

- challenging the unhealthy components of the family;
- being committed to working for the family and adapting to change.

Dealing with challenges to our family is one way of measuring how good our family awareness is. Challenge can come at various times and in various ways. One of the most common is the 'well you do it, so why can't I?' challenge. For example, your child curses, you chastise him for it and he replies nonchalantly, 'Well you say "f**k" when you are angry'. An incident like this is a good example of the family being asked to look in on itself. The implication of the challenge is that a parent is demanding one kind of behaviour and demonstrating another.

How family members deal with this type of challenge reflects their level of family awareness. If the parents accept the challenge and use it as an opportunity to assess the inconsistency of their parenting, then it is positive. We can accept this type of challenge through honesty and perhaps humour, acknowledging that there is an inconsistency and committing to everyone trying to change their behaviour for the better. If parents become defensive or pull rank, however, it reflects a poorly developed family awareness. When awareness is very poorly developed, it does not permit challenge to parents and in this context creates an environment in which parents become all-powerful. This dynamic not only places children at risk but is also not conducive to allowing parenting to evolve within an ever-changing environment.

Of course, most families strive to create such an environment by seeking to implement all of the components of the healthy family and avoiding the factors that create an unhealthy family. Nonetheless, in many families the unhealthy factors will arise from time to time as a result of difficulties, stressors or apathy. The important thing is that the family, or somebody within the family, identifies and works to address these negative factors when they arise, ensuring they do not culminate in a dangerous, unhealthy environment for the children.

In some families, the negative factors become so enmeshed that it is very hard for the family, or individuals within the family, to identify or change them. These families often need outside assistance to enable them to break the negative dynamic.

However healthy our family is, ensuring our child is kept safe within our family involves a personal commitment to doing what is best for our child plus a personal commitment to a child-centred approach to parenting. Alongside implementing the parenting skills identified in Chapter 1, we need to be committed to prioritising our child's needs and, when necessary, to be courageous for our child. For many of us this involves overcoming the personal, psychological barriers of low self-confidence and self-esteem which were ingrained in us as children. This issue is dealt with in more detail in Chapter 10.

Shared parenting, where possible, is a vital component in creating a safe family environment for our child, allowing both parents to challenge and to support each other. In the absence of one parent, constructive supports for the lone parent become vital in providing a reliable source of challenge and reinforcement.

Anna's story: An unsafe family environment

Anna's first memory of trouble was when she was six years old and her father came home from the pub one night very drunk. He beat her mother so badly that the neighbours called the Garda Síochána, who came to the house and took her father away.

From that point on she recalls many other nights when her father and mother were drunk and screaming and hitting each other. Her mother and father never got up early in the morning, so she and her sister had to get themselves to school.

Anna remembers being very frightened of her father and worrying that he would kill her mother, as he regularly threatened to do. Her mother was often absent from the house for days at a time, and Anna later discovered that she was with her sister, having received a particularly bad beating from her husband.

When she was aged eight, Anna's father started coming into her bedroom late at night when he returned from the pub. He would get into her bed and begin sexually abusing her.

When her mother had a nervous breakdown, Anna and her sister went to live with their aunt for a short period. When she was thirteen, Anna's father came into her bed one night and she began to scream at him and told him to get out. This was the last time he tried to abuse her, although she later discovered that he had already begun to abuse her younger sister. At fifteen years of age Anna dropped out of school and went to live with her aunt. Two years later she moved to Scotland, where she later married.

When aged forty-two, her sister told her that she was bringing charges against their father for abusing her and that she wanted Anna to also bring charges, which she later did. When asked why she had not reported the abuse earlier, Anna said that she had buried the abuse deep in her mind because this was the only way she could cope with what had happened to her.

When asked about her family, she said that her abiding memory as a child was feeling scared and anxious all of the time. She said that as a child she hated her father and felt she had to protect her mother. During the investigation, Anna's teachers and neighbours all said that it was obvious the family was having problems, but none of them felt it was their place to interfere. Anna said that while the abuse she experienced as a child was bad, the worst part of her childhood was not having any parents.

Chapter 4

Keeping Our Child Safe in Crèche, in Day Care and with the Childminder

Crèche, day care and childminding are relatively new concepts in Ireland. Twenty years ago, few children were cared for outside their family home because very few mothers worked outside the family home. Where the mother did work, the children were usually cared for by other family members. But Irish society has changed radically over the past decade and the majority of parents now choose, or find it necessary, to work outside the home. As a result, a dedicated crèche, day care and childminding sector has emerged.

Up until quite recently, this sector had been informal and unregulated. Many facilities were small and casually run, with little or no regulations or agreed standards of practice. Many of those running these facilities had little or no formal training. Within the last ten years, however, the government has introduced regulations governing this sector. The regulations require all staff working in day-care facilities to be vetted by the Gardaí Síochána. There is now also an obligation on those establishing day-care centres to notify their local Health Services Executive, which in turn is obliged to conduct inspections of these facilities. In addition, organisations aimed at promoting and improving standards have been established.

Despite these developments, the relative newness of the sector and the lack of adequate resourcing has made it difficult both to promote and to monitor standards. Due to the myriad demands on the Health Services Executive Inspectorate, there are significant delays in inspecting facilities. Of those premises that have been inspected, some do not adhere to even the most basic standards. As well as this, some facilities still operate within the 'black market economy', making them very difficult to monitor.

It is within this context that parents find themselves having to entrust their child to the care of others while they work – one of the most important decisions they will make as parents. It is generally accepted that the first four years of a child's life are among the most important for his/her development, so where, with whom and how our child spends his/her time during these first four years will have a significant impact on his/her emotional, social and intellectual development.

For most parents, finding somebody to care for our child while we work is not easy. Most crèche and day-care facilities are expensive and it is hard to know how to distinguish the good ones from the bad. Locating a suitable childminder is also difficult and, again, it is very hard to assess how good or bad a childminder might be. Parents can sometimes arrange for a relative to look after their child, but such arrangements can also have disadvantages given the delicate dynamics that operate within many families.

Ensuring that our child is safe when being cared for by another person is not just about preventing abuse, it is also about being sure that our child's development and welfare are not compromised by the type of care he/she receives.

WHAT DO WE KNOW ABOUT CHILD ABUSE IN PRE-SCHOOL OR DAY-CARE FACILITIES?

Research from the US and UK tells us that the risk of child abuse within nursery settings is considerably lower than the risk to which children are exposed in their own homes. Child abuse statistics in Ireland do not specifically identify abuse occurring in pre-schools or in day-care facilities because the SAVI report did not specifically identify day-care settings when examining reported abuse. Similarly, official statistics released by the Health Services Executive relating to child abuse do not create a separate category for abuses occurring in day-care settings. To date, no high-profile cases of child abuse in pre-schools or in day-care facilities have come to light in Ireland.

While no relevant statistics are available for the Irish context, other information available to us suggests that abuse can and does occur in pre-schools and day-care centres. There is evidence from the US, the UK, Sweden and New Zealand of circumstances in which persons with a disposition or desire to abuse children have deliberately targeted early-years settings and carried out multiple abuses within them. For example, in the UK in the early 1990s a male nursery student was convicted of abusing sixty children while on placement. During the 1980s in Michigan, USA, in what became known as the McMartin case, the husband of the director of a day-care centre was prosecuted for the suspected abuse of several children. When the case finally went to court, he was found not guilty. The chief prosecutor asserted that he was guilty, but had 'gained from a ponderous legal system'. Some of the jurors involved in the case later claimed that the case fell mainly because they thought the children had been led into making incriminating statements by the psychologists and other interviewers at the therapy centre at which they attended. In 1997, in Sweden, a male member of staff in a day-care centre admitted sexually abusing six children. In the 1990s in Christchurch, New Zealand, a male crèche worker, who had worked in a state-run crèche for five years and was said to be well liked by parents and children, was found guilty on sixteen charges of sexual assault/child abuse.

David Finkelhor – a leading international expert on child protection – and Linda Williams published research in 1988 on a review of 270 cases of sexual abuse in nursery settings and found that, in a certain number of cases, the abuse was committed in an organised fashion by visitors to care facilities as well as by staff. The abuse, including physical, sexual and emotional abuse, was sometimes perpetuated by single individuals and in other cases by more than one member of the care staff, or even family members of staff.

Dr Helen Buckley, a leading academic in the child protection field in Ireland, has examined types of child abuse that can occur in pre-school and day-care settings and provides the following observations:

- neglect within a day-care setting is likely to take the form of poor supervision, failure to pay attention to health and safety requirements, failure to provide adequate stimulation and failure to record, review or address persistent problems, for example the frequency and nature of accidents or mishaps. It could also mean that priority is given to the smooth and efficient running of the centre and the convenience of the staff at the expense of the quality of care provided;

- physical abuse is likely to be in the form of harsh or inappropriate discipline, sometimes rationalised in terms of a 'necessary' behavioural regime, e.g. hitting or otherwise hurting children or deliberately restricting their movement.

Research conducted in the USA found that physical abuse in day-care settings can also include more violent behaviour, such as shaking, biting and burning, most of which is precipitated by particular events, such as children fighting with each other, persistent crying that does not diminish even after efforts to comfort, conflict over mealtimes and toilet accidents. The research outlines that in these situations the carers held unrealistic expectations about the children's behaviour.

It was also found that emotional abuse or neglect in day-care settings can be associated with discipline, for example humiliating or belittling children, using sarcasm or isolating them as a means of punishment. This form of abuse is sometimes inflicted through the attitudes of care staff, who may be insensitive, racist or indifferent to the emotional needs of the children in their care. Sexual abuse in pre-school and day-care facilities can vary along a continuum of unacceptable behaviour – from inappropriate play and touching or fondling to serious and gross sexual assault.

In Ireland, the Health Services Executive started publishing *Child Care Facilities Inspection Reports* in 2005 and since then some extremely poor facilities have been identified. Some of the practices and conditions identified in these facilities was so bad, many observers considered it tantamount to abuse. Complaints documented included cases of children left wandering in public places, the administering of physical and emotional punishment, lack of proper supervision within the child-care settings and a failure to meet basic health and safety measures.

David Finkelhor and Linda Williams point out that while reports of child maltreatment involving day-care centers and foster-care homes have attracted a great deal of attention and created the perception that abuse is commonplace in these out-of-home settings, this perception seems out of line with the facts.

Statistics based on a survey conducted in the USA in 1997 by the National Committee to Prevent Child Abuse indicate that reports of abuse in day-care centers, foster homes or other institutional care settings represented about 3 per cent of all substantiated cases for that year. (This information is based on statistics from eighteen US states.) In a more recent study in Pennsylvania, in 2006, from a total of 4,125 substantiated cases of child abuse, there were 218 cases of abuse in day-care settings. In the *Canadian Incidence Study of Reported Child Abuse and Neglect,* conducted in 2003, there were no substantiated cases of child abuse in day-care settings in that year.

One of the difficulties faced by parents is understanding or defining what constitutes abuse to young children. Is it abusive to force a very young child to eat his/her lunch on their own because they make such a mess? If a child is tied into a baby chair for the entire day, is that child abuse? Whatever chance there is of a school-aged child being able to identify or tell about abuse, there is little chance that a pre-school child will be able to do either.

What is clear is that while child abuse by child carers might be relatively rare, when it does occur it can be extremely damaging to the children involved. Therefore, making the right decisions about day care is vital.

ASSESSING ALTERNATIVE CARE OPTIONS
When making decisions about what type of alternative care is best for our child, there are a number of important factors that we must keep in mind.

1. Age and personality
Different types of care will suit different types of children. When considering alternative care for our child, we need to consider our child's age, maturity, position in the family and personality.

Age: The younger our child is, the more important it is that he/she receives one-to-one care. For this reason it is important that parents wait as long as possible before returning to work after the birth of a child. When parents are placing very young babies into alternative care, it is best if a good one-to-one care situation can be arranged. The older a child is when being placed in alternative care, the better he/she is able to cope with group care, such as nurseries, crèches and playschools.

Maturity: The maturity of a child is also an important factor when choosing alternative care. Can our child speak, walk, play with other children, share or feed themselves? Is our child toilet-trained? For young babies who cannot do any of these things for themselves, one-to-one care is important. For an older child who can do some or many of these things for him/herself, group care can be effective.

Position in the family: Whether our child is an only child, an eldest child, a youngest child or a middle child is an important factor in choosing the most suitable alternative care for him/her. An only child might benefit from a group care situation where there is an opportunity to interact with other children; a middle child from a large family might benefit from a one-to-one care situation, receiving personal attention. In situations where there is more than one child, parents need to try to balance the needs of each of the children and choose a care option that best meets all of their needs.

Personality: The type of person a child is will also be important when choosing alternative care. A quiet, insecure child might benefit from one-to-one care, while a lively, outgoing child might do better in group care.

Ultimately, however, no matter how young he/she is, a child will indicate through his/her behaviour or words the type of person he/she is and what he/she is ready for. If they give themselves time, parents are best placed to understand the type of person their child is and the type of care that will best suit him/her.

2. Carer's motivation for providing the childminding service
It is important for us to assess *why* a person is interested in providing care for our child. We need to be sure that a large part of the person's motivation is an interest and commitment to our child, or children in general, and a desire to look after and nurture children. We should always be wary of people whose motivations are vague, unclear or solely for monetary gain. If the person we choose to care for our child is not a family member, it is important to ensure that he/she understands the boundaries of their role and is not seeking in any way to resolve his/her own emotional issues or needs.

3. Developmental progress
The goal for us in finding a suitable carer for our child is to find somebody who will facilitate and contribute to the growth of our

child's self-esteem and personal autonomy. This will best be achieved through valuing our child as an individual, valuing our child's contribution and work and through praise for efforts as well as for achievements.

Carers who see their role as simply minding or caring for the physical needs of our child will not benefit our child, nor will they provide a safe environment. Our child will thrive if nurtured in a holistic environment, where there is a balanced range of activities that meet his/her developmental needs. There should be adequate opportunities for:

- sensory and imaginative play, e.g. play with sand, water, clay, toy kitchens, houses, dolls, etc.;
- story and reading times;
- sleep and rest times;
- properly supervised outdoor activities, i.e. visits to parks, playgrounds, etc.;
- creative activities, such as dance, drama, singing;
- free play opportunities;
- sports activities, e.g. skipping, chasing, ball games, etc.;
- exploratory play for younger children, e.g. crawling, toddling, hiding, rolling, etc.

4. Quality of interaction with our child

One of the most important factors to consider when choosing a care option is the relationship between the carer and our child. With relatives, this can be easy to assess, whereas with more formal care, such as crèches, nurseries and non-family childminders, it can be more difficult. The quality of interaction between our child and the carer will be the single most important factor that influences how our child will develop within that setting. Aside from the core features that any good carer should demonstrate towards children, i.e. respect, love, tolerance, positive discipline and communication, another important factor will be the 'personality fit' between the carer and our child.

Assessing the interaction between our child and a carer will involve not only carefully interviewing the carer and hearing from others who have used the carer, but also observing our child with the carer. How a carer interacts with other children in his/her care or with his/her own children will give us a very good indication of how they are likely to interact with our child. All of this takes time and agreement and co-operation from the carer, but it is essential if we are to make the right decision.

5. Quality of interaction with parents
How a carer interacts and relates to parents is also an important factor to be aware of and to assess. Like a good family, open, honest communication, mutual respect, good problem-solving strategies and a shared parenting ethos are important features in the parent–carer relationship. Where there is secrecy, disrespect, conflict or unresolved parenting differences, our child will be disadvantaged.

6. Quality of interaction with other staff members
If there are other staff members working in the caring environment, the relationship between them is crucial in creating a positive environment for our child. The atmosphere and caring environment should contain the same characteristics as a healthy family, otherwise our child's welfare will be compromised.

7. Experience, qualifications and recruitment policies
While the person we select to care for our child does not have to have a professional qualification, it is important to know what experience he/she has in caring for children. With family members, this is usually easy to assess, but it can be harder with some childminders. It is important to ask carers specifically what their experience is and to seek information from others who know them or have used their services in the past.

In group-care situations, such as crèches and nurseries, it is important that some, if not all, of the staff hold recognised professional qualifications, and that the ratio of qualified to unqualified staff is reasonable. It is also important to ensure that there are practice guidelines and child-protection guidelines operating within the facility and that these are made available to parents.

Most importantly of all, perhaps, is the need to ensure that the person we choose to care for our child, and anybody else working or living in the caring facility, has been checked by the Garda Síochána to ensure they do not have a known history of being a risk to children.

8. Physical environment

The physical environment in which our child is being cared for is an important factor to consider and to assess. We need to ensure there is:

- healthy, nutritious food given to the children;
- adequate feeding arrangements, i.e. babies are fed one at a time by the same person, older children have an eating area and, if necessary, are helped when eating;
- adequate, child-friendly toilet and nappy-changing facilities;
- no overcrowding, poor hygiene or health and safety hazards;
- adequate play areas;
- no hazards existing around or near the facility in which our child is being cared for, i.e. dangerous building works, busy roads, lakes, etc.;
- the staff to child ratio is reasonable and the facility is not too big.

It is also important to know if people other than the carer have access to the facility. For example, in the case of childminders caring for our child in their own house, it is important that we know who else is in the house and who else might have contact with our child.

9. Informing the appropriate local authorities

Those running crèches, pre-schools, playgroups and nurseries are required to notify the local authorities of the existence of their service and the authority can conduct inspections of the facilities as and when it chooses. It is important for us to check with our local authorities that the carer we choose is registered.

There are also various organisations that promote standards in pre-schools, playgroups, nurseries and childminding facilities. It is important to check that the carer we are choosing is a member of such an organisation. Many of these organisations produce guidelines and standards which are available to parents and should be read before choosing a care facility.

It is important to remember that the best way for us to ensure our child does not experience any form of abuse or trauma while being cared for by another person is to ensure that we seek the very best care available.

IDENTIFYING ABUSE

Most crèches, playgroups, pre-schools and childminders provide a safe and secure environment for children. In some facilities, however, children do not have positive experiences, and in a small number of others they are at risk of being subjected to abuse. Due to the young age of most of the children in such facilities, they are particularly vulnerable to abuse because they would find it very difficult to tell anybody if they were being abused.

Many children attending care facilities will be too young to speak. Those who are able to speak will not be advanced enough to be able to discuss complex things, like how they are feeling, and will not have the vocabulary to describe bad or hurtful things they may be experiencing. For this reason, with younger children child protection involves monitoring and being responsive to their behaviour because although they have not yet developed the capacity to express emotions clearly, they will use behaviour to express themselves. How children behave and interact with their parents, with alternative care workers and with other children illustrates how they are feeling. Unhappiness, sadness and insecurity will be expressed and evident in their interactions.

How would we know if the care facility in which we have placed our child is unsafe? How could we tell if the carer with whom we entrusted our child is abusing our child? There are a number of indicators to be aware of.

- **Developmental problems:** One indication that our child is unhappy, stressed or traumatised is the emergence of problems in his/her development. A delay in talking or walking and eating difficulties, including unwillingness to eat, and over-activity/non-focused behaviour are all indications that our child's development is being interrupted or blocked by something. Of course, there could be many explanations for such delays, but when they arise, we should not rule out the possibility that they are resulting from unhappiness or trauma of some kind.
- **Expressions of unhappiness:** Although most young children will find it difficult to express their unhappiness verbally, they will often have the ability to say things that will give us a general impression that things are not right. We need to listen carefully to what our child says to us and follow up on even the smallest of issues. This way we will ensure that we pick up on things that are

serious and worrying, as well as things that are not so serious but that may be very important to our child.

- **Interaction with parents:** If our child is experiencing unhappiness, stress or trauma, this will inevitably impact on his/her relationship with us. Our child will want us to know that he/she is unhappy. So if our child:
    + begins to show excessive difficulty separating from us, or a sudden lack of attachment to us,
    + becomes excessively aggressive, compliant or withdrawn,
    + becomes overly upset or appears fearful when attending the caring facility,

  we need to find out why this is occurring.

Remember, children want to be loved and they want to please their parents, so if their behaviour starts to become difficult or problematic, there is always a reason.

- **Interaction with other children:** Another indication that our child could be unhappy, traumatised or stressed is difficulties arising in his/her interactions with other children. Such difficulties might include over-aggressive behaviour, overly compliant behaviour, inappropriate/over-sexualised play, periods of detachment or a reluctance/withdrawal from interactions with others. Again, when these difficulties arise there may be many explanations for them, but it is important for us to assess and explore what might be causing them.

- **Interaction with care staff:** If our child is experiencing difficulties within the caring environment, these difficulties will emerge in the interactions he/she has with the carer. If we find our child becoming inappropriately or overly attached to a carer, or carers, or excessively compliant towards a carer, we need to assess why this might be happening. If we find our child is particularly fearful of a carer or of something in the caring environment, or appears to have a lack of attachment to the carer, we should be concerned. Similarly, if the carer appears to be apathetic towards our child, is consistently frustrated/angry/disappointed or generally negative towards our child or lacks basic understanding of our child's needs, we should be concerned.

Remember, our child has a right to be happy when being cared for by others and we have a right to be confident that our child is receiving the best care possible. While there can be many factors that can cause our child to be unhappy or traumatised, we need to be sure that the carer to whom we have entrusted our child is not the cause.

WHAT CAN I DO TO PROTECT MY CHILD?
As with all forms of risk to children, the best way for us to safeguard our child is to be consistently vigilant. However, there are also a number of practical principles we should keep in mind when choosing a care option for our child.

1. The older our child is when placed in alternative care, the better
In general, the longer we can care for our child ourselves, the safer and more secure our child will be. Of course, there are many factors that impact on our ability to care for our child ourselves, e.g. financial and career considerations, our willingness and ability to parent and the availability, willingness and capability of a second parent to share in the parenting. However, unless a parent is a threat to his/her child or is emotionally incapable of parenting, a child will not only be better cared for in their own parents' care, but will also benefit emotionally and psychologically. In addition, the older a child is when entering an alternative care environment, the better he/she will be able to cope with this new setting. We should therefore seek to:

- take as much maternity and paternity leave as possible. Remember, no parent looks back on their baby's lives and wishes they had returned to work earlier;
- take as much unpaid leave as you can when the children are young;
- negotiate to work the shortest day possible for as long as possible. Parents should not feel guilty about working as short a day as possible if it means spending more time with their children;
- Expect, and demand, to be treated differently by your employer. Whenever the opportunity presents itself to work from home, take it, and take all your leave and request extra days if they are available;
- involve your child in as much of your lives as possible: bring him/her shopping with you, involve them in household chores, bring them with you when visiting friends, etc.

Remember, childhood is shorter than you think. As children grow up they will be happy to, and will want to, spend more and more time away from their parents. We need to enjoy and make the most of the times when they want to be with us.

2. Listening to our child

Actively listening to what our child is telling us through both his/her language and behaviour is the most effective way to ensure our child is kept safe. Often, what may seem silly or childish to us is actually our child's way of telling us something very important. Behaviour that we find annoying or irritating can in fact be telling us that something is not right. At all times, what is important to our child needs to be important to us.

One good example of this is when our child challenges us about why he/she must go to a carer. This challenge usually comes at a time when we least want to hear it, or are least able to cope with it. 'Mummy, why can't I stay home with you like Sophie does with her mum? Why do you have to go to work? Why can't you stay with me? I don't want to go!' This verbal challenge can be accompanied by crying, tantrums or clinginess. Our child might start refusing to go into the care setting or become upset at night before bed, saying that he/she does not want to go to the care setting the following morning.

Almost all parents who place their children in alternative care are presented with this difficulty at some stage. What is important is how we listen to and respond to this complaint. The best way is to try our best to empathise with our child, i.e. to see things from his/her perspective. If we can do this, we can work out how best to deal with the situation. We need to be brave enough to explore *exactly* why our child does not want to go to the carer. We may find that what is upsetting our child relates to something that is happening in the care setting or something that is happening at home. This might be something small that can be fixed easily or something more complex that requires more work.

Exploring the problem might present us with a greater difficulty, however: we might find that our child is simply missing us and is becoming aware of what he/she is missing by not being with us. What our child might be doing is challenging our life choice, saying that he/she does not like this particular choice. How we respond to this will depend on our options. Some of us might opt to change our life choices either permanently or temporarily. We might decide to take time off work until our child has gone to school, to give up work altogether or start to work part-time. Some of us may not be in a position to do this, however. We might need to discuss with our child why the situation is as it is, then try to find ways to make it easier for our child to accept.

Our response to this issue is determined by a lot of factors, but the important point is that we are prepared to listen, to empathise and to understand how our child is feeling. If we become defensive and close down communication with our child when this challenge is made, we not only deny him/her the opportunity to be heard and understood, we also discourage him/her from telling us about things that are upsetting or difficult to hear.

3. Communication with the carer

Consistent communication with a carer is crucial to ensuring our child receives good care and adequate protection. Many carers encourage regular communication, but others avoid it because they feel it adds to the pressures of the job. It can happen that parents feel lucky to have obtained a particular carer for their child or a place in a particular care facility and are therefore reluctant to ask questions or to communicate their wishes.

Parents can also feel intimidated by the expertise of the carer. It is important to remember that while the carer may have professional knowledge, as parents we have the most important knowledge about our individual child. It is through the sharing of this knowledge that our child will benefit most. For example, we should ensure that:

- at least once a week we have some discussion with our child's carer about what is happening on a day-to-day basis, i.e. important events occurring at home or in the care setting, news, special events and upsets that our child has experienced during the week;
- at least once a month we have a formal meeting with the carer to discuss our child and how he/she is changing and developing. Such a meeting should involve a sharing of information and knowledge and we should be prepared to challenge and to be challenged;
- there is a formal process of mutual feedback established between the carer and ourselves, where we discuss both positive and

negative feedback about how the caring arrangement is progressing and how well we are communicating with each other;
• at least once every three months we spend some time in the care setting with our child, or accompany our child on a trip with the carer/carers.

It is important that we do not get into the habit of communicating with our child's carer only when there is a problem. A constructive channel of communication must be established that discusses all aspects of our child's welfare.

4. Agreed parenting strategy

If our child is to be secure and safe, he/she needs to receive consistent parenting. The parenting approach being used in the alternative care environment needs to be the same as our parenting approach. In particular, we need to agree with the carer about the important components of parenting, about how we discipline our child, how we support and reward our child and how we communicate with our child. A common parenting strategy will benefit our child greatly.

The question of how to deal with discipline is perhaps one of the most important components of parenting that we need to agree with our child's carer. For our child, learning about discipline is key to his/her healthy development. We need to decide how we are going to discipline our child, then we need to ensure that our child's carer agrees to this approach. This should be quite easy if we are dealing with an individual carer who is prepared to take direction from us. It becomes more difficult if we are dealing with a number of carers, as in a crèche or nursery situation, where there might already be an established disciplinary regime in place, or where there might be great variance between the carers within the facility.

Dealing with this issue should be made easier by our initial assessment of and decisions about the facility we have chosen for our child. It is also made easier if the facility is a registered facility that adheres to established regulations and guidelines defining the importance of positive discipline and the unacceptability of punishment-based discipline. Nonetheless, it is still very important that we discuss and agree a disciplinary strategy with our child's carer and ensure that policies are followed through into practice.

If our child's carer is good at his/her job, we will learn something from him/her about positive discipline. We will be able to co-ordinate our efforts with their efforts, giving our child the benefit of shared care. If we do not agree a disciplinary strategy with the carer, we risk a number of things: our child will inevitably receive mixed messages, may find it difficult to develop self-discipline and, most worrying of all, will become vulnerable to exploitation as a result of the uncertainty and lack of self-discipline.

Although discipline is one of the more important parenting strategies to be agreed with the carer, the real challenge is to have a cohesive parenting strategy so that we can be assured our child obtains the maximum benefits from the shared parenting arrangements.

5. Mutual respect

It is important for our child's well-being that there is mutual respect between us and our child's carer. If we are constantly questioning, criticising or competing with our child's carer, our child will not have confidence in the carer and will become insecure. Similarly, the carer needs to have respect for us and should not involve our child in any conflict or disagreements they might have with us. In this regard, it is worth noting that problems of one kind or another will arise between parents and our child's carer. Instead of striving to avoid such disagreements, we need to work to ensure that the way we resolve these conflicts is healthy and constructive. For example, to attain mutual respect with our child's carer, one of the first obstacles we must overcome is the issue of money. Money can, and often does, characterise our relationship with our child's carer. This relationship is unusual in that it is a business relationship, yet in order to protect our child's welfare it must also be a personal relationship.

Many good childcare arrangements become fraught with tension and bad feeling because of the financial arrangements, e.g. parents believe they are being over-charged or are being charged for time they are not using, while carers feel parents are slow to pay, etc. Even when the arrangement involves family or more informal set-ups, money can cause a problem, e.g. parents not leaving money for food, carers using food money for other things. It is very often the financial arrangements that challenge the mutual respect we need to have.

As in all aspects of the relationship with our child's carer, the financial arrangement must reflect the principles of mutual respect.

We need to be happy that the amount we are paying is fair and we ought to pay on time, without animosity. Similarly, our carer needs to keep the financial dealings absolutely separate from the day-to-day dealings with our child. He/she needs to have a professional attitude towards fee increases, explaining when they are likely and why, and should also ensure that fee increases are not so significant that they impact on the continuity of care. If challenge is necessary, it should occur in a non-emotional manner and our child should not be aware of what is happening.

Although it may seem unrelated to child protection, the financial arrangements with our child's carer can and will compromise our child's welfare if it is a source of tension or animosity. If such feelings exist, our child will be aware of them and will feel conflicted and confused.

6. Demand the best

To ensure our child is kept safe and to reduce the possibility of our child experiencing any form of abuse while being cared for by somebody else, it is important that we demand the best care for our child. Settling for less than the best compromises our child's welfare and provides the potential for an abusive environment. Yet demanding the best from a carer is perhaps one of the most difficult things for parents to do. Nonetheless, it should start when choosing the carer and should continue throughout the caring relationship.

In reality, most parents' childcare choices are limited by financial considerations or availability. But even where choices are limited, it is important that we invest in obtaining the best option for our child, not the only available option. We should try and remember that:

- the easiest option is not always the best option;
- good childcare does not necessarily have to be the most expensive;
- even if our child's carer is a family member, we still need to expect and demand high standards;
- once we choose a carer, it is very hard to change;
- facilities that are not registered with the Health Authorities should be avoided;
- while 'black economy' arrangements might seem attractive, they do not facilitate accountability or high standards and place us in a compromised position;

- child carers and childcare facilities change over time, so we need to ensure that we continually monitor standards;
- we need to continually invest in the relationship with our child's carer.

Financial pressures and life demands place immense pressure on us, forcing us to make many compromises. However, we *cannot* compromise on choosing a carer for our child.

What do we do if we discover there is a problem?

When we become worried about our child's welfare or become aware of the fact that our child might be experiencing abuse, it is important to take immediate action to ensure our child is safe. What form this action takes will depend on the type of concern we have and the type of risk to which we believe our child is exposed. It is extremely important not to act rashly.

Before taking any action, we need to reassure and support our child and make sure that he/she knows and understands that he/she has done nothing wrong. We need to try to discuss the situation in an age-appropriate way with our child, listening to what he/she thinks should be done and explaining to him/her what we are going to do and why.

In some instances, it will be enough to discuss the situation with the carer and resolve what is making our child unhappy. Where we have serious concerns for our child's safety, however, we need to remove our child from the carer's jurisdiction and discuss our concerns with the appropriate authorities.

Usually we get on well with our child's carer, and cannot contemplate that he/she, or somebody in the caring environment, would hurt our child. It is often the case that our child has formed an attachment to the carer and therefore will become upset if the caring arrangement is altered in any way. It is important to remember that our primary priority is our child's welfare and that it comes before any of our personal relationships or friendships. Whatever action we decide to take, it is necessary to keep our child informed, in an age-appropriate manner, and to ensure we support him/her through any changes our actions might necessitate.

Michelle's story: Assessing the care environment

Arriving early one evening to pick up her son, Rory, from the crèche, Michelle was surprised to find that he was not in the playroom where he usually was. Antoinette, the care worker, seemed embarrassed when she noticed Michelle and said that Rory was in the toilet. Antoinette brought Rory in from the toilet and he looked like he had been crying. Michelle was in a hurry, so she did not have time to discuss Rory's red eyes with Antoinette, but as she walked to the car she asked Rory if he was okay. Rory said he was, but nonetheless seemed quiet. Michelle let the incident drop because Rory quickly became distracted with the book she had bought him.

Later that evening, Peter, Rory's father, mentioned to Michelle that he felt Rory was becoming more tearful at bedtime and that it was getting harder to get him asleep. He felt that Rory would have to start going to sleep earlier, as he used to do, because he was four and was starting school next year. The following morning, Rory started to cry the minute his mother put him into the car to take him to the crèche. He sobbed all the way there, saying he wanted to go to work with her. While there had been other times when he did not want to go into the crèche, this upset was different.

On arriving in the crèche, Michelle told Antoinette that Rory was upset and did not want to go in, but Antoinette reassured her that he would be fine. Michelle was uneasy for the entire day in work. She rang the crèche twice and was told Rory was fine. That evening, when she was collecting Rory, she met one of the other parents and in conversation mentioned that Rory had been very upset going into the crèche that morning. The parent at first did not seem to want to discuss the issue, but then told Michelle that although it might be nothing, her daughter had told her that 'teacher had left Rory in the toilet for a long time because he was a bold boy'.

Michelle was furious and confronted Antoinette, who said that Rory had bitten another child and that as a punishment they had put him into the toilet. Antoinette explained that biting another child could not be tolerated and that Rory could not continue to attend the crèche if he continued to bite. When Michelle asked how long Rory had been put into the toilet for, Antoinette was vague. Michelle was very upset leaving the crèche, but was not sure what to do.

That evening, Michelle received a phone call from Paula, one of the other workers in the crèche. She was upset and said that she wanted to tell Michelle that she had put Rory into the toilet the day before for biting the other child, but that she had then taken a break and had forgotten that Rory was in the toilet. She said that Rory had spent most of the afternoon in the toilet and was only taken from the toilet when Michelle had arrived to collect him.

Michelle rang five parents who had children attending the crèche to discuss with them what had happened. Each of the parents expressed different concerns about things that had happened in the crèche, ranging from staff shouting at each other in front of the children, a staff member grabbing and shaking a child, and one child being called 'pooy pants' because he was not toilet-trained.

Michelle decided to remove Rory from the crèche and the next day, having discussed what had happened with a friend, informed the local health authority. Three months later, following an inspection by the local health authority, the crèche was closed down. Having interviewed staff, the health authority discovered that in addition to the issues complained about by parents, on many occasions children had not been given lunch as punishment and that at many times during the day there was only one staff member supervising the children.

Chapter 5
Keeping Safe in School

Our children will spend approximately one-third of their childhoods in school and the experiences they have there will impact immensely on their development. In particular, our children's experiences in school will have a major bearing on how they view themselves socially and intellectually and will often determine if they believe they are clever, good at achieving things and popular. Furthermore, their experiences in school teach them how to get on with others, how to work and how to compete.

Most schools provide good educational experiences for children. All schools are governed by standards developed by educational authorities and are subjected to inspections to check that these standards are being met. Most schools have procedures governing discipline, child protection, health and safety and teaching practice. Most schools seek to employ good-quality teachers and most teachers are committed, dedicated professionals who seek to do the best they can for their pupils. Parents have a say in the running of most schools through the Parents' Council and the Board of Management, and in many schools pupils have a say through the Student Council.

In spite of everyone's best efforts, there are still risks for children in school. In an environment where so many adults and children interact on a daily basis, difficulties will arise. In addition, some schools, for a variety of reasons, do not provide a safe environment for children. For this reason, it is very important that the schools to which we send our children are safe and provide the best opportunity for them to achieve their potential.

RISKS IN SCHOOL

There are four main risks that arise in school for our children:

- bullying or abuse by other pupils;
- abuse by an adult working in the school;
- self-abuse;
- our children bullying or abusing other children within the school.

Bullying

Within a school, our children can be at risk of being bullied by other children or by teachers. Bullying of children by other children probably occurs in all schools and is best described as the continuous physical, verbal or psychological intimidation of one child by another child or by a group of children. Bullying of children by teachers can also occur, particularly when teachers do not have the ability to keep control or teach. Bullying can take many different forms, ranging from physically hurting a child to continually 'slagging' or calling a child names or excluding a child. Bullying can impact on our children's physical and emotional well-being and on their educational and social development.

The dynamics underpinning bullying within schools are complex and involve the personal, emotional and psychological problems of the perpetrator, the psychological make-up of the victim and the school environment, which facilitates the abuse or bullying.

Abuse by teachers, other staff or other children

As in all situations where children are entrusted to the care of adults, there will always be a small number of adults who will exploit this trust. A school will be an attractive environment for a person wishing to hurt or abuse a child. The abuse of children by teachers or other staff can take many forms, including sexual exploitation, physical abuse and intimidation or exclusion of a child. Due to the position of authority and trust any adult holds in a school, it makes it easier for them to exploit a child and harder for a child to disclose when they have been exploited.

Although not as common an occurrence as abuse by adults, older children can sometimes sexually or physically abuse younger children within a school. Stark examples of this would be where a sixth-year student pressurises a first year into engaging in sexual activity, or where a much older child physically assaults a younger child. The difficulty with this form of abuse is that children may not see it as abuse and are therefore less likely to disclose it. For example, a young girl being sexually assaulted by an older student might believe they are in a relationship.

Self-abuse

Within a school environment, a child can begin to self-abuse for a variety of reasons. Self-abuse can take a number of different forms, as are outlined in Chapter 8. Self-abuse within school can take the form of getting into trouble with teachers deliberately or excluding oneself from other children in the school. What is important for parents to remember is that behaviour that we view as disruptive or bold may be an indicator that our child is self-abusing and has begun not to care about him/herself. The actions of self-abuse are often underpinned by feelings of insecurity, anger, sadness or despair.

Abuse or bullying of other children by our children

Children bully or abuse other children for a variety of psychological and emotional reasons. Sometimes they feel insecure, inadequate or humiliated and want to take out their anger, frustration or sadness on somebody else. Sometimes they may have been abused in some way themselves, or are being scapegoated or bullied somewhere else. Sometimes they feel under pressure of some kind, perhaps to succeed. Sometimes they feel they don't fit in with others, or they expect everyone to do what they say because they like the feeling of power. For a variety of reasons, our children can sometimes abuse or bully others in school.

HOW COMMON IS ABUSE IN SCHOOLS?
Bullying

It is only in the last fifteen years that the problems of violence and bullying in Irish schools have begun to be recognised and addressed. Recently, we have seen a growing body of research and growing public awareness of this issue. This has led to changes in educational policy, with a variety of different guidelines being published, such as *Guidelines on Countering Bullying Behaviour* (1993) and *Guidelines on Violence in Schools* (1999). Following the publication of a report examining student behaviour in second-level schools, a number of new measures have been announced to assist schools in dealing with behavioural difficulties, including:

• new regional behaviour support teams to work with schools that have significant discipline problems;
• behaviour support classrooms to be piloted in schools.

There have also been various pieces of legislation passed, including the Safety, Health and Welfare at Work Act 1989 and the Education (Welfare) Act 2000. Bullying is also being tackled through the SPHE and CSPE courses in schools, while Trinity College Dublin has established a specialised unit called the Anti-Bullying Centre: Research and Resource Unit.

The *State of the Nation's Children* report indicates that, according to a study conducted in 2002 called the *Health Behaviour in School-aged Children Survey*, Ireland ranked twenty-seventh among thirty-five WHO countries participating in the study for the percentage of eleven-, thirteen- and fifteen-year-olds reporting that they had been bullied within the last couple of months.

This report indicated that:

• 23 per cent of children reported to have been bullied at school in the last couple of months (the WHO average was 33.5 per cent);
• a higher proportion of boys (26 per cent) reported being bullied than girls (21 per cent);
• there was a consistent downward trend by age in the percentage of children who reported being bullied at school: 28 per cent of children aged ten to eleven reported to have been bullied compared with 18 per cent of fifteen- to seventeen-year-olds.

A nationwide survey conducted in 1997 by Dr Mona O'Moore and her colleagues from the Anti-Bullying Centre provides some indication of the type of bullying and violent behaviour prevalent amongst pupils. Dr O'Moore's studies indicate that:

• bullying involved physical violence (being 'physically hurt e.g., hit and kicked') for 15 per cent of the primary schoolgirl victims, for 32 per cent of the primary schoolboy victims, for 11 per cent of the post-primary girl victims and for 34.5 per cent of the post-primary boy victims;

- besides 'being hit or kicked', other types of physical bullying that appeared in the victims' comments included being spat at or urinated upon, being hit with fruit, having one's head held in the toilet bowl, being kissed against one's will and having one's clothes ripped off. Thirty post-primary pupils reported having been sexually harassed.

In 2006 the ISPCC/Childline service received 5,477 calls and 6,904 automated texts relating to bullying.

In addition to this research, there have also been some distressing, high-profile cases of bullying in Ireland and in other countries. In April 2000 a fourteen-year-old Belfast girl took an overdose in her bedroom and died. She had been a pupil at a local girls' school, and according to her sister had been bullied by another pupil at the school during the last month of her life. Her sister was reported as saying: 'We did know she was being bullied but she led us to believe that she was coping better with it. We had no idea she was in such despair. I don't know how we're going to cope. I'm angry that she has gone, but I'm not blaming anyone.'

Despite the tragedy, teachers at the school had recently won an award for their work in combating bullying. Staff had worked extensively with the young girl and with her family to try to address the bullying situation. The Acting Principal at the school said that the young girl 'was always a popular girl, who had a lot of good friends, and she was a good friend to them'. Following this young girl's suicide, the Northern Ireland Education Minister announced a major study into the causes of school bullying in the region.

In March 2001 a fifteen-year-old Californian high-school student brought a gun to school and shot and killed two schoolmates and wounded thirteen more, as well as several adults. Friends said that he was constantly picked on. One said: 'He was so skinny that some people called him "Anorexic Andy".' His older brother said that he was used to being taunted: 'He has big ears and he's real skinny. People liked to pick on him. It was like that as long as I can remember.' 'He was always getting picked on,' said another friend. 'He's scrawny, he's little. People think he's dumb. Recently, he had two skateboards stolen.' Another teen admitted: 'We abused him pretty much, I mean verbally.'

These cases, while rare, indicate the worst consequences of bullying if it is not addressed.

Physical and emotional abuse in schools

Official child abuse statistics do not specifically identify physical and emotional abuse perpetrated in schools. Over the last number of years, however, there have been numerous revelations of extreme physical violence, under the guise of classroom 'discipline', perpetrated on 'hundreds, if not thousands in the care of religious orders or in State institutions'.

These revelations have highlighted the type of physical and emotional abuse that can be encountered in educational and care settings, such as schools. Many of these instances of abuse dated back to the 1940s, for example those revealed by past residents of Goldenbridge orphanage and industrial schools in the *Dear Daughter* and *States of Fear* television documentaries. But others took place as recently as the 1990s. The 1996 report into Madonna House documented not only sexual abuse, but other practices by staff that failed to meet the emotional and psychological needs of the children in residence there.

In addition to these revelations, a number of recent studies give us some indication of the level of physical violence still existing in schools. In a study conducted by the Anti-Bullying Centre in 1998, it was reported that forty-nine post-primary pupils (out of a total of 1,767 post-primary victims of bullying) reported that they had been bullied/physically assaulted by teachers.

A number of studies also suggest that children, young people and their parents can behave aggressively towards teachers:

- the Irish National Teachers Union found that in 1998 just under 9 per cent of teachers had been victims of physical abuse. In this study, the majority of the perpetrators of the abuse were pupils, with the next most frequent perpetrators of violence towards teachers being parents. In a similar survey amongst second-level teachers, commissioned by the Teachers Union of Ireland, it was found that one in five (21.9 per cent: 9.1 per cent male and 12.6 per cent female) school staff had been bullied in the previous twelve months. Of those teachers who were bullied, 4.8 per cent were bullied by pupils;
- in a similar study, the ASTI found that some 32 per cent of teachers (of whom 42 per cent were female) had suffered physical abuse during their teaching careers (ASTI, 1999). The perpetrators of this abusive behaviour were most commonly pupils and parents.

While the prevalence of emotional abuse by teachers and other educators has not been studied in any great detail in Ireland, some international studies indicate that a proportion of teachers regularly use physical and emotional abuse, in conjunction with other punitive disciplining practices, as a means of exerting control. In *Child Protection: A Guide for Teachers and Child Care Professionals* (1996), Briggs and Hawkins, two Australian researchers, cite studies which found that teachers emotionally abused children by:

- overly restricting access to toilets for very young children;
- threatening to tell parents of a child's misbehaviour or unsatisfactory work;
- rejecting the child or his/her work;
- verbally abusing children, harassing or allowing other children to harass children;
- labelling children as 'uneducable', 'dumb' or 'stupid';
- screaming at children till they cried and providing a 'continuous experience of failure by setting tasks that are inappropriate for their stages of development'.

Briggs and Hawkins describe other 'emotionally abusive' actions recorded in two studies: pinching, shaking and pulling children by the ears; using fear-inducing techniques to control children; and tipping or pulling chairs out from under seated children. Such behaviours would seem to be more appropriately labelled as physical abuse, which highlights the difficulties inherent in developing clear definitions of emotionally abusive acts.

Finally, Briggs and Hawkins also label as emotional abuse the failure of teachers to deal with allegations or suspicions of child maltreatment, along with the experience of bullying by peers.

Sexual abuse

As most official statistics do not identify the profession of those who sexually abuse children or the location in which they are abused, it is difficult to assess the extent of sexual abuse perpetrated by teachers or staff in schools. Often termed 'educator sexual child abuse', the term 'educator' usually refers to any person older than eighteen years who works with or for a school or other educational or learning organisation. Such persons may be paid, unpaid, professional or volunteer and may include teachers, sports coaches, bus drivers, school principals and teacher's aides.

The revelations emerging of sexual abuse in religious and state-run institutions over the last number of years illustrate how vulnerable children can be to sexual abuse within schools. The Irish SAVI report (2002) identified that of those respondents who reported that they had been sexually abused as children, 6.3 per cent identified the perpetrator as a teacher, i.e. 3.9 per cent reported that the perpetrator was a clerical/religious teacher and 2.4 per cent reported that the perpetrator was a non-clerical/religious teacher.

While it is widely acknowledged that 'educator sexual abuse' is woefully understudied internationally, research conducted in the USA and Canada gives us some insight into the risks for children of educator sexual abuse within schools. Defining it as unwanted contact and/or non-contact sexual behaviour by an educator, these studies indicate that:

- 9.6 per cent of students are targets of educator sexual misconduct at some point during their school career. This figure was outlined by Dr Charol Shakeshaft, a professor at Hofstra University in Huntington, New York and a leading national authority on sexual abuse and harassment. It is based on a review of twenty-four international research studies on educator sexual abuse;
- in Canada, research has found that the most common reason why students do not report educator sexual misconduct is fear that they will not be believed. This is because the sexual misconduct takes place in the context of schools, where students are taught to trust teachers and where teachers have more power and status than students.

Other US research has looked at the prevalence of sexual harassment of students in schools, which is defined as unwanted and unwelcome sexual behaviour that interferes with one's life. A study (2001) undertaken by the Harris Interactive Foundation for the American Association of University Women found that 83 per cent of girls and 79 per cent of boys reported that they had been sexually harassed in a school setting. Of those, 18 per cent said the harassment came from an adult who worked in their school; the remainder reported that they experienced harassment by fellow students. Examples of behaviours encountered by the respondents included sexual comments, jokes, gestures or looks; showing the student sexual pictures, photographs or illustrations; writing sexual messages and/or spreading sexual rumours about the student; spying on the student as he/she dressed or showered at school; pulling at clothing in a sexual way, 'flashing'/exposing genitals; rubbing up against and/or touching or grabbing the student in a sexual way; forcing the student to kiss; blocking or cornering student in a sexual way.

In addition to this research, there have also been a growing number of high-profile cases of sexual abuse by teachers in Ireland and other countries. In January 2004 a North Dublin private grinds teacher who introduced young boys to cannabis and pornography and sexually abused them while recording the abuse on video received a suspended four-year sentence. The Garda Síochána said that when giving private lessons to his students, the man gave them drugs and made them watch pornographic videos. The Garda Síochána seized videos of the teacher performing indecent acts on young boys, and he volunteered the names of three victims to the investigating officers. Only one boy was willing to speak to the Gardaí. This boy said that he had taken grinds with this man for his Junior Certificate and that during these grinds the man had sexually abused him. This man had previously taught Maths and Junior Certificate Science in two schools before retiring due to ill health.

In 2002 a California high school teacher ran off to Las Vegas with one of her fifteen-year-old students; in the same year a Louisiana teacher was accused of having an affair with a fourteen-year-old student; a Washington State teacher was convicted of ten counts of sexually exploiting minors by persuading them to pose nude for him and then uploading some of the images to a website.

IDENTIFYING ABUSE IN SCHOOLS

It is not easy to identify abuse within schools. Signs that could indicate that our child is being abused could also indicate lots of other things. However, in addition to the general signs of abuse identified in Chapter 2, there are a number of common indicators related to school that should cause us to be concerned if our child displays them.

The following is a list of the common signs that might arise if our child is experiencing trauma, abuse or unhappiness in school:

- frightened of walking to or from school;
- unwilling to go to school;
- begs parent to drive him/her to school;
- changes route to school;
- begins doing poorly in school work;
- regularly comes home with clothes or books destroyed;
- comes home hungry (because lunch money or lunch was taken);
- becomes withdrawn, starts stammering;
- becomes distressed, stops eating;
- cries him/herself to sleep;
- has nightmares;
- has unexplained bruises, scratches, cuts;
- possessions start going 'missing';
- has possessions or money from unexplained sources;
- asks for money or starts stealing money (to pay the bully);
- continually 'loses' pocket money;
- refuses to say what's wrong;
- gives improbable excuses to explain any of the above;
- engages in self-harm or attempts suicide.

It is important to remember that parents are best placed and usually first to know when their child is unhappy or upset. Any behaviour or moods that are out of character for our children and cannot be explained should be explored with them in order to get to the bottom of what is happening.

WHAT CAN I DO TO PROTECT MY CHILD?
We can safeguard our children in school by:

- making the right decisions when choosing a school;
- involving ourselves in an active way in our children's education, staying vigilant and aware;
- resolving our own school experiences.

ASSESSING SCHOOLS
How do we distinguish good schools from poor schools? Parents often pick a school for their child on the basis that one or other of them attended the school or because another of their children attended or attends the school. Many parents will judge a school solely by overall

academic achievements, while others pick the school simply because it is local. In fact, picking the right school for our child should involve consideration of a number of factors.

Our child's personality

Different schools will suit different children. Some children do very well in schools that are very focused on academic achievements, while others will do better in less academic schools. Some children will respond well to strict discipline, while others will prefer a less tightly controlled regime. Some children will find it difficult to make new friends, others will find it easy.

As a result, knowing our child's personality is the key to picking the right school for him/her. Most parents know the type of person their child is and, with a little bit of thought and consideration, will have a fair idea of the type of environment that will best suit their child. The child's age, social skills and emotional maturity should have a big bearing on the choice of school. For example, younger, quieter children will benefit from a smaller school with the opportunity for more individual attention. Of course, as children get older they will be able to tell us what type of school they feel will best suit them.

Educational Ethos

Our children will benefit most if they receive a rounded education, which includes academic, social and physical education. Most importantly, a good education will help a child to achieve his/her individual potential in these three areas, enhancing his/her sense of self-worth, self-esteem and opinion of him/herself as an achiever.

There is an important distinction to be made here: children should not have to do well academically to feel they are achievers. An over-emphasis on academic achievement or competitiveness in a school is not healthy. The school we choose for our children should have an educational ethos that values different skills, abilities and achievements and seeks to ensure every pupil is valued in his/her own right.

Assessing this ethos in any given school can be difficult, but the task can be made easier by reading all the material available about the school, talking to other children who attend the school, talking to the teachers in the school and talking to other parents who have sent their children to the school. At all times, we must ourselves remember the importance of the various facets of education and not be put off by schools with an all-encompassing ethos just because their students do not reach the higher levels academically or their students exhibit more individualism.

Part of the educational ethos of the school we choose for our child should involve:

- all school staff being vigilant for early signs of distress in pupils, such as deterioration of work, spurious illness, isolation, the desire to remain with adults and erratic attendance. While this behaviour may be symptomatic of other problems, it could be the early signs of bullying or abuse;
- all accessible areas of the school being supervised at break, lunchtime, between lessons and at the end of the day;
- all pupils being actively involved in countering bullying.

It is also worth checking if the school facilitates peer counselling or has a buddy system for new or shy children, as these can be very helpful.

Child-friendly environment

A school that has a child-friendly ethos will be a safer and more secure environment for our child. A school is child-friendly if it incorporates systems that emphasise the inclusion and participation of all children. The more children are encouraged to take an active role in the school through school councils, organising committees and consultation forums, the more likely it is that the school will have an environment that is conducive to their development. The school that promotes consultation with children will be a safer environment, and the school that values positive interactions with children will promote the students' well-being and development. As parents, we can best assess this by talking with the children, parents and teachers involved in the school.

Disciplinary regime

One of the most important factors to consider when assessing and comparing schools is the way in which discipline is taught and maintained. For our children to feel and to be safe and secure, the school must have a strong, positive approach to discipline, whereby children co-operate and support one another and act in a way that gives due consideration to the welfare of others.

In addition, a school should contribute to a child's understanding of what is right and wrong to them, should encourage the child to think about right and wrong and to question, challenge and take personal responsibility for his/her own actions. The hallmark of positive discipline is teaching children how to understand the importance of valuing others and how to make decisions that will benefit the greater good.

In a school where discipline is weak, our children will feel unsafe and will not be able to learn to be self-disciplined. Equally, in a school with a negative or punishment-based disciplinary ethos, our children will be fearful and will learn to do as they are told, regardless of their own opinions or intuition.

Experience, qualifications and recruitment policies of staff

While most schools are careful to employ only qualified teachers, it is important that parents enquire as to the quality and experience of the teaching staff in their children's school. The criteria some schools employ for appointing teachers is simply that the teacher has the necessary qualification. It is important that the school we choose for our child has a strong recruitment ethos and seeks to employ the very best teachers it can obtain.

When researching a school, parents should ask members of the Board of Management and other parents what the school's recruitment policies are and how they monitor the performance of teachers and staff. It is also recommended that parents ask whether the school has practice guidelines, child protection guidelines and an anti-bullying strategy, and that these are made available for the parents to study. Most important of all, parents should check whether all of the staff working in the school have been vetted by the Garda Síochána to ensure they do not have a known history of posing a risk to children.

Physical environment

The physical environment in which our children are taught is an important factor to assess. Parents should enquire about:

- the condition of classrooms, canteens, etc.;

- hygiene and health and safety;
- class sizes;
- overcrowding;
- availability of adequate play areas;
- hazards existing around or near the school;
- that school transport meets the highest standards of health and safety.

While few schools provide a completely safe physical environment, it is important for us to know in advance what the physical dangers might be and to arm our children with the necessary information or skills to avoid these dangers.

Quality of interactions between staff

The quality of interaction between staff working in the school will not only impact on the type of environment created for the students, but will reflect on how the staff will interact with our children.

In a school where staff interact with each other in a respectful, positive manner, it is likely that our children will not only benefit from the positive environment this creates, but will be treated in the same manner. Where staff are disrespectful, critical or negative towards each other, it is likely that the atmosphere will promote this sort of interaction among the student body and therefore will not contribute positively to our children's well-being and development. Of course, just because staff interact positively with each other does not automatically mean that they will interact positively with children, but it does make this much more likely.

Quality of interactions with parents

How staff in a school interact with parents is an important indicator of the type of atmosphere existing in the school, and of the quality of interactions with the students. Again, disrespectful and antagonistic interactions will create a negative atmosphere and engender this sort of behaviour in the student body. School staff should be willing to meet with parents, to listen to their concerns and to work with them to ensure a child's welfare is promoted at all times.

Getting to and from school

One of the most important things to consider when choosing a school for our child is how he/she will get to and from the school. While this might seem quite a basic issue, it is perhaps the one component of our child's schooling that can present a significant risk. Therefore, we need to carefully think through the following.

- **Who is supervising our child and when?** Due to work pressures, many parents find themselves in a situation of having to leave their child at school very early to ensure that they themselves get to work on time. Similarly, they may arrive late to collect their children from school for the same reason. Teachers, on the other hand, are obliged to supervise and take responsibility for children between certain defined hours. As a result, there may be times at the start or end of the school day when young children are left unsupervised. This presents significant risks and needs to be considered and prevented where possible.

- **Is the mode of transport to the school safe?** Getting our child to and from school can be a complicated matter and one that should be given consideration when we are assessing schools. If we cannot walk to school with our child or allow our child to walk there by him/herself, then we need to consider how exactly he/she is going to get there. If we intend to use a school bus, we need to ensure not only that it is fully compliant with the new health and safety measures, but also that supervision on the bus is adequate, that the bus company is a recognised company and that our child is accompanied by friends, where possible, when using school transport.

  If we are going to establish a school run with other parents, we need to ensure that there is an explicit understanding about how this will work, i.e. the number of children that will be in a car at any one time, where exactly the children will be collected and dropped off, who exactly will be doing the runs, what our child should do if there is a sudden change of plan, etc. To this end, it is useful to give our child a mobile phone so that he/she can contact us should any problems arise. If we intend our child to cycle to school, we need to make sure that the route is generally safe, i.e. does not involve cycling through isolated areas, is safe for a bicycle, that our child has received adequate training to use a bicycle, that his/her bicycle is equipped properly and capable of transporting all of his/her school equipment, books, sports equipment, etc.

Related to this is the necessity of assessing whether our child's attendance at the school requires that he/she must get out of bed very early in the morning or return home very late in the evening. These factors are of concern because tiredness and exhaustion can have a significant impact on our child's physical and emotional well-being.

- **When is it safe for our child to go to and come from school without adult supervision?** One of the key considerations for parents is when to allow their children to walk or cycle to and from school on their own, or with friends. This decision is best made on the basis of our child's age and maturity. It should *not* be based on circumstances, e.g. we want to have a lie-in, nor on what others are doing. If children are too young or too immature to be capable of going to or coming from school without adult supervision, then allowing them or forcing them to do so will impact on their welfare.

  Aside from the obvious dangers of the child being unable to cope with aggressive or threatening approaches by adults or other children, our child's emotional well-being will be adversely affected by the experience. No matter what the inconvenience to us or our employer, we need to ensure that we or another trusted adult accompanies our child to and from school for as long as our child wishes us to do so.

BEING INVOLVED IN OUR CHILD'S EDUCATION
Listening to and communicating with our child about his/her experiences at school
Sometimes our busy lifestyles can make it difficult to find the time to discuss the everyday happenings of work and school with our children. But it is only through regular communication and listening to them about their school activities that we will identify problems when or before they arise. If we are listening to what they are doing on a daily basis in school, that will help us know quickly if they start to become unhappy.

Teaching personal safety skills
Although the responsibility for keeping safe should never rest solely with our children, it is important that they are taught the necessary

personal safety skills to enable self-protection. Most schools have personal safety programmes running as part of the school curriculum, but in addition to this it is important that parents teach their children, in age-appropriate ways, about the dangers that can arise in school and how they can protect themselves.

We must explain clearly to children the difference between good and bad touches, good and bad secrets, about treating others with respect and being treated with respect. Our children need to know that we are responsible for sorting out major difficulties, not them, and that they can come to us to discuss any worries or problems. The best way to do this is to integrate it into everyday parenting, making self-protection a normal part of the parent–child relationship.

Getting to know our child's friends

School is first and foremost a social environment in which our children learn to communicate, to co-operate and to socialise with other children. Getting to know who our children's friends are, how they support and reinforce each other and how they can hurt each other is important. For example, we should encourage our children to bring their friends home and to have social events in our home so that we can get to know their friends.

Their friends will often be the first source of support for our children when they start to experience difficulties in school. When our children start to become distant from friends or start to change friends, we need to find out why this might be happening. Friends can sometimes become the source of bullying for our children and if we know these friends, we can more easily deal with the problem.

Communication with the school

Consistent communication with the school is crucial to ensure our children receive a good education and are protected adequately. Many schools and teachers encourage regular communication, but others avoid it as they feel it simply adds to the pressure of their work. It is important to look at this aspect of the school's ethos when researching the education options for our child.

Sometimes parents can feel intimidated by teachers, believing they are more educated or more intelligent. This is particularly true when a parent feels that he/she did not perform well academically in school. It is important to remember that while the teacher may have professional knowledge, we have the most important knowledge about our individual child.

Agreed educational strategy

If our children are to be secure and safe in school, they need to be receiving consistent educational messages. In particular, we need to agree with the school and the teacher about the important things: how we believe our children can best learn, our attitude to homework, how we discipline our children, how we support and reward them and how we communicate with them. A common educational strategy will benefit our children greatly.

Working in partnership with the school

It is important for our children's well-being that we view our relationship with the school as a partnership, that we are working together to achieve the best outcome for our children. If we are constantly questioning or criticising the school or our children's teachers, our children will not have confidence in them and will become insecure. Similarly, the school should treat us as educational partners, so that when problems or conflicts arise our children are not involved and the school deals directly with us in a positive, constructive way.

Resolving our own school experiences

Our views of school are greatly determined by our own experiences of school. For some the old adage held true and school days were the best days of our lives. Indeed, some of us may attribute our successful lives to our schooling and to particular teachers. For others, however, they were some of the worst days of their lives. Depending on how old we are, we may have experienced a significant degree of physical punishment at the hands of our teachers. Some of us may have been subjected to treatment in school that we now consider to have been abusive. We may have been bullied by other pupils or we may have bullied our classmates.

Whatever our experiences, they have inevitably impacted on how we view and manage our child's involvement in school. For this reason it is important to acknowledge and resolve the legacy of our own school experiences.

Each of us will have our own very personal legacies, but it is necessary to realise that there are a number of unhealthy legacies that can make it extremely difficult for us to support our child in school:

- **The 'Doormat' legacy:** Because of our experiences in school, some of us continue to feel intimidated by teachers and by the school system, even though we are now adults ourselves. No matter how hard we try, we cannot resolve the feelings of inferiority and fear we carry with us from our school days. Such feelings can result from having been treated badly in school or by seeing others being treated badly. Perhaps these feelings have been engrained in us by our own parents, who may have felt lucky to have been able to send us to school.

   This legacy can have a significant impact on our ability to support our child in school. We may avoid conflict with teachers or with school authorities at all costs, avoid becoming involved or raising any issues in the school and accept, without question, what school personnel decide to do or say. If we carry this legacy, we may discourage our child from questioning anything or anybody involved in the school system and may impress upon him/her that 'doing what you are told' is the most important thing in school. Such a legacy will disempower us and can disempower our child as well, thereby making him/her vulnerable to exploitation and abuse.

- **The 'Green Eyed Monster' legacy:** For some of us the idea that our children may do better in school than we did, or may be academically 'cleverer' than we are, can be very difficult to accept. For some of us the idea that school can be fulfilling or enjoyable is difficult to comprehend and if our child feels this way about school, we may begin to feel very challenged. Such feelings sometimes lead us to disengage from our child's schooling and to become apathetic about what our child is doing and how he/she is getting on in school. At other times we can become unconsciously destructive, presenting obstacles to our child's happy and successful participation in school.

   These sorts of feelings leave our child vulnerable because as parents we are not fully committed to ensuring our child thrives in school. In addition, our child may become secretive about what is happening in school in an attempt to hide his/her achievements or success.

- **The 'Che Guevara' legacy:** Arising from our own school experiences, some of us adopt a revolutionary attitude towards school. Perhaps we spent our time in school fighting against the system, or perhaps we look back on our time in school and wish we had rebelled against the system. Those of us with this legacy can sometimes use our children to fight against a school system that we believe failed us or that we feel needs to be changed.

  This legacy can cause significant difficulties for our child within the school system because he/she might not share our views and is unlikely to have the same experiences we had. This is not to say that we do not do everything to ensure our child has a beneficial school experience and that we act if there are problems. However, we should never use our child to fight battles that are essentially our own and that will impact on our child's school welfare.

- **The 'Pathologist' legacy:** Some of us approach our child's schooling looking for problems. Like a pathologist, we spend all of our time trying to identify what is, or might be, going wrong. We over-analyse or negatively interpret all of the information we obtain about our child's education and school experience, expecting and finding problem after problem. Of course, most children experience some problem or other in school and good parenting necessitates that we work to identify and resolve problems, ideally before they arise. But this is very different from expecting and continually seeking out problems.

  This legacy is usually borne out of bad experiences in our own schooling or from over-anxiety about our child's welfare. The problem with this approach to schooling is that it can have an adverse impact on our child's welfare, causing him/her to be overly anxious as well and therefore continually unsettled. The children of parents who take this approach to school often move classes or schools and can become disliked by teachers and other pupils. Children need to be given the confidence and security to integrate, enjoy and benefit from school, believing that the majority of people they encounter will nurture, protect and empower them.

It is crucial that we do not allow our own experiences of school to impact or interfere with how we perceive and manage our child's experiences. For most parents, being aware of how our own experiences could impact is enough to ensure that these experiences do not affect our child. For others, whose self-awareness is perhaps not so well developed or whose experiences were particularly traumatic, it may be necessary to obtain support or counselling to resolve some of these issues. Being able to accurately assess schools and involve ourselves in an active, positive way in our child's schooling will depend on how well we have resolved our own experiences of school.

Private tuition/grinds

In Ireland, many children receive extra private tuition of one sort or another. While this is more common when children reach secondary-school age, it is a small, but growing, phenomenen among primary school children, too. It is necessary to ensure that these private tuition arrangements are safe. Not only do we need to apply the same criteria to these situations as we would to regular schooling, but we also need to be extra vigilant, given that most of these arrangements involve one-to-one, unsupervised contact with our child. It is therefore important that we ensure that:

- we have thoroughly assessed the private tutor and at the very least ensured that he or she has been vetted by the Garda Síochána;
- we have explained all of the safety principles to our child and have reminded him/her of the importance of telling us if anything occurs that makes him/her feel unsafe or threatened;
- the tuition occurs in a location that is appropriate, safe and convenient for our child.

In addition to these measures, we should also be careful that we do not overly depend on private tuition or overly pressurise our child by employing private tuition. Given the length and intensity of the school day, private tuition should be used only when absolutely necessary and in full agreement with our child. Remember, there is far more to school than just educational achievements.

WHAT DO WE DO IF WE DISCOVER THERE IS A PROBLEM?

When we become worried about our children's welfare or become aware of the fact that our children might be experiencing abuse or bullying, it is important to take immediate action to safeguard our child. What form this action will take will depend on the type of concern we have and the type of risk to which we believe our child is exposed.

Before taking any action, it is important to:

- reassure and support our child;
- ensure that he/she knows that he/she has done nothing wrong;
- discuss the situation with him/her in an age-appropriate way;
- listen to what he/she thinks should be done; and
- explain to him/her what we are going to do and why.

In some instances it is enough to discuss the situation with the teacher or school principal in order to resolve what is making our child unhappy. However, in the most serious cases of abuse or bullying, it may be necessary to seek to get a teacher or other child removed from the school, to remove our child from the school or to inform the relevant authorities.

It can sometimes be difficult to take action to protect our children in school because we do not want to create trouble within our community, nor do we want other parents or children to know what is happening. It will often be the case that our child has formed an attachment to the school, to teachers or to other pupils and therefore will be very upset if there is a major upheaval. However difficult it might be, our first priority at all times is our child's welfare. We cannot deviate from that primary concern, which should guide all our actions. Whatever action we decide to take, it is important to keep our child informed in an age-appropriate manner and to ensure that we support them through any changes or actions that prove necessary.

Bullying in school
Every child should experience a happy school life, therefore it is important that adults take immediate, appropriate action if they discover that their child is being bullied.

The following is a list of measures we should consider to tackle bullying:

- if we are worried that our child is being bullied, ask him/her directly;

- be aware of the signs and symptoms of bullying;
- take bullying seriously and find out the facts when told about an incident of bullying;
- keep a written diary of all bullying incidents;
- help our child to practise strategies to deal with the bullying, such as shouting no, walking with confidence and running away;
- do not encourage our child to hit back, as this will only make matters worse. Such behaviour could be contrary to our child's nature;
- more positively, encourage our child to recruit friends or join clubs: a child who has friends is less likely to be bullied;
- give our child a chance to vent his/her feelings about being bullied;
- get other parents together and discuss ways to stop the bullying;
- if the bullying is happening on the way to or from school, arrange to meet our child to accompany him/her;
- invite other children over to help our child make friends;
- do not agree to keep the bullying a secret from the school authorities.

Where we feel the bullying is too serious for us or our child to deal with, we should talk with the teacher or principal about the situation and agree how it can best be dealt with. If we are not satisfied with this, we should write to the Secretary of the School Board of Management and ultimately to the education authorities. Remember, if our child is being bullied in school, it is likely that other children are also being bullied. It is very important that for our child's sake, and other children's sakes, the bullying is stopped.

Abuse by another child or adult within the school
If we become aware that our child is being subjected to any form of abuse within the school, the first thing to do is to discuss with him/her what is happening and listen to how he/she would like the situation to be handled. It is also important to get advice from somebody we trust.

While our child's safety is our priority, where possible we should try and reach an agreement with him/her as to how the situation will be handled and then keep him/her informed about what is happening. As with all other forms of abuse, it is crucial that we reinforce for our child that he/she has done nothing wrong. Where we have a strong reason to believe that our child is being abused, we should inform the school principal and the appropriate authorities. We should insist that the persons who are allegedly abusing our child are removed from the school pending an investigation. Failing this, we may have to remove our child from the school temporarily.

Self-abuse

When children start to engage in self-abusive behaviour in school, we need to find out why they are doing this. All children want to impress their parents and teachers and be successful, so if they start getting into trouble deliberately or distancing themselves from other children, we must explore why this is happening.

Again, talking to our child is the best way to get to the bottom of these issues. It can be easy to view self-abusive behaviour as bold or defiant, but it is important to remember that there are often emotional worries or difficulties underpinning such actions. If this behaviour is accompanied by more serious self-abuse, such as drug abuse, self-harm or inappropriate early sexualisation, then it is extremely important to get the difficulties resolved as quickly as possible. In these situations, it may be necessary to seek support from counsellors or social workers.

My child is abusing other children

If we discover that our child is bullying or abusing other children in school, we need to explore with him/her why he/she is doing this. We must listen carefully to his/her explanations and try to understand his/her behaviour. We need to find out if the children who are being bullied or abused by our child are the same age, younger or older, and we need to check out the nature of the relationships our child has with these other children.

It will be necessary to discuss with our child the trauma and upset his/her behaviour is causing to others and how important it is that the behaviour stops immediately. We need to ensure that our child is not being manipulated or exploited by someone else, and that he/she is not re-enacting abusive behaviour that he/she is also experiencing. We also need to ensure our child is not part of an exploitative circle.

It is likely that even where our child is abusing or bullying others, he/she is a victim of his/her own confused sexuality, of unresolved frustration, anger or dissatisfaction, or is the victim of another person's confused sexuality, exploitation or manipulation. If we become concerned that our child is abusing others or is grooming other children for abuse, it is very important that we discuss our concerns with the school and seek support from a social worker and a counsellor.

It is important to remember that for most children, school is a happy, safe place, most of the time. However, due to the impact of school experiences on our children's educational, social and emotional development, it is vital that we do everything we can to ensure they do not experience any form of abuse while in school and that if they do, we do everything possible to stop it and to protect them.

Garrett's story: An unsafe school environment

When Garrett came home from school on his first day of fourth class and announced his new teacher was Mr Morrisey, his older brother Dominic said, 'Be careful he doesn't feel you up.' Garrett did not really know what Dominic meant, but during the first month he started to notice that Mr Morrissey was always hugging and pinching the boys in his class. He also noticed that Mr Morrissey would take particular boys into the toilets from time to time and that they would usually return to the class crying.

Then one day Mr Morrissey tried to put his hand down the front of Garrett's trousers. Garrett's immediate reaction was to push Mr Morrissey's hand away and tell him to 'f**k off'. Mr Morrissey was temporarily shocked, but later found an excuse to shout and punch Garrett. When Garrett went home from school, he told his mother what had happened. She went up to the school the following day and confronted Mr Morrissey, who told her that Garrett was telling lies to deflect from the fact that he was being troublesome and lazy and was very poor at reading and spelling.

Garrett's mother had left school at the age of thirteen and was eager for her son to get a good education. She did not want to cause trouble in the school because she was worried that Garrett would be thrown out. She did not pursue the matter any further with Mr Morrissey, but told him not to touch her son again. When she went home she told Garrett to stay away from Mr Morrissey and to stay out of trouble.

The following day, Mr Morrissey started calling Garrett names and told the class that he was the most stupid boy in the class. Every week, he would make Garrett read in front of the class and would encourage the class to laugh at him. The rest of Garrett's class started calling him names. They began taunting and pushing him in the schoolyard and some of them started chasing him and beating him up on his way home from school. Garrett started arriving home from school upset, with his books missing and his clothes torn.

Worried about her son, Garrett's mother discussed what was happening with his father, who lost his temper and told Garrett and his older brother that they were to 'sort it out'. The following day, on their way home from school, the two brothers had a fight with the six boys who were bullying Garrett and his brother broke one boy's nose. Garrett's parents were called to the school and were told that both boys were being expelled.

Garrett's mother became very upset and lost her temper, asking the principal why he would expel her sons for defending themselves while he did nothing about Mr Morrissey, who was molesting the boys in his class. The principal ignored her outburst, but later that evening began to become concerned about what she had said. While nobody had ever formally complained about Mr Morrissey, he had picked up innuendo and suggestion about him in the staff-room.

This was a tough school, in a deprived area, and the principal had difficulty getting good teachers. However, he was aware that a principal in a nearby school had experienced serious trouble for failing to deal with an incident of sexual harassment between two staff members. The following day, he rang the local authorities. A week later, following an interview with Garrett, the authorities commenced an investigation into Mr Morrissey's behaviour. The investigation took eight months and resulted in sixty-three serious complaints of sexual abuse being made against the teacher.

Chapter 6
Safety in Leisure, Sport, on Holidays and with Babysitters

For children to have balanced lives and develop healthily and fully, it is important that they get regular opportunities to engage in leisure and sports activities. While younger children are usually accompanied by their parents to such activities, as they grow older we will allow our children to engage more and more in activities that we are not directly supervising.

Similarly, children and parents benefit from going on holiday where they get the opportunity to relax, experience another way of life and spend quality time together. Most children go on holidays with their parents until they are in their teens, at which time they may start going on holidays without their parents. However, many children now travel without their parents at a younger age, to go on school trips or holiday with a friend's family.

While family time on holiday is very important, parents also benefit from time socialising together and will need time engaging in relaxing or social activities as a couple. This usually means parents will have to entrust their children to babysitters.

Unlike crèches, childminding facilities and schools, there are few regulations to govern babysitters, organisations providing sports and leisure activities or holiday resorts and facilities. As we associate these services and organisations with pleasure and relaxation, we can sometimes forget to ensure that they are safe for our children. And, of course, because we are relaxed and enjoying ourselves, we can be less vigilant than we normally are. Although we pay for many of these services and activities, some are provided and run by volunteers, such as uniformed organisations, sports clubs and youth groups. Similarly, although we often pay for babysitting services, we sometimes turn to friends or family for unpaid help. Whether we are paying for these services or not, it is important to be sure that they are safe for our children.

WHAT ARE THE RISKS IN LEISURE, SPORTS AND HOLIDAY ACTIVITIES?

Aside from the potential risk of physical, sexual or emotional abuse attached to various activities our children engage in, there are some specific risks associated with leisure sports and holiday activities.

Physical injury

The physical nature of many sports, leisure and holiday activities means that physical injuries to children can occur if proper safeguards are not put in place. It can be difficult for parents to assess how safe certain activities are, particularly when lots of other children are participating in them. But we should never be afraid to ask questions: good organisations will welcome the opportunity to outline their health and safety measures.

Psychological risks

Sports, leisure and holiday activities often impact on children's emotional well-being and self-awareness. Activities to which parents do not attribute much significance can often be very important to children. For them, being acknowledged for even the smallest achievement can be thrilling, while, likewise, being criticised or made fun of for any reason can deeply upset them. That is not to say that children do not need to learn to deal with constructive criticism, disappointment and failure, but when they are subjected to continuous negative feedback that is presented in a destructive or personalised manner, it can have an adverse affect on their self-image, self-esteem and psychological well-being.

Sexual abuse risks

As with any activities our children engage in, there is always a possibility that they will be confronted with the risk of sexual abuse. Sports, leisure and holiday activities carry some additional risks because many of them involve physical interaction, dressing and undressing and building close relationships between adults and children. None of these factors are problematic in themselves, but we must be aware that they do offer the opportunity for exploitation should a person wish to sexually abuse a child.

Burn-out

Burn-out occurs when an activity that was once a source of fun and personal satisfaction becomes associated with progressive physical and psychological distress. It usually results from the sheer number of hours involved in activities, coupled with high expectations and pressure from staff, volunteers or parents/guardians.

Burn-out is characterised by a loss of energy and enthusiasm for an activity, along with increasing anxiety and stress. Children no longer have fun and become overwhelmed by the demands of competition and training. This is usually caused by:

- stretching children to perform at a level beyond their capacity, which is related to age or maturation level, i.e. placing excessive pressure on children to win;
- over-training or making continuous demands on children;
- knowingly permitting injured children to participate in a sporting activity.

Burn-out is often displayed in children in the form of sleep disturbance, irritability or tension. Sometimes it appears as a lack of energy and a loss of interest and enthusiasm for the activity. Children who are burnt out can become sad and depressed, or begin to avoid the activity by complaining of illness or arriving late and leaving early.

WHAT DO WE KNOW ABOUT CHILD ABUSE IN SPORTS AND LEISURE SETTINGS?

The *Sexual Abuse and Violence in Ireland* study (SAVI, 2002) found that of those respondents who had been sexually abused as children, 1.8 per cent had been abused by sports coaches/instructors. The

Canadian Incidence Study of Reported Child Abuse and Neglect (2003), on the other hand, does not specifically identify coaches/instructors when categorising perpetrators of child abuse, instead using general categories such as 'other professional' and 'other acquaintance'.

To date, there have been very few specific research studies assessing child abuse occurring in sport or leisure activities. As a result, there are insufficient statistics available to give an accurate estimate of the extent of the problem. In addition, available statistics give an incomplete picture because:

- harassment and abuse in sports and leisure often go unreported for a wide variety of reasons;
- some abuse that is identified may not be recognised as sports- or leisure-related;
- professional definitions of what constitutes harassment or abuse have been introduced only relatively recently.

The limited evidence available shows that sport and leisure activities do not present any more risk than a wide range of other activities in which children participate. However, some high-profile cases of child sexual abuse occurring in sport in recent years have raised public awareness of the issue. In Ireland, one of the most distressing cases involved two coaches of the national swimming team.

In 1993, an investigation by the Gardaí revealed that a former Irish Olympic coach had been allegedly raping young male and female swimmers under his control for a number of years. Attempts to prosecute this man failed because he was successful in seeking a judicial review, therefore the case against him did not proceed. He subsequently fled to Scotland, where he continued coaching. When the Scottish club was contacted and made aware of his career in Ireland, he left Scotland and went to the USA, where he coached children in Colorado. The police in Colarado were alerted and the coach, who was by then married with three children, moved on once again.

In 1998, the man appointed to take over from him as Olympic coach was sentenced to twelve years in prison for sexually abusing swimmers, some as young as ten years old. One of his victims described how swimming had been her life and that this coach had become her closest 'friend'. She believed that the abuse was an integral part of her training.

Similar cases have occurred in many other countries. In Australia, for example, a well-known international cricket umpire was jailed for child sex allegations made when he was a schoolteacher. In 2001, a UK-based tennis coach was jailed for seven years for child sexual abuse, while in America a number of junior baseball and football coaches have been jailed for similar offences.

While there are no official statistics available to indicate the amount of abuse occurring in leisure or holiday facilities or perpetrated by holiday or leisure personnel, there have been a number of high-profile abuse cases in this sector. In early 2000, the Australian authorities received complaints of a number of cases of suspected child sexual assault that had occurred in childcare centres at two exclusive holiday resorts in Bali. In 2007, the disappearance of three-year-old Madeleine McCann from a holiday apartment in Portugal and the murder of a Swiss student in Ireland raised awareness worldwide of the risks posed to children and young people on holiday.

These high-profile cases have made children and parents more aware of the dangers of abuse in sports, leisure and holiday activities, and also appear to have increased the number of young people reporting abuse. These cases have also prompted many sporting, leisure and holiday organisations to address the problem by developing positive steps to reduce risk of abuse and improve their response to allegations of abuse.

ASSESSING LEISURE, SPORT AND HOLIDAY ACTIVITIES

The first step in ensuring our child is kept safe while engaging in sports, leisure or holiday activities is to make sound judgments about the types of activity and organisation with which our child becomes involved. To do this, we need to have good criteria on which to base our decisions. The ISPCC has identified some of these criteria in a booklet entitled *Have Fun Be Safe*. When deciding on leisure, sport or holiday activities for our children, it is important that we keep the following in mind.

1. A good organisation will welcome questions about their activities and the safety of their environment. All organisations should have a child protection policy, including a statement on and guidelines about keeping children safe.

2. All staff and volunteers should have gone through a proper recruitment process, which includes interviews and references and, where appropriate, police checks. In addition, the staff should be competent and qualified for the activity they are running, should be positive and enthusiastic in their approach to children and should be able to maintain control and discipline in a constructive and encouraging manner. Above all, they should recognise the importance of fun in children's activities and should always be encouraging fair play. This is not to say that staff and volunteers will not make mistakes, lose their temper or want, at times, to win above all, but the overall attitude of staff and volunteers should be positive and child-friendly.

3. The organisation should encourage the participation and involvement of parents as much as possible.

4. All organisations should have a written code of behaviour that outlines good practice when working with children and discourages bullying, shouting, racism and sexism. Apart from skills training, all workers should have training in child protection and health and safety.

5. There should be someone in charge who supervises staff and volunteers.

6. The organisations running the activities should be able to tell you where to go and what to do if you or your children have any worries.

7. In the case of very young children, or those with a disability, you should check out routines for toileting, feeding and administering medication.

8. Find out if there is a leader qualified in first aid, a first aid box and whether the premises have passed fire regulations.

9. You should be informed of arrangements for every outing, including transport to and from the pick-up point, no matter how long or short, and your consent should be requested for all such outings.

It may also be helpful to read the Department of Health and Children's 2002 publication, *Our Duty to Care – The Principles of Good Practice for the Protection of Children and Young People*. This document is aimed at community and voluntary organisations, of any size or type, including sports and leisure organisations. It is a practical guide on developing safe practices when working with children and young people. It describes a good-quality organisation as one that values children and centres its activities around their safety, enjoyment and comfort. This means that organisations should:

- adopt the safest possible practices to minimise the possibility of harm or accidents happening to children;
- create an environment in which the self-esteem of children and young people is developed and where they are not subjected to bullying and other aggressive behaviours;
- develop a child protection policy that raises awareness about the possibility of child abuse occurring and the steps to be taken if it is suspected. This includes issues such as clear methods for recruiting staff and volunteers, health and safety policies, staff/volunteer supervision, etc.

It may be useful to ask if the sport or leisure facility you are considering has read this document and has sought to implement the policies and practices outlined therein.

Physical safety
In addition to these general criteria, it is important that all activities being undertaken by children should meet the following physical safety requirements:

- activities should be suitable for the age, experience and ability of the participants;
- where protective equipment is deemed necessary, it should be used;
- there should be first aid expertise and equipment available where the activities might require these and a procedure should be in place for informing parents/guardians of all injuries their children could incur;
- children wishing to participate in the activities should be adequately prepared and made aware of their personal responsibility in terms of safety. Children should be taught the rules of the activity and encouraged to abide by them, as many rules are based on safety;
- if the activity involves trips, then children and parents should be

made aware of the safety and supervision rules attached to these trips. Adequate insurance cover should be in place and adults transporting children in their own cars should be familiar with the provisions made in their motor insurance policy in relation to acceptable numbers and liability;

- the use of drugs, alcohol and tobacco should be actively discouraged as being incompatible with a healthy approach to child-friendly activities.

Psychological safeguards

To reduce the possibility of emotional difficulties arising for our child, we need to check for a number of factors:

- the staff and volunteers running activities respect the rights, dignity and worth of every child and treat everyone equally, regardless of sex, age, ability, ethnic origin, religion or political persuasion, and maintain the highest standard of personal conduct;
- all children are given sufficient opportunity to participate in the activity and are made to feel and to believe that they all have an equally important contribution to make to the activity. For example, no matter how good a footballer a child is, he/she should get the same opportunity to play in matches as others;
- effort and enjoying the activity are emphasised rather than winning at all costs, and children are encouraged to treat others with due respect, both in victory and defeat;
- discipline is positive in focus and is administered through praise for effort and social skills as well as activity skills. There should be no place for fighting or over-aggressive or dangerous behaviour in the activities;
- sanctions are used in a corrective way and any that may be interpreted as being humiliating or improper are not used. Children must not be exposed to embarrassment or disparagement by use of sarcastic or flippant remarks.

Safeguarding against sexual abuse

It is also important that alongside the other safeguards outlined in previous chapters, we also consider the following factors:

- sports, leisure and holiday activities should be held in recognised, appropriate venues and not at personal premises. Situations where a staff member or volunteer and a child cannot be observed should be avoided;
- there should be clear boundaries between a working relationship and friendship with staff, volunteers and children;
- staff and volunteers should avoid situations where they are alone with children in changing rooms. Wherever practicable, there should always be two or more adults present in changing rooms;
- staff and volunteers running the activities should not be exerting too much influence over children.

While many activities are run by volunteers or by people within our communities, it is still important to try and ensure that as many of the above criteria are met when choosing activities for our children. Remember, these criteria will not only help keep our children safe, but will also add to the enjoyment and security of the staff and volunteers running the activities.

IDENTIFYING ABUSIVE SITUATIONS
Identifying abuse in leisure, sport and holiday facilities is not easy. In addition to the indicators discussed in Chapter 2, there are a number of other indicators that should cause us concern:

- activities where parents are discouraged from staying to watch or becoming involved;
- behaviour that encourages rough play, sexual innuendo or humiliating punishments;
- individuals who take charge and operate independently of organisational guidelines;
- individuals who show favouritism or personally reward specific children;
- encouragement of inappropriate physical contact;
- poor communication and lack of parental involvement, which leaves you feeling uneasy.

Parents should also become concerned if a child suddenly decides to drop out of an activity or stops going for no apparent reason. If our children begin to get invitations to spend time alone with staff or volunteers or to visit them in their own home, we should assess why this is happening and what the purpose of this activity is. Most importantly, we need to listen to our child, ask questions about the activities and take expressions of unhappiness seriously, no matter how silly or trivial they may seem to us.

WHAT CAN I DO TO PROTECT MY CHILD?

Making adequate preparations

Before picking activities for our child, we need to do our homework. With the many demands on our time and the numerous decisions we have to make as parents, it sometimes seems just too much to ask that we thoroughly research every activity our child participates in. But it is worth it for the sake of his/her safety. Similarly, when we are on holidays, the last thing on our mind is to check out the activities, but again it is imperative that we do so. This is best done by talking with other parents and children who have participated in the activities, checking out any literature available and talking to the people who are running the activities.

Most clubs, organisations and holiday complexes welcome the opportunity to tell you about the activities they offer. If they are reluctant to give you information or become agitated or defensive when asked particular things, go somewhere else. Remember, the better the organisation, the less likely it is that our child will experience difficulties or abuse.

Once we have checked out the activities, the next step is to make sure we prepare our child adequately. This involves discussing and agreeing the rules of the activity. These should be simple rules, but the child must understand that he/she must adhere to them. For example, if the activity involves water, then we might agree with our child that no matter what anybody else does or says, he/she does not go into the water without a buoyancy aid or does not go out of his/her depth. These rules should include basic personal safety skills, such as explaining to our child that nobody should touch him/her without consent, that he/she should not travel on his/her own with adults and that he/she is entitled to personal privacy when undressing. We should remind our child that he/she needs to treat others with respect and courtesy at all times and that, in turn, he/she should expect to be treated in the same way.

Lastly, we should agree with our child what he/she should do if he/she feels unsafe. This might include agreeing that he/she can phone us on our mobile phone at any time, or agreeing with other parents a rota for staying to observe the activity.

A good example of how well we prepare or fail to prepare is provided by the holiday 'kiddies' club'. Many holiday resorts now have such clubs, which run various activities throughout the day and evening. These clubs are a big attraction for children and often provide a welcome opportunity for parents to get some free time while on holiday. However, despite all of the research and preparations we put into choosing a holiday destination, picking accommodation and making travel arrangements, we rarely check out who exactly is running the kiddies' clubs, what activities our child will be participating in and what health and safety measures are in place. Sometimes we allow our child to run off to the kiddies' club immediately on arrival at a holiday resort and may never ourselves get the chance to go and see where the activities are happening or what exactly is happening.

In most situations, the kiddies' club is safe and provides an enjoyable experience for children. However, in some cases the activities are dangerous or inappropriate for our child's age, or children are subjected to bullying or abuse by the organisers or other children. Furthermore, if we have not thought about what we want to achieve from our family holiday and have not prepared accordingly, our child might spend most of the holiday in the kiddies' club, which could result in us missing an opportunity to spend valuable quality time with our child.

Communicating our expectations

When we decide to leave our children in the care of another adult or young person, no matter what the circumstances, it is important that we communicate our expectations to them as clearly as possible. This will reduce the chance of any misunderstandings and will also give them the opportunity to tell us if they are not in a position to meet these expectations.

Although well-trained and well-intentioned, staff and volunteers working in leisure, sports or holiday organisations sometimes see their roles and responsibilities differently from the way parents might see them. They might, for example, see their primary role as ensuring the activity is exciting or competitive rather than that it is safe and enjoyable. They might find it difficult to maintain control, or tend to gear the activity to one particular age group. No matter what the circumstances, we need to get agreement from the people running the activity about how we expect our child to participate in and be cared for during the activities. If we cannot get this agreement, we should find a different activity for our child to pursue.

For example, do we communicate adequately with the football club or dance class? Although we appreciate how beneficial our child's involvement in a dance class or football team might be, because we are time-pressed we might find it difficult to build up a relationship with the dance class teacher or football coach. Aside from the times once or twice a year when we are paying the fees or attending the displays or medals ceremony, we often do not really get a chance to talk to them about how our child is getting on. If we do contact the coach or teacher, it is usually because a problem has arisen. In fact, we might not even be sure who is in charge at the dance class or at football.

However, when we think about the amount of time our child will spend at these activities and the impact they can have on our child's self-confidence and self-esteem, it seems clear that we need to make contact regularly with those who run the activities. We need to check out how things are going and how our child is getting on. Aside from the need to check on things, we run the risk of missing out on some of our child's most important achievements and successes if we do not keep regular contact. In addition, most coaches and teachers will welcome the contact and interest, as they often get little recognition for their efforts.

Monitoring and staying vigilant

One of the biggest attractions with sports, leisure and holiday activities is that they provide us with an opportunity to get some free time away from our children. Therefore, having to stay and observe what is happening seems to defeat one of the main attractions. While we don't need to be there for every minute of the activity, it is important to monitor it from time to time – not only to check out how our child is doing, but also to show our child that we are interested and that we support his/her involvement in the activity.

Ideally, we should agree a rota with other parents where one parent will stay and watch the activities and support the children from time to time. Again, good organisations will support this. It is also a benefit if we can offer support to the staff and volunteers or take an active role in the organisation of the activity. That said, it is important to achieve a balance and not to become too involved, which might stifle our child's independence and enjoyment. We should let the level of our involvement be determined by our child and by how comfortable he/she feels with us being present.

A good example of this is youth clubs, most of which are community-based, with the activities generally occurring at weekends and evenings. Most youth clubs are viewed by adults as 'no go' areas, as solely the domain of young people. Supervision in these clubs is often conducted by other young people or young adults, therefore parents rarely get an opportunity to monitor or observe what is happening. Some of us may opt to become actively involved in the club by becoming a leader, etc. if we have the time and feel our direct involvement will not discourage our own child from attending. However, there are other simple ways to monitor what's happening without having to give a great deal of time or risking being seen as interfering. We can become involved in those activities that occur parallel to the main club activities, i.e. making the sandwiches, repairing broken equipment, opening or locking up, etc. Even dropping our child to the club or collecting him/her gives us an opportunity to get a flavour of what is happening. At all times, though, we must strive to get the balance between over-involvement and appropriate monitoring; it might not be easy to do so, but it is important.

While on holiday, it is particularly important that we apply the same level of vigilance and monitoring that we would apply at home. Sometimes being on holiday gives us a false sense of security and lulls us into taking short cuts and risks with our child's safety that we would never take at home, e.g. leaving a young child unsupervised or unmonitored while we socialise. No matter how safe we believe a holiday environment to be, we must apply common-sense parenting principles at all times and never compromise our child's safety.

Listening and getting feedback from our child
Like all other areas of our children's lives, the most effective way to keep them safe while engaging in sports, leisure or holiday activities is to listen to what they are saying about the activities and to seek

constant feedback. This not only helps us to recognise and praise our children's efforts and achievements and thus build their self-confidence, but also to identify problems before, or soon after, they arise. If our child begins to express concern or unhappiness about an activity or begins to refuse to talk about it, we need to take this seriously and find out what is causing this reaction.

How often do we talk to our child about what he/she is doing at basketball, tennis or karate? When he/she is telling us about these activities, do we sometimes 'turn off', putting the information into the category of the 'unimportant'? How many times can we listen to how the goal was scored, who got to dance the solo or who is a 'show-off' at basketball? It is impossible to actively listen to everything our child tells us or wants to talk about. Often, the leisure and sports updates are the least likely pieces of information to filter through to us. But we have to realise that, at times, these events may be more important to our child than what is happening in school or at home, therefore we need to accord them the same importance.

Resolving our own attitudes to sport and leisure
As with many other activities our children engage in, we often carry preconceived ideas and expectations about sports and leisure activities stemming from our own personal experiences. In general, these will be constructive and will serve to facilitate our child's enjoyment and safe participation in these activities. Sometimes, however, our preconceived ideas and expectations can be problematic and can compromise our child's healthy participation in these activities. Our attitudes and beliefs about sport and leisure will vary, depending on a number of factors, but there are some unhealthy attitudes that can be particularly problematic and should be resolved.

- **'I could have been a champion'**: We might be tempted to try to relive our sporting or leisure ambitions through our children. As a result of our own successes, near successes or failures, we can place great emphasis on our child achieving certain things at sport or leisure pursuits. In this way, we become completely immersed in his/her progress and begin to manage and dominate their participation. Of course, ambition and competition are not problematic – it is when these attitudes lead to too much pressure or expectation on our child that they can interfere with his/her welfare. No matter how good or bad our child is at a particular sport or leisure activity, we must step back enough to allow him/her to participate at his/her own pace and level of commitment. We cannot relive our past glories or compensate for our past failures through our child. If we try to do so, we will not only compromise our child's welfare and happiness, but will most likely cause him/her to burn out very quickly.

- **'It's all a waste of time'**: Some of us dislike sport and leisure activities. Perhaps we were never good at them in our youth, or perhaps we prefer what we view as more 'intellectual' activities. Maybe we feel that members of our family were, or are, too involved in sports and therefore are determined to ensure that our children do not become overly involved.

  For a number of reasons, we may feel that sports and leisure activities are simply a waste of time. If we do, this attitude can impact on our child's welfare and happiness. It can lead us to disengage from our child's involvement in these activities, leaving him/her to fend for themselves. We may even actively discourage our child's involvement or become jealous of his/her successes.

  Once again, it is important to remember that, in general, involvement in sport and leisure is good for children and helps their physical and psychological development. More importantly, if our child chooses to engage in such activities, it is essential that we support and reinforce his/her involvement so that they obtain the maximum benefit and are kept safe.

- **All or nothing**: Many people are inclined to approach sports and leisure activities with the attitude that unless we are good at the activity, there is no point being involved. Thus we end up evaluating our child's involvement in sports activities on this criteria alone. This attitude can be transferred to our child: we cannot settle for second best or just being average, and as a result neither can our child. At the slightest disappointment or setback we become disillusioned, and so does our child. He/she gives up the activity or moves to another club or class, and we support this in the quest to find an activity in which our child will excel.

  As a result, our child misses out on the most important benefits derived from sports and leisure activities, i.e. participating, learning to lose, being a team player, enjoying the fun and making new friends. Instead of gaining in self-esteem and self-confidence, our child becomes increasingly less confident or insecure because there are always others doing better. In the end, our child just gives up trying.

It is essential that we allow children to participate in sports and leisure at their own level and on their own terms. Imposing our attitudes and ambitions will not only have a negative impact on our child, but will compromise his or her welfare.

WHAT DO I DO IF I DISCOVER THERE IS A PROBLEM?

Child safety: A priority

If we become concerned about our child's welfare or safety, it is important that we take these concerns seriously. There can be factors that deter us from pursuing the matter. For example, because sports, leisure and holiday activities are sessional, we might not take as much notice as we would if they were daily activities. As these activities are often run by volunteers or people we know from our community, we might not want to cause trouble for these people. However, negative experiences in any of these activities can impact significantly on our child's self-confidence and self-esteem and can place his/her welfare in danger. This means it is not a matter of choice: we have to prioritise our child's welfare.

Listen and consult with our children

While prioritising our child's safety, we need to discuss our concerns with our child and find out what he/she would like us to do. We may not be able to do what they want, but sometimes they can see solutions we have not considered. If, for our child's safety, we need to do something that will upset him/her, we need to prepare our child for this and explain why it is necessary.

Seek support

Where we have concerns for our child, it is useful to discuss them with the staff and volunteers running the activities. It can also be useful to speak to other parents or to our child's friends. It may be necessary to talk to somebody in the organisation who occupies a higher position of authority. It is important to discuss our concerns in a sensitive and confidential manner, remembering that our child will not want his/her difficulties discussed openly.

Likewise, we should remember that most organisations will want to ensure children's safety and will welcome being informed if there are difficulties. If we have serious concerns about our child's welfare, we need to remove him/her from the activity and contact the appropriate authorities.

Remember, removing our child – while essential – is not enough because it is likely that he/she will need additional support, plus it is also possible that other children could still be at risk.

BABYSITTING

Babysitters are persons who care for children temporarily, usually in the child's home, in return for payment. While the majority of babysitters will provide safe, good-quality care, as with all people to whom we entrust our children, there are risks that can arise and about which we need to be aware.

There are no criteria or standards governing babysitting, which means it can be very hard for parents to distinguish good babysitters from bad ones. In addition, parents often find it hard to get babysitters and therefore often find themselves in a position where they have to settle for what they can get. This can lead to using a babysitter whom the parents don't really know that well, or even a person whom they don't know at all but who has been recommended to them by friends or family. This particularly arises during holidays, when parents might use local babysitters recommended by hotels.

Unlike many other situations when we entrust our child to the care of others, babysitters have unsupervised, one-to-one care of our child for a particular period of time. In this context, it is crucial that we take the necessary precautions to ensure that our child is safe.

What do we know about abuse by babysitters?

In Ireland there have been few studies conducted on abuse perpetrated by babysitters. However, *Sexual Abuse and Violence in Ireland* (SAVI, 2002) found that of those respondents who reported having been sexually abused as children, 8.8 per cent claimed they had been abused by a babysitter. (This was reported by 4.2 per cent of males and 4.6 per cent of females.) Most of those who abused children while babysitting them were lone males (73 per cent) and the majority (58 per cent) were relatives of their victims.

The *Canadian Incidence Study of Reported Child Abuse and Neglect* (2003) indicated that of the reported cases of sexual abuse, 2 per cent involved sexual abuse by a babysitter or a member of the babysitter's family.

In the USA, the 2006 *Annual Report of the Pennsylvania Department of Public Welfare* identified that in 4,152 substantiated cases of child abuse in that year:

- 12 per cent of perpetrators were babysitters;
- 22 per cent of abusive babysitters were between the ages of twenty and twenty-nine;
- babysitters were responsible for the third largest number of injuries to children and students (13 per cent);
- most of the abuse committed by babysitters was sexual abuse (86 per cent).

An article entitled 'Crimes Against Children by Babysitters' (2001), written by David Finkelhor, one of the world's leading experts on child abuse, found that babysitters account for approximately 4 per cent of crimes committed against children aged less than six years – a rate below that of complete strangers. The article based its findings on the FBI's National Incident-Based Reporting System.

Finkelhor's study also found that among babysitters:

- male offenders outnumbered female offenders by 63 per cent to 37 per cent;
- males were disproportionately involved in sex offences perpetrated against children (77 per cent of sexual offences);
- females committed the majority of the physical assaults (64 per cent);
- of babysitters who committed sex offences, males were more likely than females to target female victims and victims aged six and older. They were also more likely to be adults (58 per cent), whereas female sex offenders were predominantly juveniles (67 per cent), mostly aged thirteen to fifteen years.

Finkelhor concluded that it is likely that the percentage of abuse committed by males masks the true disproportion in the risk of male offending, in that most children are exposed to more female than male babysitters, both in terms of numbers and the amount of time spent in their care.

In addition to these statistical findings, there have also been a number of high-profile cases of abuse by babysitters, which have caused great distress and anxiety for parents. The most famous of these cases occurred in 1997 in the USA and involved a nineteen-year-old British *au pair* who was convicted of second-degree murder of an eight-month-old boy. (A Massachusetts Superior Court Judge later reduced this sentence to involuntary manslaughter.)

In the UK in 2005, a forty-year-old man and his nineteen-year-old girlfriend pleaded guilty to rape and making indecent images. The offences had been committed against a baby the couple babysat. The man was given a life sentence and his partner was jailed for five years. International law enforcers alerted police after the man downloaded 7,000 indecent images from the Internet. The baby's mother was unaware of the abuse until detectives visited her home after finding photographs detailing the abuse, which took place at the man's home.

In 2007, police in Alabama in the US charged a nineteen-year-old babysitter with raping one boy and sexually abusing another she was caring for over a period of three weeks.

Although these high-profile cases are very disturbing, the research studies indicate that given the large number of children exposed to babysitters, a relatively small percentage are abused by them. However, it is important to bear in mind that most of the research is based on the most serious criminal acts, i.e. those reported to the police, and therefore might not accurately reflect the full scale of babysitters' misconduct towards children in their care.

As Finkelhor wrote, although sexual acts toward children are usually considered very serious and reported to police, many acts of physical assault by babysitters, even those resulting in injury, are unlikely to be reported. In addition, episodes of babysitter neglect and emotional abuse are rarely reported to police. Parents are probably more inclined to simply terminate a babysitter's services than bother with official police or child protection reports. In addition, babysitter crimes may be disproportionately obscured because younger victims are often unable to communicate this abuse to their parents.

Assessing babysitters
When assessing babysitters, there are a number of factors we need to consider.

1. Age, maturity and experience

It is important that when we are asking a person to babysit, we are sure that he/she is old enough to understand the responsibility he/she is taking on and mature enough to deal with difficulties or problems should they arise. While different children will mature and develop at different rates, in general babysitters should be at least sixteen years old. The ISPCC advises that it is generally unsafe to leave children in the care of a babysitter who is aged less than sixteen and that it is unfair to the babysitter, who is likely to find the experience difficult and maybe traumatic.

Alongside the person's age, we need to be sure that he/she has the necessary maturity to take on the responsibilities of minding a child. Some sixteen-year-olds simply would not have the maturity for this task. Combined with age and maturity, it is useful if a babysitter has some experience of minding children, although this in itself may not be necessary.

Assessing a person's maturity and experience can be difficult, but is best achieved by meeting with the person, talking with him/her about your expectations and exploring with him/her how he/she might handle certain situations. While this sounds quite formal, it can be achieved through casual, non-threatening conversation. It is also important to talk to others who know the person and know what they are like with children. If the babysitter is a teenager, it is useful to talk to their parents.

It is usually unwise to accept babysitters on the basis of a recommendation from somebody else, unless the person is prepared to give you some guarantees about the babysitter's suitability. This particularly applies to babysitters provided or recommended by hotels or holiday complexes, where it is extremely important that we ensure the babysitters have been properly interviewed and vetted.

2. Motivation to babysit

We need to ensure that a person's motivation to babysit is not solely financial. Of course, most people who babysit do so for financial reasons, but it is important that they also enjoy babysitting and like children. If a babysitter is motivated solely by money, he/she will not try to make the babysitting experience enjoyable for our child.

Children can be demanding and a babysitter who is only interested in money will find it difficult to meet these demands. Many abusive situations arise when a child's needs or demands are viewed as intrusive or irritating.

3. Quality of the relationship with our child and with us
The essential component of assessing a babysitter is how good a relationship he/she has with our child. This is hard to assess without seeing the babysitter and our child together. Therefore, it is important that before we leave our child in the sole care of a babysitter, we create an opportunity where the babysitter, our child and ourselves spend some time together. In addition, we should see the relationship with a babysitter as an evolving one, where we start by leaving our child with the babysitter for short periods and gradually increase this time as we become more confident.

As this relationship progresses, we need to monitor how well it is going through seeking and hearing the feedback from our child and continually assessing our relationship with the babysitter. If we find that our child is becoming unhappy or information about how the babysitting session went is getting more difficult to obtain, we need to reassess the situation.

4. Making our expectations clear
Making our expectations clear to the babysitter and hearing what his/her expectations are is an important aspect of the babysitting relationship. We need to ensure our expectations are reasonable and involve only the core components of good babysitting, minding our child and giving him/her a good experience.

We need to hear and agree with the babysitter what he/she is prepared to do and what he/she expects from us in turn. If we cannot come to an agreement, yet we believe our expectations are reasonable, then we need to find another babysitter. For example, sometimes we hear from others about babysitters who, in addition to minding the children, do some housework. While this may sound attractive, we need to remember that the most important characteristic of good babysitters is that they care for children first and foremost and make them happy.

We also need to establish whether the babysitter is going to be accompanied by anybody, such as a friend, sister, boyfriend or girlfriend. If we agree to this arrangement, we need to be sure that we apply the same assessment to this person to ensure he/she is safe for our child.

5. Staying objective

In principle, assessing and choosing suitable babysitters seems straightforward. In reality, it can be a little more complex. We may find ourselves under pressure to use friends, a friend's children or family members. In most cases the babysitters we use are local, so ideally we will know them and their family. If difficulties arise, however, the fact that they are local or that we know their parents can make things awkward. We may use a person once, be unhappy with that person, but be afraid to cause offence to him/her or his/her family by not asking them to babysit again.

Although these situations can be difficult to handle delicately, it is important that we remember to prioritise our child's welfare above our discomfort or embarrassment. Once we are guided by this principle, we will find an appropriate way to deal with these situations. It can be the case that short-term discomfort is preferable to a long-term difficulty.

Equally, even if our babysitter is good but is unhappy babysitting or feels under duress to babysit, it is important that we do not pressurise him/her into accepting the task. Remember, if he/she is unhappy babysitting, it is likely that he/she will cut corners or communicate this lack of interest to our child. Additionally, if the babysitter is a young person we have an obligation to ensure that we consider his/her welfare and safety.

6. Keeping our babysitter safe

While adult babysitters are usually in a position to care for and keep themselves safe, it is important that we are aware that when it comes to young people babysitting, we have a responsibility to make sure they are safe. This is important whether it is our child who is babysitting or we are using a young person to babysit our child.

We need to remember that a young babysitter should never be asked to do something he/she is incapable of doing, such as care for too many children or for a very young child. He/she should not generally be expected to feed children, mind other people's children, bathe children or to carry out other personal care needs other than in exceptional circumstances, where they have agreed and have received the necessary training.

Babysitters should not be subjected to any form of harassment or inappropriate behaviour and should be guaranteed a safe environment in which to babysit. They should also be assured of a safe way of coming to and going home from babysitting. We need to treat our young babysitter as we would expect our child to be treated when he/she is babysitting for someone else.

Dealing with problems

The one-to-one nature of babysitting makes it important for us to deal promptly and effectively with any problems that arise. These problems can often be dealt with through discussion with the babysitter; if they cannot be resolved this way, we need to stop using the babysitter and find another. Again, if we know the babysitter well, if our child likes the babysitter or if we know his/her family, it may be difficult to take such steps. But unresolved difficulties will not go away and will ultimately place our child in an uncomfortable, and perhaps unhappy, situation. If serious difficulties arise and we become concerned about our child's safety, we need to stop using the babysitter immediately and seek support from the appropriate authorities. Remember, while the thought of taking such action might make us feel very anxious, we could be placing our child, and other children, at further risk if we do not take the necessary steps.

Susan's story: Abuse of power

Susan had always loved swimming. She had won many medals and was one of the best swimmers in the club. She was delighted when she was informed that she was going to be coached by Ted, who was considered the best swimming coach in the club, and that if she worked hard, she might make the national team.

At eleven, she would be the youngest swimmer to have been coached by Ted. Her father, who had been a swimmer himself, was really proud of her and boasted to everybody about her achievement. Susan had to train every morning and evening and the coach did not allow parents to watch the coaching sessions because he felt they distracted the children. Susan found the training tough. She was afraid of Ted, who shouted a lot and kept telling her she wasn't as good as everybody said.

Sometimes he would race her against the older swimmers

and ridicule her in front of them when she lost. Many nights she would get upset and would ask her father to change her coach, but he said that this type of tough training was what she needed to make her a better swimmer. Then one evening Ted rang Susan's father and told him that he had decided to give Susan individual coaching because she had great potential and that he had arranged for the individual training sessions to occur early every morning.

Susan's father was delighted, although she was a little sceptical. During the first week Ted praised Susan a lot, telling her how special she was. Then during the second week he came into the dressing room while she was changing and started to ask her about her periods, explaining that this was important information for the training programme. He also said that he had to measure her and told her to undress. Susan was very embarrassed and could not bring herself to tell anybody about these incidents.

As the weeks progressed, Ted started coming into the dressing room and sexually abusing Susan on a daily basis. He told her that if she told anybody, she would not be believed because he was the best swimming coach in the club and had a lot of power. Susan could not tell anybody about what was happening because she was ashamed and knew how important Ted was in the club.

Then one evening, on her way home from school, Susan fainted and was brought to the hospital. When the doctor examined her, she was grossly underweight and had bad bruising around her genital and breast area. At first, she would not tell how the bruises had occurred, but following reassurance from her mother she told the doctor about Ted. Following a police investigation, it emerged that Ted had sexually abused more than twenty young girls in five different swimming clubs.

Chapter 7
Internet and Mobile Phones – Safe Use of Technology

The last ten years have witnessed one of the greatest transformations in the way humans communicate with each other with the development of the Internet, mobile phones and text messaging. These advances have impacted most significantly on children.

As with all new developments, children have embraced these new technologies very quickly, using them as everyday modes of communicating with friends, parents and strangers. Most children aged ten and older now have a mobile phone and the vast majority of children have access to computers, either at home, in school, in friends' houses or in Internet cafés.

All advances in communications systems present great opportunities, but also pose risks. For example, the development of worldwide letter postal systems saw the advent of 'poison pen' and abusive 'chain mail' letters. The development of landline telephone systems brought anonymous, hoax and threatening phone calls. Now the development of mobile phones and the Internet present a whole new range of risks and concerns.

As with all communication advances, it is those who stand to gain the most who are at the greatest risk: our children. They will grasp these advances with energy, enthusiasm and skill, putting them to use to share, promote and enjoy life. They will also be the most susceptible to being the victims of their misuse. It is within this context that the risks and misuse of such media need to be understood and addressed.

MOBILE PHONES AND THE INTERNET

Mobile phones are not only a convenient and extremely effective way to communicate, they are also an asset to parenting. Mobile phones allow immediate and personalised communication, allowing parents and children to stay in constant touch and enabling children to text or phone a friend any time of the day or night.

Parents can give many instances where mobile phones have been extremely important in the parenting process, e.g. a child that isn't picked up from school (due to a confusion) can simply phone on the mobile, or a child that is not home on time from the disco can be contacted by phone or text. There is certainly an argument to be made that all children, once they start leaving home without their parents, should be given a mobile phone.

For children, the Internet is an unrivalled source of information and communication. It provides an instant and easy means of obtaining information on almost any subject, and also provides a way for children to communicate with others anywhere in the world. The Internet opens up the opportunity to expand children's thinking and outlook on life and to communicate with people who have the same interests as they have.

For socially isolated children, the Internet provides an opportunity to communicate with others in a less threatening way, while for other children it provides the opportunity to access alternative belief systems and life choices. The Internet has effectively opened up an unlimited spectrum of opportunity and ideas for the world's children.

However, despite the many advantages of mobile phones and the Internet, most parents are still uneasy about the reach and influence of these media. Realistically assessing the risks posed by this new technology can be difficult, especially if parents have only a rudimentary understanding of it. This is not helped by the fact that the technology is continually being updated and advanced. Once a parent falls behind, it can be very challenging to catch up. On top of our own incomplete knowledge about these advances, the media is constantly telling us things about mobile phones and the Internet that worry us.

THE RISKS OF TECHNOLOGY

The effectiveness and attractiveness of new technology can lead children to over-use them, to the extent that they can damage their physical or emotional development. Through these technologies, children can discover, be sent or willingly access material that:

- is unsuitable for them;
- can distort their views of sexuality and gender relationships;
- can lower their threshold for violence;
- can traumatise them.

As has been widely documented, people who wish to hurt or abuse children can utilise these technologies to access, groom and meet them. The dangers posed are very real, so parents need to be fully appraised of them.

1. Physical damage

Since the introduction of mobile phones, there have been growing concerns that the radiation generated by them can cause damage to our bodies and, in particular, to our brains. These concerns are more significant for children given that their bodies and brains are only developing and are therefore more vulnerable to damage. The research conducted thus far on this issue is inconclusive: some studies indicate that mobile phones can cause physical damage, others conclude that they do not.

For parents, the most important thing to remember is that the mobile phone is still too new for us to be sure beyond doubt that it does not cause any physical damage. It is also reasonable to surmise that if mobile phones do cause physical damage, such damage is more likely to occur through excessive usage. In this regard, we need to take reasonable precautions to ensure that our children use their mobile phones safely and responsibly.

2. Compulsive usage

Anybody familiar with using mobile phones and the Internet will know how compulsive they can become. Constantly making and receiving calls, texting, checking messages, checking e-mails, surfing the web or chatting in chat rooms can swallow a large amount of our time and can become addictive. For children, the danger of becoming addictive is even greater given their hunger for novelty and excitement.

Research on the impact of compulsive use of new technologies on children's intellectual development is still somewhat contradictory, with some indicating a negative impact and others indicating a positive impact. However, there is no doubt that compulsive use of these technologies has a negative impact on a child's social and emotional development because a child can miss out on those extremely important social and emotional experiences that can only be obtained through face-to-face contact with others. It has a detrimental effect on physical activity, peer interaction, imaginative and exploratory play. In addition, some children, if they are spending too much time in a virtual world, can begin to become detached from reality, with their involvement in everyday activities becoming even more limited.

3. Bullying through technology

It is an unfortunate reality that mobile phones and the Internet are extremely effective bullying tools because they:

- enable bullying to be carried out any time of the day or night;
- enable the quick and extensive spreading of nasty messages or pictures; and
- protect the anonymity of the bully.

There are many kinds of bullying that can take place. Bullies might take pictures or videos of the bullying incidents and disseminate them to others through their mobile phones or over the Internet. Being in possession of a mobile phone can put a child at risk, as there have been many cases of children being beaten up and robbed of their mobile phones. Sometimes, children are bullied because they do not have a mobile phone or computer, or they have one that is out-of-date or not as technically sophisticated as others. Bullying through technology can also be more subtle, with some young people refusing to allow others to interact with them over the Internet, or a group of children refusing to visit a particular child's personal web space.

Children might find it very hard to tell their parents if they are being bullied through their mobile phone or the Internet because they worry that they are doing something wrong, that their phone or computer might be taken away from them or that their parents will over-react.

When it comes to our children and technology, we have two responsibilities: to ensure, as best we can, that our children are not bullied via this medium and to ensure that our children do not bully others via this medium.

4. Pornography and technology

Talk to anybody who uses a computer and they will tell you how often they receive unwanted pornographic material across the Internet. Primary-school principals will tell you that pornographic images on children's mobile phones, even those of quite young children, are becoming more and more common. In the main, the source of these pornographic images are X-rated websites, although a very small minority consist of pictures taken by older children, teenagers or adults using their camera phones. These images, particularly those downloaded from pornographic websites, tend to be sexually graphic in the extreme and many can be hardcore in content and theme.

Children who unexpectedly receive such images through their mobile phones or over the Internet can become very traumatised and distressed. They often think they have done something wrong and are reluctant to tell their parents in case they get into trouble or are prevented from using their mobile phone or computer in future. Others who download such material from the Internet or receive it willingly from somebody else may keep it on their mobile phone or computer and pass it to others.

Whatever the circumstances, the discovery that our child has viewed or is storing, downloading or passing on such images is likely to be extremely distressing for us. Most parents are not accustomed to such sexually graphic material and find it disturbing that their child has viewed such material. Their initial reaction is shame and anger, particularly when another adult, a teacher or a friend's parent brings the possession of the images to their attention.

This reaction is normal because viewing such images is not healthy for a child and indeed for many children it is distressing in the extreme. A child will not have the maturity to understand the nature of the material and could, with continued exposure, become inappropriately sexualised and confused about their sexuality and the nature of healthy sexual relationships.

5. Child abuse and technology

Research indicates that increasing numbers of children are engaging in communications with people, on the Internet or through their mobile phones, that become abusive. Any communication mechanism that allows direct contact with children can and will be exploited by those wishing to hurt and abuse children. The anonymity afforded by mobile phones and the Internet provides a strong attraction for such people and a further risk for children.

Those wishing to hurt and abuse children often use mobile phones and the Internet in order to pose as children, to groom a child for abuse and to lure children to particular places. Grooming commonly involves building a secretive and emotionally dependent relationship, gradually introducing sexual content into this relationship and then progressing the relationship to a face-to-face contact.

Given the personal nature of mobile phones and the Internet, it is very difficult for parents to detect when this is happening. Those wishing to abuse children will coerce and threaten a child to discourage him/her from disclosing the nature of the communications. These people will be very good at reinforcing in a child the view that he/she has instigated the communications and that he/she will be blamed if his/her parents find out about it.

6. Violence and technology

Technology is often used to disseminate and promote violent messages. There are many websites depicting and encouraging violence and there has been substantial growth in the number of violent computer games available. While research on the impact of such violent messages on children is still inconclusive, it seems likely that some children will be deeply affected by such messages and become more aggressive in their behaviour.

The interactive nature of violent video games increases the impact on children. Consistent exposure to violent images and messages will lower a child's threshold for violence and will normalise violence in a child's mind. Unlike pornography, parents often do not see the damaging effect violent messages can have on children and are therefore less likely to monitor their child's exposure to such material.

7. Chat rooms, social networking sites and personal web diaries (blogs)

Among the most popular new innovations available are chat rooms, social networking sites and personal web diaries. There are various names used to describe these facilities, the most common of which are MSN, Bebo and MySpace. General chat rooms are areas on the Internet where people with a common interest can chat with each other via typed messages. Common types of chat rooms are those that provide forums to discuss things like football, pop stars or hobbies.

Up to 2005, most chat rooms were unmonitored and therefore were increasingly being utilised by those wishing to hurt or abuse children. Stories of young people meeting and running away with adults they met in chat rooms were becoming more commonplace, and as a result Microsoft closed all of its unmonitored chat rooms in 2004. What has emerged since is the development of closed chat rooms, most notably MSN. These are more secure sites in that young people can control, to some extent, with whom they choose to interact.

Similarly, personal web diaries, blogs and social networking sites provide a forum for people to post a diary of their activities, thoughts, opinions, photos and other material for browsers to read. The best known of these are Bebo and MySpace. Access to these sites can be made safe and secure, but many of them still carry significant risks for children.

Despite attempts by service providers to make chat rooms, social networking sites and personal web diaries safer, most can be infiltrated by those wishing to hurt and abuse children. Where age or identity verification is not required, people can pose as children and change their identity. Where children are making personal information available on the Internet, there is a risk that people wishing to exploit them can misuse this information to their own ends.

WHAT DO WE KNOW ABOUT CHILDREN'S EXPERIENCES OF TECHNOLOGY?

Since the emergence of mobile phones and the Internet, a number of Irish and international bodies have been established to monitor people's usage of these technologies. In addition, many governments, including the Irish government, have established organisations that are responsible for promoting and monitoring the safe use of these technologies.

Ireland has an Internet Advisory Board, an Internet Hotline, to which complaints about unsuitable content or communications can be made, and a service established by the Department of Education and Science called Webwise. These organisations also produce regular research data outlining the pattern of young people's usage and experiences of these technologies. What does this research tell us?

Research published by Webwise in 2006 indicates that:

- 97.8 per cent of children aged between nine and sixteen years have used a PC or a computer;
- 91 per cent have a PC at home: 43 per cent of personal computers in the home are located in a public room and 33 per cent are in bedrooms;
- 90 per cent of children with a PC at home stated that they had an Internet connection at home;
- 21 per cent said they had Internet access via a personal device, such as a mobile phone or a games console;
- 24 per cent of those using the Internet use it almost every day at home, while 52 per cent use it at least once a week at school;
- over 50 per cent said that their parents spoke with them very rarely or not at all about what they did on the Internet;
- 27 per cent said they met someone new on the Internet who had asked for information like their photo, phone number, street address or the name of their school;
- 26 per cent had visited hateful websites: boys were three times more likely than girls to have visited hate sites frequently;
- 35 per cent had visited pornographic websites;
- 23 per cent had received unwanted sexual comments on the Internet, with boys being twice as likely as girls to receive such comments frequently;
- half of the teenagers questioned said they had chatted on the Internet, while a quarter of the pre-teens said that they had chatted;
- one in ten of those using the Internet used instant messaging every day or almost every day;
- 19 per cent of those who chat said they had been harassed, upset, bothered, threatened or embarrassed by someone when chatting online;
- 7 per cent have met someone in real life that they had first met on

the Internet, and 24 per cent of these said that someone who introduced themselves to them as a child on the Internet turned out to be an adult.

While there is little specific information regarding the use of mobile phones to abuse children or how frequently mobile phones are used by children to access unsuitable material, a discussion paper published by the European Telecommunications Standards Institute in 2006 highlights some of the current concerns within the telecommunications industry regarding the use of information and communication technologies by young children, particularly those under the age of twelve.

The paper specifically discusses risks identified with mobile phone usage, including physical risks such as repetitive strain injury caused by very small hands using a keypad designed for adult hands, children communicating with unknown or undesirable contacts, children gaining access to harmful content and children using the phones to misuse or abuse others. The paper recommends that, in addition to educating parents and children on the safe use of technology, there is a need to develop corporate responsibility in the area and to give some consideration to developing specific industry protocols for phones designed for young children.

Over the last number of years, a number of high-profile cases in different countries, including Ireland, have highlighted the risks for children associated with technology.

In Ireland in February 2007, the mother of a fourteen-year-old boy discovered, through checking the texts on his mobile phone, that he was being sexually abused by a number of men. The boy was communicating with and arranging to meet these men through his mobile phone. It later emerged that the boy had met these men on a website aimed specifically at homosexual men. Some of the men suspected of abusing the boy included a teacher, a Garda and a scout leader. The case sparked a nationwide debate about how parents should monitor their children's usage of mobile phones and the Internet.

In 2006 in New Zealand, a twelve-year-old girl who had been a target of text and e-mail bullying was found dead in her back garden the day before she was due to return to school after the summer holidays. Following her death it emerged that she had been bullied relentlessly for several months by a group of girls not much older than herself. Her mother described it as an orchestrated campaign by e-mail and text. The girl's mother had informed the school about the bullying and the school had made an attempt to deal with it. However, by using mobile phones and the Internet, those bullying the young girl had continued to harass her throughout the summer holidays, warning her not to return to school.

It later emerged that this young girl's death was not an isolated case in the small town in which she lived. In the year before her death, three young people in the town had died in similar circumstances. As a result of the girl's death and these findings, the New Zealand authorities and the technology service providers began an extensive review of strategies to prevent bullying through text and e-mail.

In 2003, a twelve-year-old British schoolgirl ran away from home with a former US Marine whom she met over the Internet. The girl arranged to meet the man and the two flew to France. As a result of international publicity and a search by police forces in a number of countries, the girl returned on her own to her family and the man was later arrested in Germany. He claimed that the girl had misled him about her age, while the girl claimed that he had initially presented himself on the Internet as a teenager.

HOW CAN WE PROTECT OUR CHILDREN WHEN USING THESE TECHNOLOGIES?

Integrating technology into parenting
The best way to protect children from the risks presented by technology is to make discussing technology with them an integral part of parenting. As soon as children become aware of mobile phones and computers, we need to start listening to them about what they know about these technologies and what their experiences have been when using them. Using age-appropriate language, we need to talk to our children about the advantages and the risks involved. In other words, rather than seeing technology as an addition to our lives, we need to integrate it fully.

For example, many parents tend to keep their computers and mobile phones away from young children to ensure that they do not damage them. However, given the key role technology plays and will play in our child's life, it is important that our child becomes comfortable and familiar with the technology as soon as is practical.

For this reason we should allow our child to play with and explore the technologies in our home as soon as he/she is old enough to understand the importance of not damaging them or hurting themselves. This will not only allow our child to see these technologies as a normal part of everyday life, but will also allow us to talk about the benefits and the pitfalls of technology at an early stage in our child's development.

The more familiar our child is with technology at a young age, the better equipped he/she will be to deal with any challenges presented at a later stage. Some parents will remember that when television and radio were first introduced into homes, they were often locked away from children, to be used only when parents were in attendance to supervise. Parents now allow even the youngest of children to play with the TV remote control, to press the buttons on the TV and to put on videos as part of everyday learning because they realise that these technologies are now integral to people's lives. Taking a similar approach to computers and mobile phones will help to integrate them into the parent–child relationship.

Building our knowledge

Before deciding to buy a computer or a mobile phone or allowing our child to purchase them, we need to know exactly what they can do. Different models will have different capabilities and we need to know what these capabilities are. The best place to get this information is from the person selling the technology. If they cannot explain the technology in simple, understandable language, then we should shop elsewhere. Some mobile phone companies have simple explanatory leaflets that outline exactly what mobile phones can do.

If possible, it is important to ensure that at least one parent is knowledgeable about mobile phones and computers so that we will understand how various programmes work and can keep up-to-date with the programmes our child is using. As soon as we have purchased our first computer, or our child has purchased his/her first computer or mobile phone, we need to learn about them with our child.

It will be necessary to come to an agreement with our child about the safe and responsible use of these technologies. For example, we need to explain to our child that he/he should hold phones slightly away from their ear, not pressed to it, and that when carrying phones they should put them in their handbags or coat pockets rather than in clothes directly in contact with their bodies, i.e. shirt or trouser pockets.

Learning about computers and mobile phones is beneficial to parents because they are becoming more and more important in a general context. Whether we like it or not, we are becoming increasingly reliant on technology and are being encouraged to utilise it in a number of different ways. Most banks are now eager to get us to bank on the Internet, and the easiest way to book flights is online. Many clubs and organisations send notices via texts rather than by post. For all these reasons, parents should feel encouraged to become more knowledgeable about technology.

The difficulty is that many of us only know what we have to know. While we might use the Internet and mobile phones to conduct business, we often have no idea how these technologies work, or how other components of the computers and mobile phone work. The reality will quite often be that our children know more about them than we do. Yet it is important that we become familiar with the basics and learn the essentials.

What do we need to know? With regard to our child's mobile phone, we need to know whether the phone can connect to the Internet and whether it can store and send pictures. If it can do these things, we need to have some idea how it does them. Similarly, if the computer our child is using has access to the Internet and e-mail, we need to know how this works, what a website is, what a chat room is, what a blog is and what a social networking site is. One of the essential things to know is if our child, either via the mobile phone or the computer, can have, or has, access to strangers rather than a defined number of friends or acquaintances. For example, is our child using Bebo? If so, is he/she allowing strangers access to his/her Bebo site?

Learning about these things is relatively easy as long as we are willing to do it. If we have the time, we can complete a basic computer course. If this is not possible or practicable, we should talk to friends, other parents or work colleagues about these technologies. Remember, many parents find technology daunting, so don't be afraid to admit what you don't know and be willing to learn.

Establishing the rules

As with all activities, we need to agree the rules of usage with our child *vis-à-vis* using communications technology. The rules that are most important are those that impact directly on their safety. For example, we need to impress upon our child the importance of being careful who he/she gives their telephone number or e-mail address to and of never responding to intimidating or nuisance calls, texts or e-mails. We need to explain to our child the importance of never engaging in communications with individuals he/she does not know, no matter how nice or reasonable they seem, and we need to reinforce for our child the dangers of going to meet somebody he/she knows only through communications on their mobile phone or on the Internet.

It is advisable to agree a schedule for mobile phone and Internet usage with our child. We would not, for instance, allow our child to play football or listen to music any time he/she wishes. In the same way, our child should be encouraged to limit individual calls on mobiles to under ten minutes and to text or use a land-line as alternatives to calling on mobile phones. This is an easy principle to implement, as most young people like to text and are eager to save their call credit. Children should be encouraged to spend no longer than forty-five minutes a day on the Internet or playing computer games.

As part of the rules of usage, computers should be placed in family areas of the house, where they are accessible to everybody and where use can be monitored at all times.

It is important that the rules we establish are appropriate to our child's age and maturity. We should be flexible and open to challenge, while at the same time ensuring the rules we set down will serve to protect our child. For example, while we might be happy for a young child to have a mobile phone or to use a computer, we may not wish him/her to have access to the Internet. The decision to give our child access to the Internet should not be taken without careful consideration, and even then should not be taken until our child is old enough to cope with and understand the many things he/she might come across. We also need to be sure that our child has the maturity not to misuse technology before allowing him/her to use it. While we may be happy to allow an older child to use the mobile phone or computer any time he/she wishes and to have a computer in his/her bedroom, it is not appropriate to allow a younger child this freedom. In general, the rules we apply in other aspects of parenting should be applied to the use of technology.

Discussing the dangers

As with all other risks, the best way for parents to protect their children is to discuss with them the dangers associated with technologies like the Internet and mobile phones. We need to ensure that our child knows that he/she can come to us if he/she gets worried about anything happening on the Internet or via their mobile phones. We need to explain to our children that:

- they might receive messages from unknown sources, which they should not open;
- there is unsuitable material available and that if he/she comes across any, or is sent any, it is important to tell us;
- sometimes people pretend to be other people or children and that some of these people want to use mobile phones or the Internet to hurt or abuse children.

If our child is too young to discuss such matters, then he/she is too young to have a mobile phone or to have access to the Internet.

Equally, we need to communicate to our child the importance of not misusing the phone or computer. Many children engage in 'pranking' – passing on nasty messages, pictures or e-mails – not realising how damaging or upsetting this could be. Sometimes our child might be bullying another child through his/her mobile phone or through the Internet. If he/she has the facility to take or receive pictures on his/her mobile phone or with a digital camera, we need to explain the importance of not taking pictures of others without their permission, and of not passing on pictures of others or posting them on the Internet without their permission. We need to explain that he/she should not try to access or distribute unsuitable material on the Internet, no matter how curious he/she is, and that he/she should delete any unsuitable material sent to him/her by others.

Many parents take the view that there is no point alarming children unnecessarily by outlining all of the dangers they might, but are unlikely to, encounter while using technology. In many ways this is understandable, given that most children will not encounter any problems. The downside of this approach, however, is that many children will find it very difficult to talk to their parents when they do encounter difficulties. This is not a reflection on their relationship with their parents, but rather is a normal reaction by children who feel they may have done something wrong, or may feel too embarrassed or shocked about what they have come across or what has happened. It is usually the case that children simply do not want to worry their parents.

For this reason, it is important that we are proactive in discussing the potential dangers with our child. In a balanced, sensitive and age-appropriate manner, we need to raise and explore with our child the types of dangers that exist. We need to reinforce that these difficulties are manageable and containable, but also that our child can and should come to us if such difficulties arise. By proactively raising and discussing such topics, we show that we are not only in tune with technology, but are also not going to become inappropriately embarrassed, distressed or angry if our child presents us with such issues.

Taking an overly alarmist approach to the dangers is not helpful. While it is important not to turn a blind eye to the dangers, it is necessary to strike a balance and to discuss the potential pitfalls in a matter-of-fact way. Remember, our child needs to know that there are dangers but that, in general terms, he/she is safe to use technology and has the necessary supports if he/she should run into any trouble.

Giving our child responsibility

When it comes to technology, the ultimate goal for parents should be to allow their children to take as much responsibility for their own safety as possible. This means we should strive to give our child as much responsibility as possible, taking into account his/her age and maturity.

Where possible, we should give our child responsibility for his/her own call credit and Internet costs. If he/she is responsible for the cost, this will reinforce for our child responsible and safe use of mobiles and computers. How children negotiate or earn the money to buy their call credit or Internet time is a matter for each individual child and parent, but the key point is that our child is responsible for obtaining and spending his/her own call credit and Internet time. If our child is too young to take responsibility, then he/she is probably too young to have a mobile phone or to have access to the Internet.

As our child becomes more technologically proficient, we should invest more trust in him/her. Asking our child to show us how to use our own mobile phone or computer not only helps us develop a common ground, but indicates that we trust him/her. Another example of this might be dealing with pop-ups or unwanted e-mails: instead of us trying to continually monitor and check for these, we can ask our child to take responsibility, giving him/her the freedom to obtain and operate a firewall and to take on the technological challenge of blocking them. With very technologically proficient children it can be useful to set challenges to ensure their energies are focused on constructive projects. For example, asking them to establish a database for us, or to set up a blog or website, gives them responsibility and at the same time indicates that we trust and value them.

Appropriate monitoring

Monitoring children's usage of the Internet and their mobile phones is important. This should not infringe their privacy, but should be done in agreement with them and as part of the deal struck with them when we agreed to purchase the technology. Such monitoring will highlight very quickly any secretive or compulsive usage and any patterns of upset following texts or calls received or Internet usage. If our child becomes overly secretive or possessive of the mobile phone, computer, calls, texts or e-mails, we need to discuss this and explore with him/her what is happening.

In the absence of satisfactory explanations, we need to ask to see the texts and e-mails, to view the call register on the mobile phone and to view the history folder on the computer, explaining that we are not seeking to infringe our child's privacy but are interested in ensuring his/her safety. We need to be aware that our child might be using a computer in school, in a friend's house or in an Internet café. For this reason we must monitor our child's activities as best we can and communicate as best we can with their friends and friends' parents, ensuring that we have some idea of how they are spending their time when they are not at home.

Many parents view their children's mobile phones and e-mails as personal diaries and letters and are reluctant to infringe their children's privacy by monitoring them. But it should be remembered that there are significant differences between mobile phones, e-mails, diaries and letters. Mobile phones and the Internet put our child in communication with a wide range of individuals and offer them a staggering range of information and images. A diary is a personal document that is not shared, and it is extremely unlikely that our child will receive letters from unknown people.

So, how do we resolve the privacy and monitoring dilemma? The easiest way to tackle this situation is as part of the rules of usage that we agree with our child before he/she begins to use a mobile phone or the Internet. This agreement should explain why it might be necessary, from time to time, to monitor calls, texts, e-mails or websites and should also outline how we intend to do this, if and when it becomes necessary. For example, we might agree that we will check from whom texts and e-mails are received and read only those that are from people we do not recognise. This way, our child knows in advance that while we are prepared to respect his/her privacy, this privacy is not absolute. It also gives our child some security and sets some boundaries.

Of course, there might be times when, in order to protect our child, we need to check out what is happening without his/her consent. If we feel our child is showing serious signs of distress, alienation or withdrawal and we have good reason to suspect it is related to texts, e-mails or websites, then it is important that we check these out. All we can do in these situations is to exercise our best judgment on the matter.

WHAT DO WE DO IF WE DISCOVER THERE IS A PROBLEM?
If we discover that our child is experiencing a problem on the Internet or via the mobile phone, the first thing we need to do is stay calm and not panic. We should keep foremost in our minds the fact that our child will need our help and support, and that our key priority is to protect him/her. We need to remember that, whatever the problem, we should discuss it with our child and give him/her the opportunity to outline how he/she believes the problem could best be resolved. Most times, he/she will know best what to do, but will need our reassurance and support to express it.

Bullying
If we discover that our child is being bullied or intimidated via his/her mobile phone or the Internet, it is important to react appropriately, that is to support him/her and to emphasise that he/she has done nothing wrong and will not lose out because of others' actions.

If we discover our child is receiving bullying texts, calls or e-mails, we should record the times and dates of these communications and the sources of them. We should discuss the problem with our child and see how he/she would like to handle it – he/she may feel he/she can deal directly with the bullies. However, it is important to ensure that he/she does not respond to the texts, calls or e-mails in an aggressive manner.

If we feel our child is not able to handle the situation, we should discuss it with the parents of the people sending the bullying communications, assuming we know or suspect who they are. Again, this needs to be handled assertively, but sensitively. It may also be necessary to discuss the bullying with teachers in our child's school or, in severe situations, with the Garda Síochána.

At times it may be necessary to turn off the mobile phone for a period, obtain a new telephone number or obtain a new e-mail address. If we discover the bullying is of a more subtle form, such as excluding our child from chat rooms or boycotting our child's Bebo site, we should seek to address it with the parents of the people involved.

As with general bullying, it is important that we strike a balance between involving our child in resolving the problem and taking the appropriate action to protect him/her.

Pornography

If we discover pornographic images on our child's mobile phone or computer, we need to stay calm and not jump to conclusions. On most occasions these will prove to be unwanted images, received without our child's instigation or consent. In these situations we need to support, reassure and comfort our child, explaining in an age-appropriate manner the nature of such images. Younger children may not have any idea of the significance of the image and may be more distressed by the fact that the image shows people who are nude, whereas teenagers would most likely understand the full significance of the image.

If we discover that our child has downloaded the images from the Internet or has willingly received them from friends, we need to:

- discuss the exploitative nature of the images;
- discuss the unrealistic impression the images give;

- reinforce healthy sexual messages; and
- where possible, discuss the matter with the friends' parents.

It is important that we find out from our child where he/she has received the images from in order to ensure that they were not sent by a person who may have been trying to exploit or groom our child for abuse. In such situations it is important to remember that our child is a victim of his/her own confused sexuality or of another person's confused sexuality, exploitation or manipulation. If we become concerned that our child received the images from a person who could be exploiting or grooming him/her, it is important to involve and inform the appropriate services (HSE and/or Garda Síochána).

If we discover that our child has passed on pornographic images to other children, we need to explore why he/she did so. We need to find out if these children were the same age, younger or older than our child and we need to check out the nature of the relationship with these other children. As in other circumstances, we need to discuss the exploitative nature of the images and the unrealistic impression they give and to reinforce healthy sexual messages. We need to ensure that our child is not passing these images on to other children whom he/she is exploiting or grooming for abuse and that our child is not being manipulated or exploited by someone else, perhaps as part of an exploitative circle.

Child abuse

If we become aware that our child is involved in inappropriate communication or is in an inappropriate relationship with another person through use of a mobile phone or the Internet, we need to investigate and explore this relationship with him/her. We need to listen to what he/she thinks about the relationship and how he/she thinks the relationship developed. We need to be particularly concerned if the individual with whom our child is communicating is unknown to us or is somebody our child knows only through the phone or Internet.

We also need to be extremely concerned if the communications involve explicitly violent or sexualised content, or if there is undue pressure on our child to meet with the person. Assessing the relationship may not be easy to do, given the secretive nature of such communications, but it is very important that we carefully assess whether we think our child is being unduly influenced or exploited. If we have any concerns, we should explain to our child that we need to end the relationship and why, and we need to report the matter to the appropriate services.

Most children will never run into serious problems while using mobile phones or the Internet. However, technology does carry risks, so educating our children about the dangers and monitoring their usage will help prevent them from becoming one of the unlucky ones who has a bad experience.

Ray's story: Exploiting vulnerability

Ray was thirteen when his family got their first computer, which was bought to allow his father do some work at home in the evening. His father showed him the Internet and explained to him the types of things that it could be used for, like getting football results, e-mailing friends and doing school projects. Ray's father told him he could use the Internet whenever he wanted to, but also warned him about unsuitable material and what to do if unwanted things started popping up on the screen.

One evening, while Ray was checking the football results, he followed a link to a chat room where people were discussing the team he supported. He got involved in the chat, discussing how his team were performing. He started to go into the chat room every Sunday night to discuss the weekend matches. Although lots of people were using the chat room, he started to have most of his chat with another boy called Nick, who was the same age as him but who lived near the football stadium in which his team played and who said that he had gone to see the team play a few times.

Nick and Ray agreed on most things about the team and after a while Nick suggested that he could e-mail Ray some good pictures he had of the team players. Ray got some really great pictures from Nick and they began exchanging e-mails about the team and each other. Ray mentioned to his father that he had gotten some great pictures of the team on the Internet, although he did not mention that Nick had sent them.

Then one Sunday evening Nick sent some pictures that included one image of two men having sex. When Ray opened the picture, he was shocked and upset. He did not like it and knew it was the type of unsuitable material his father had warned him about, but he did not know what to do. He knew that if he told his father he would get into trouble and would probably be banned from using the computer. He knew if anybody else found out about the picture, they would think he was gay. He decided to delete the picture and stop e-mailing Nick.

Later that evening he got another e-mail from Nick saying that he was really sorry, that he had accidentally sent him the picture, which his older brother had stored on their computer. Nick begged him not to tell anybody because he would get into trouble. Ray responded saying that he had just deleted the picture and would not tell anybody. Nick and Ray continued to communicate about football, but the e-mails also began to discuss the picture, with Nick saying that his older brother and all of his friends had lots of this type of thing and were always sending them to each other.

Nick started sending Ray more pictures, just to show him the type of thing his brother had, but told him he had to keep them a secret because they would both get into trouble if anybody found them. Nick explained how to move the pictures into a special folder on the computer. Ray began to feel bad about the pictures, but nonetheless felt compelled to look at them. Some of them began to make him feel aroused.

Then one Sunday evening Nick suggested to Ray that maybe he could come and see a soccer game. He told Ray that he could get the tickets if he could organise to get to the venue. Ray was not sure how he would get to the match without asking his father, but he also did not want his father to know about Nick and what they were doing. When Ray said he could not come to the match, Nick was very angry, saying that he had paid for the tickets and thought that Ray was his friend. He said that he was not going to e-mail Ray any more.

Later that evening Nick e-mailed Ray and said that he was sorry for getting angry and that he understood. He suggested that instead of going to the match, perhaps they could arrange to meet up somewhere near where Ray lived. Nick said he would e-mail Ray the following week to see if they could make an arrangement. Two days later, Ray's father came home from work with a friend who was going to set up an e-mail facility on their computer to enable him to access his work e-mails from home.

Before leaving, the friend told Ray's father that he had come across some very disturbing pornographic images in e-mails, which had apparently been sent to his son. Ray's father was horrified. He looked at some of the images and was sickened. His first reaction was anger. What would his friend think, and was his son gay? He lost his temper with Ray and started shouting and screaming at him. He told him he was banned from using the computer.

The following morning, when Ray's father had left for work, his mother started to discuss with him what had happened. Ray became very upset, but began to disclose his relationship with Nick.

Chapter 8

Drug and Alcohol Misuse, Early Sexualisation, Self-harm and Preventing Self-abuse

When we consider child abuse, most of us consider it to be actions perpetrated by others on a child. There is another form of child abuse, however, namely behaviour that children engage in which hurts or damages themselves. There are many examples of such behaviour, but the ones with which we are most familiar are drug and alcohol misuse, self-harm, such as cutting oneself or attempting suicide, and premature early sexualisation.

While most of us are very familiar with such behaviours, we tend not to consider them as abuse. Discussion about such actions tends to focus on the criminal or anti-social nature of the activities, or on the societal factors we believe cause children to engage in such activities. For example, there is a great deal of focus on how we might control the supply of drugs and alcohol, how we can reduce the sexual messages children are receiving or the opportunities children have to engage in sexual activity and how we can act more quickly when children are feeling suicidal. But in many ways drug and alcohol misuse, self-harm and premature early sexualisation are best understood, and best prevented, if seen and considered within the framework of self-abuse.

What is self-abuse and is it reasonable to consider these behaviours as self-abuse? Self-abuse is behaviour or an action a person engages in even though he/she knows or suspects that this behaviour or action will cause him/her harm and will impact negatively on his/her physical, psychological and social well-being. There is little doubt that drug and alcohol misuse, self-harm and premature early sexualisation cause significant harm to children. There is also little doubt that children know or suspect that these behaviours will, or are likely to, cause them harm. Understood in this way, it is reasonable to consider such behaviours as self-abuse.

Understanding children's involvement in these behaviours is a little more complex, however. Although children might know or suspect that such behaviour can cause them harm, they usually do not have the maturity or intellectual understanding to give full, informed consent to such behaviours and are often unaware of the full consequences of engaging in them. In situations of self-abuse, children are both the victims and the perpetrators of the abuse, making it very difficult to prevent and therefore even more damaging to children.

Of course, viewing drug and alcohol misuse, self-harm and premature early sexualisation as self-abuse should not minimise the role others might play in encouraging or manipulating children into participating in these behaviours. Those who knowingly sell drugs or alcohol to children are contributing to the abuse of these children. Those older children or adults who seek to involve children in premature early sexual behaviour are contributing to the abuse of these children. Many feel that the persistent sexualised messages promoted by advertising and the media contribute to the abuse of children, and there is no doubt that those who glamourise self-harm and suicide contribute significantly to the abuse of children.

However, the availability of drugs and alcohol, the promotion of sexualised messages and the glamorisation of self-harm are not the primary or sole factors that cause a child to engage in such behaviours. A child who does these things ultimately makes a decision to do so. The key to prevention is understanding why a child makes this decision and the psychological factors that underpin this decision. Understanding these behaviours as self-abuse helps us to apportion appropriate responsibility to our child as the perpetrator of this abuse and yet to balance this by offering appropriate support and compassion to our child as the victim of this abuse.

What do we know about self-abuse and children?

DRUG AND ALCOHOL MISUSE

There are essentially three factors that give us some indication of the extent of misuse of drugs and alcohol among children:

- the extent of usage of these substances by children;
- the age at which children start using these substances;
- damage caused to children by the usage of such substances.

Research in Ireland indicates that drug and alcohol usage are becoming more and more prevalent among children.

Alcohol Intake

The 2006 Irish government report, *State of the Nation's Children*, indicated that 57 per cent of fifteen-year-olds admitted that they binge-drink (i.e. consumed five or more alcoholic drinks in a row in the past thirty days, which is considered problem alcohol intake). This represented a 15 per cent increase on the numbers found to be engaging in binge-drinking in 1995. This statistic was based on the *European School Survey Project on Alcohol and Other Drugs* (ESPAD, 2003).

The study compared the usage of alcohol and drugs among fifteen- and sixteen-year-olds in a number of different countries and found that Irish children reported the third highest levels of binge-drinking among the thirty-three European countries surveyed. In addition, while Irish boys reported the fourth highest levels of binge-drinking, Irish girls reported the second highest level. The percentage of young Irish girls who report binge-drinking has increased significantly from 42 per cent in 1995 to 57 per cent in 2003. Other findings from the *European School Survey Project* indicate that young people are mixing alcohol with other substances and that drunkeness is seen by young people as an end in itself.

Two reports published by an Irish strategic task force established to tackle alcohol usage by children indicate a significant but decreasing amount of alcohol usage by children younger than fifteen. The task force reported that in 1998, 26 per cent of boys and 17 per cent of girls between twelve and fourteen years were current drinkers. In the 2002 report, 16 per cent of boys and 12 per cent of girls in this age group were current drinkers. There was no reported change in drinking patterns of fifteen- to seventeen-year-olds: about half of the boys and girls in this age group reported that they were regular drinkers, with drunkeness prevalent in 60 per cent of boys and 56 per cent of girls.

Illicit Drugs
The *European School Survey Project on Alcohol and Other Drugs* (2003) found that 40 per cent of Irish children aged fifteen reported using an illicit drug in their lifetime. While Ireland ranked third among thirty-six countries surveyed, Irish girls ranked first. The percentage of young Irish girls who reported using an illicit drug increased from 32 per cent in 1995 to 40 per cent in 2003. Additionally, 9 per cent of the Irish children surveyed reported that they had used an illicit drug other than marijuana.

Research conducted in the USA in 2005 on the use of illicit drugs by children and young people indicates that:

- 11.2 per cent of adolescents aged twelve to seventeen years reported using illicit drugs in the past month;
- the use of illicit drugs within the past month increased with age. Among twelve- to thirteen-year-olds, 3.8 per cent reported past-month use, compared to 19.2 per cent of sixteen- to seventeen-year-olds;
- alcohol is the most commonly used drug among adolescents, with almost 18 per cent of twelve- to seventeen-year-olds reporting past-month use in 2003;
- marijuana is the most commonly used illicit drug (7.9 per cent), followed by the non-medical use of prescription psychotherapeutic drugs, such as pain relievers, tranquilisers and stimulants (4 per cent);
- marijuana use is more common among male adolescents than their female counterparts (8.6 per cent versus 7.2 per cent), while prescription drug abuse is more common among females (4.2 per cent versus 3.7 per cent);
- in 2003, 48.4 per cent of twelve- to seventeen-year-olds who smoked cigarettes in the past month also used an illicit drug, compared to only 6.1 per cent of adolescents who didn't smoke.

Adding to these studies on current usage is a growing body of research reflecting the difficulties caused by alcohol and drug usage by children. The *State of the Nation's Children* report indicates that the most common reason for Irish young people to be referred to the Garda Juvenile Diversion Programme were alcohol-related offences.

The report compiled by the strategic task force suggests that children who begin drinking before the age of fifteen years are four times more likely to develop problems with alcohol than those who begin drinking at age twenty-one. There is also a growing acknowledgment that alcohol usage by children impacts on their ability and motivation to learn and on their ability to remember what they have learned.

What the research clearly indicates is that Irish children are among the highest users of drugs and alcohol in Europe, and that the younger a child starts to use drugs or alcohol, the more likely he/she is to develop problems. Particularly worrying is the extent to which young Irish girls are using alcohol and drugs.

The research findings are supported by anecdotal evidence from parents, teachers and young people themselves. Discussions with these three groups indicate that drugs and alcohol are readily available in most communities, and that many children come into school on a regular basis suffering the after-effects of drug and alcohol misuse.

It is important to remember that not all drug and alcohol usage can be considered self-abusive behaviour. Children will take drugs and alcohol for a variety of reasons. Some will experiment once and never take them again. Most children will take some form of alcohol or drug before they have reached the age of eighteen and will continue to take them on a 'social basis'. It is when a child starts to take drugs or alcohol on a continuous basis, starts to have difficulties as a result of taking them or becomes addicted to them that the behaviour can be considered self-abuse.

EARLY SEXUALISATION

In most Western societies, children are bombarded daily with a tremendous number of sexualised messages and images. Digital television, magazines, advertisements, media reporting and peer behaviour all portray sexualised images and messages on a regular basis. Whether or not these impact on our children and how they might impact are difficult questions to assess. It is likely, however, that unless our children are capable of dealing with them, these messages will inevitably affect their thinking and behaviour. It is also likely that children experiencing other difficulties in their lives and children who have low self-esteem or are socially isolated will be most affected by these messages.

While many of us might suspect that children are becoming more sexualised at a younger age, is there evidence of this?

A report published by the Crisis Pregnancy Agency in 2004 reviews the Irish and international research on teenage sexual activity. This report suggests that in Ireland:

- 20 per cent of young people have sexual intercourse before the age of seventeen and that the average age of first intercourse for these young people is between fifteen and sixteen;
- in the year 2000, there were ninety-three conceptions to girls under the age of sixteen and that 29 per cent of these girls travelled to the UK for terminations.

Referring to a study conducted in 1997 that surveyed 2,754 young people aged between fifteen and eighteen in the West of Ireland, the report found that 70 per cent of the young people surveyed used condoms or other contraception the first time they had intercourse, with a third reporting inconsistent use thereafter. The report suggests that 30 per cent of young people did not use contraception because they were too embarrassed, did not know about contraception, worried about possible side effects, felt unable to negotiate its usage or were having sex impulsively.

The State of the Nation's Children (2006) report indicates that in 2004, 654 babies were born to girls under the age of eighteen. This represented a decrease compared to the year 2000, when the corresponding number was 777. The ISPCC/Childline service received 20,794 calls relating to sexuality and sexual issues in 2006.

How do the Irish statistics compare to international statistics? The research indicates the following.

1. A five-year study of 1,300 pre-teen girls, aged thirteen to eighteen, in several countries, including the UK, USA, Australia and Canada, who use chat rooms shows that three-quarters of the girls claimed to have had sexual intercourse; only a small number had not performed some sexual activity. Of the pre-adolescent girls who discussed sexual activity, nearly 33 per cent were younger than twelve and 8 per cent were under ten years of age.

2. Research conducted by the World Health Organisation indicates that the percentages of fifteen-year-olds who report having had sexual intercourse ranges from 15 per cent in Poland to 75 per cent in Greenland. In nine countries and regions, mainly in Eastern and Central Europe, fewer than one-fifth of young people report ever having had sexual intercourse. At the upper end of the spectrum, in England, Greenland, Scotland, Ukraine and Wales, one-third or more reported to have had sexual intercourse.

3. In England, the Teenage Pregnancy Unit's teenage conception statistics indicate that:

   • in 2005, 39,683 children under the age of eighteen became pregnant;
   • 46.9 per cent of these ended in legal abortion;
   • 7,462 of these conceptions were to under-sixteens;
   • 57.4 per cent of conceptions to under-sixteens ended in legal abortion.

4. In the USA in 2003:

   • the birth rate among adolescents aged fifteen to nineteen was 41.6 births per 1,000 females;
   • there were 6,661 births to adolescents aged ten to fourteen, representing 0.6 per 1,000;
   • 46.7 per cent of secondary school (high school) students reported having had sexual intercourse;
   • 63 per cent of sexually active students reported using a condom during their last sexual intercourse. Condom use by male students was reportedly higher than condom use by females.

A study conducted by UNICEF in 2007 comparing rates of births to women aged fifteen to nineteen in thirty-one different countries indicates that Ireland ranks nineteenth; the USA tops the poll with the highest rate.

Research published in Ireland in 2007 by the Department of Education and Science and the Crisis Pregnancy Agency indicates that in 11 per cent of secondary schools, the Relationship and Sexuality Education programme was not being taught. The research further indicated that over 40 per cent of schools did not teach this programme to fifth- and sixth-year students. The research found that there are still many blocks to effective relationship and sexuality education, including an overcrowded curriculum, teacher anxiety and pupil discomfort.

Research published by the American Psychological Association in 2007 indicates that sexy and sexualised images could be:

- damaging the mental and physical health of young women;
- leading to a lack of confidence in women about their bodies, as well as depression and eating disorders;
- encouraging older children and adults to relate to younger children as sexual beings, sometimes with tragic consequences.

What seems clear from all of this research is that children are being subjected to more and more sexualised messages and we are failing to prepare them adequately to deal with these messages. Teenage pregnancy is high in Ireland, children are reporting more sexual activity and interactions between children are becoming more sexualised. While in many ways this trend is reflecting a growing sexualisation of society in general, it is vulnerable children who will be most affected by this trend.

The difficulty with the premature sexualisation of children is that it impacts significantly on their lives. It deprives children of their right to have an innocent, carefree childhood and often forces them into communication and behaviour patterns that they do not fully understand. Early sexualisation will also make children more vulnerable to sexual abuse: many teenagers enter into abusive relationships with older adults, not realising they are being exploited.

The Crisis Pregnancy Agency report draws on international research and concludes that compared to women aged twenty to thirty-five, teenagers who become pregnant have a higher risk of experiencing adverse health and obstetric outcomes and of experiencing adverse educational, social and economic outcomes as well.

When we are considering the sexualisation of children, we need to be careful not to get distracted into discussing what young people are wearing or what music they are listening to. While some would argue that even children's fashion and music is serving to sexualise children, the research indicates that the key factors impacting on the early sexualisation of children are family instability or break-up, mental health difficulties, low educational attainment, sexual and physical abuse, social isolation, a family history of teenage pregnancy and early sexual initiation.

Many children wearing what adults might perceive as sexually provocative clothing or listening to sexually provocative music are not seeking to transmit sexual messages – they are simply trying to be fashionable. Some children wear particular clothes to be attractive or to look 'sexy', but they do not intend nor are they ready to engage in sexual activity. It is only when children begin to exhibit sexual messages, begin to act in a sexual manner and become sexually active that the child has become inappropriately sexualised.

SELF-HARM

One of the most distressing ways that children can self-abuse is by inflicting physical harm on themselves. There are many ways that they can do this, including cutting with implements, refusing to eat or committing suicide. Self-harm by children, particularly teenagers, is not uncommon and is usually driven by psychological and emotional factors.

Suicide is the most serious form of self-harm, and is underpinned by a deep sense of despair, unhappiness and extremely low self-worth. Many children who commit suicide have a history of self-harm, poor mental health, hopelessness or experiencing suicidal thoughts, although some will have no such history at all.

Irish research indicates that, as in many Western countries, suicide and deliberate self-harm represent a significant and growing problem among children. The 2005 annual report of the National Office for Suicide Prevention indicates that:

- Ireland has the fifth highest rate of youth suicide in the European Union (among fifteen to twenty-four-year-olds);
- the suicide mortality rate among children aged ten to seventeen is higher for boys (six per 100,000) than for girls (1.8 per 100,000);
- the highest rates of cases of self-harm presenting to hospitals is among girls aged fifteen to nineteen.

The *State of the Nations Children* (2006) report outlines that:

- the suicide mortality rate among children aged ten to seventeen is higher for boys (six per 100,000) than for girls (1.8 per 100,000);
- in 2004, there were eighteen suicides by children aged between ten and seventeen years, accounting for 22 per cent of all deaths in this age group;
- in a study conducted in one part of Ireland by the National Suicide Research Foundation in 2004 involving 3,830 teenagers aged fifteen to seventeen years, 12.2 per cent reported a lifetime history of deliberate self-harm.

How do these figures compare with the figures available from the UK? A report produced by the British Medical Association Board of Science in June 2006 on child and adolescent mental health outlines that:

- the incidence of self-harm is increasing among young people;
- 6.9 per cent of young people commit an act of self-harm, with 11.2 per cent of those being girls and 3.2 per cent being boys;
- the average age of onset of self-harm is eleven;
- boys and young men aged fifteen to twenty-four are most at risk;
- attempted suicide is more frequent: 2–3 per cent of girls attempt suicide at some point in their teenage life.

The report found that young people who have already tried to kill themselves, or who know someone who has tried to kill themselves, are at greater risk of attempting suicide. It was also found that self-harm and suicide are poorly understood by parents, teachers and child welfare professionals.

It is important to note that rates of self-harm reported by parents are much lower than the rates of self-harm reported by children. This suggests that many parents are unaware that their children are self-harming. In addition, it is very difficult to get a true figure for self-harm because research definitions of self-harm vary, plus the level of taboo surrounding the subject is so high that most people are very secretive about it, which normally omits them from any research being conducted.

WHY DO CHILDREN SELF-ABUSE?

There are five main reasons why children engage in self-abusive behaviour.

1. Developmental, psychological and emotional difficulties

If a child become distressed, sad or anxious and these feelings persist for a long time, he/she can become vulnerable to self-abuse. Drug and alcohol use or sexual activity can provide short-term relief from negative emotions, while self-harm might be a way of showing distress.

Similarly, if a child is developing at a slower rate intellectually or emotionally than other children, this can also cause vulnerability to self-abuse. A child who is experiencing developmental delay will be less capable of dealing with the emotional effect of drugs and alcohol, will be less likely to see the consequences of inappropriate sexual activity, less likely to identify exploitation and less capable of dealing with frustration and disappointment.

2. Low self-image, self-worth and self-esteem

One of the main reasons a child engages in self-abusive behaviour is because he/she has a confused or extremely low self-image. This is usually characterised by a belief that he/she is not a nice person, that nobody likes him/her, that he/she is useless at everything, that he/she has done something terrible or that there is no point in continuing with his/her life. Sometimes these feelings are caused by other psychological problems and sometimes they are caused by events in a child's life. The one common feature among children who misuse drugs and alcohol, become involved in premature sexual activity or self-harm is that they do not value or like themselves and therefore do not consider the consequences of their behaviour.

3. Social isolation

If a child begins misusing drugs or alcohol or becomes involved in premature sexual activity, we tend to assume that he/she has lots of friends and lots of social outlets. While taking drink and drugs may occur in groups and be part of socialising, children who misuse them tend to be the ones who have difficulty forming social relationships or who have been ostracised from social groups because of their misuse. Likewise, children who are engaging in premature sexual activity will most likely have few friends and will also be ostracised if other children become aware of their behaviour.

Children who are socially isolated are vulnerable to drug and alcohol misuse and to premature early sexualisation because these activities not only give them short-term gratification, but make them feel socially attractive; however, engaging in these activities can lead to their exclusion from their social grouping. Children who become socially isolated may engage in self-harm as a means of communicating their distress and unhappiness.

Sometimes, for a variety of reasons, it is not a child but the child's family that feels socially isolated. Children from socially isolated families are particularly vulnerable to self-abuse.

4. Family stability

An important factor in the lives of children who self-abuse is the healthiness and stability of the family in which they live. (The factors contributing to the healthiness of a family are discussed in Chapter 3.) When children are confronted with alcohol, drugs or sexual messages, they will need somebody to help them understand and assess what they are being presented with and to help them make the right choices. The safest and most effective place for this to occur is within the family. If families are experiencing difficulties or are functioning in a negative way, then a child may not have anywhere to resolve and explore issues regarding alcohol, drugs and sexual activity.

If someone in the family is misusing drugs or alcohol or has themselves engaged in premature sexual activity, then a child is even more likely to engage in the same behaviour. If a family is experiencing difficulties, then drugs, alcohol and sexual activity can provide a child with short-term relief from this and a means of communicating his/her upset.

5. Availability/opportunity

While distress, unhappiness and low self-worth may underlie a child's decision to engage in self-abuse, the availability of drugs or alcohol and the opportunity to engage in sexual activity or self-harm will undoubtedly contribute to the likelihood that he/she will engage in these forms of behaviour. In the absence of opportunity or availability, a child might choose a less damaging way to express distress.

HOW WOULD I KNOW IF MY CHILD WAS SELF-ABUSING?
It might not be easy to ascertain whether a child is self-abusing. Along with the general indicators of abuse discussed in Chapter 2, the following may also indicate that a child is self-abusing:

- sudden/regular mood changes;
- very low mood episodes;
- loss of appetite;
- loss of interest in school;
- lying and secretive behaviour;
- money/valuable objects missing;
- unusually tired;
- unable to sleep;
- new friends;
- bouts of exciteable, talkative or over-active behaviour;
- poor hygiene and deterioration in self-care;
- unexplained scarring on arms or legs.

While none of these indicators in itself would signify that a child is self-abusing, they are all signs that should be explored further once observed. As parents, we will begin to notice if our child starts to become extremely negative and self-critical or begins to lose interest in him/herself. If this occurs, it is important that we find out why this is happening.

HOW DOES SELF-ABUSE AFFECT MY CHILD?
Self-abuse will impact on our child's physical, emotional and social well-being. The physical risks associated with self-abuse are numerous: there is often a gradual deterioration of physical health and sometimes permanent physical damage. Self-abuse can lead to death, either through physical damage or suicide.

In addition to physical damage, self-abuse can cause substantial psychological and emotional damage. Drug and alcohol misuse, premature early sexualisation and self-harm will all contribute to a child's feelings of guilt and shame and will further reduce his/her self-worth and self-esteem. Self-abuse will also impact negatively on our child's relationships with us, with friends and with his/her social and educational development.

WHAT DO I DO IF I DISCOVER MY CHILD IS SELF-ABUSING?

While self-abuse by a child is extremely worrying, it is important for us not to over-react. What our child will need is understanding and support. While we may feel extremely upset, losing our temper or breaking down will not help him/her. What we need to do is to ask our child how he/she feels the situation would be best dealt with, and to hear from him/her what he/she wants us to do.

Remember, if our child is self-abusing, he/she will find it very difficult to be aware of or to accept that this is what he/she is doing. Children who are self-abusing will often deny they have a problem, believing that they can handle it themselves. So while listening to and hearing what our child would like us to do, we may also have to make decisions that he/she will neither like nor support.

Where a child is misusing drugs and alcohol, a physical or psychological dependency may have developed, making it even more difficult for him/her to handle the situation. However, as one of the contributing factors to self-abuse is low self-worth, it is important that we try and involve our child in the decisions we are taking to tackle the problem. Where possible, we need to work in partnership with our child, making his/her welfare our priority, while continually listening to and communicating honestly with him/her. We might need to seek outside support, such as counselling or social work help, for both our child and ourselves. Often the most difficult decision facing parents in this situation is knowing when to seek outside support.

It is common for parents to discover that their child is using drugs or alcohol, is becoming involved in premature sexual activity or is self-harming, but not to know how serious the problem is. A child involved in such activities will most likely underestimate the problem. In these situations, we have to assess our knowledge of our child carefully and ask ourselves whether we feel he/she has the self-awareness, confidence and emotional strength to cope with this situation, with our support. If we feel he/she does not, we have to seek outside support as soon as possible.

As discussed earlier in this chapter, if it is not addressed, self-abuse can cause serious physical and psychological damage to our child. If it is tackled through support and intervention, we can prevent it from causing such damage.

HOW DO I PREVENT MY CHILD FROM SELF-ABUSING?
The best way to prevent children from self-abusing is to ensure they
stay psychologically healthy by building their emotional intelligence,
self-image, self-worth and social skills. They also need us to ensure
that they have the necessary supports and capabilities to deal with
peer pressure, personal and social difficulties and setbacks. One of the
most effective ways of achieving this is to establish a strong, healthy
relationship with our child and to integrate the management of
drugs, alcohol, sexuality and self-worth into this relationship.

Communicating about alcohol, drugs, sexuality and self-worth
Communicating with our child about drugs, alcohol, sexuality and
self-worth needs to become a core component of our parenting role.
We need to listen carefully to what our child is telling us about how
he/she is learning, seeing and experiencing these challenges. We need
to communicate to our child the attractions and dangers of engaging
in drug and alcohol usage, sexual behaviour and self-harm and we
need to ensure that we are the people with whom our child assesses
his/her choices and options. We need to:

- begin our discussions about drugs, alcohol, sexuality and self-
  worth long before the teenage years;
- instead of taking the 'big talk' approach, we need to look for
  opportunities in everyday conversation to develop a dialogue with
  our child. Mounting personal attacks, delivering sermons or
  convening family conferences is not helpful;
- letting our child talk, confide and trust in us is important, as is
  staying cool and trying to keep any negative reactions until later,
  when we have had time to think them out;
- it is not enough to stress an abstinence-only message, rather it is
  best to try for abstinence-based education, which will leave room
  for conversation.

Giving our child accurate information
If we are to ensure that our child makes the right decisions about
drugs, alcohol, sexuality and self-harm, it is important that we give
him/her as much accurate and appropriate information as we can. We
need to take a lifelong learning approach to educating our child on
these issues, starting as early as possible and continuing throughout

childhood and adolescence.

The amount and type of information we give our child and the way we present it to him/her should be determined by his/her age and maturity. While we should only ever give our child the information he/she is capable of handling, we should be careful not to limit the information we are giving because of our own prejudices or discomfort. We should remember that:

- we can't prevent children from being curious about drugs, alcohol, sex or death and we can't shield them from social pressures. We *can* encourage their self-worth, give them the hard facts, establish firm limits and keep open the lines of 'communication without condemnation'. For example, many older children have a fascination with death and things related to death. When upset, some of them will say that they wish they were dead. Most parents become distressed by such statements or preoccupations when in fact it is at these times that we need to engage and communicate with our child, giving him/her the facts about death and dying;

- a child needs to know how his/her body works, how to prevent pregnancy, how drugs and alcohol can effect him/her and how self-harm can cause lasting damage. Such communication is a process, one that is far more than one brief, uncomfortable conversation. It is a process of building trust with our child, of listening and not penalising him/her for telling the truth about his/her body;

- we need to explain that desire is one of the joys and wonders of being human, and that sadness, guilt and self-criticism are also part of being human. We need to explain that it takes a long time to know how to handle these feelings (and many people never learn!). We need to follow our child's lead in this. If the conversation is going in a direction we didn't expect, we should take a deep breath and go there. Staying calm is important. We should try and avoid romanticising sex ('Like the smell of blooming roses, like fireworks, transcendent, spiritual') or frightening our child ('The first time you'll bleed, it hurts, you'll feel terrible', 'You'll get AIDS');

- it is important to explain that any sexual involvement or drug and alcohol usage should be by consent. As parents, we should not be afraid to express our values: our child will be strongly influenced by where we stand on such matters. For example, we need to emphasise to our child that he/she may come under a great deal of peer pressure to become sexually active or to use alcohol or drugs and that engaging in such behaviour just to be in with girlfriends or boyfriends is not advisable;

- we need to teach our child healthy ways to deal with stress, sadness or feeling bad about themselves. For example, we need to encourage talking about feelings, engaging in relaxing activities, finding distractions and challenging negative, self-defeating beliefs.

Monitoring our child's behaviour

Getting the balance right between appropriately monitoring our child's behaviour and not smothering our child is one of the hardest things for a parent to do. When it comes to alcohol, drugs, sexuality and self-worth, this balance is extremely important. For example, the research on drug usage indicates that children who are over-controlled or under-controlled by their parents are more likely to misuse drugs.

While most parents strive to achieve that balance, it is a difficult thing to do, particularly if we suspect that our child is using alcohol or drugs or engaging in sexual behaviour. It is even more difficult if we discover that our child is self-harming. It is important to remember that, short of locking up our child, there is actually no way of completely monitoring what he/she is doing all of the time. The best and most effective way of monitoring our child is to invest in our relationship with him/her and to trust them until trust becomes impossible.

Most children want parents to monitor what they are doing. They want the security of knowing that their parents care enough about them to check on them and set limits. Remember:

- trying to reduce our child's exposure to inappropriate sexual messages, drugs and alcohol is important. We should try, at an age-appropriate level, to monitor magazines, the Internet, the TV and social environments and we should not be afraid to challenge messages being presented by friends or others;
- trying to monitor and advise on the types of clothing or make-up our child is wearing is also important. We should explain to our child how others might perceive him/her, without being overly

dramatic. We should try to be understanding of fashion trends and peer pressure, but also hold to some basic standards of what is or is not acceptable to us;

- if our child starts using drugs and alcohol or starts to become sexually active, we need to try to supervise and monitor his/her usage and activity and try to set limits, e.g. allow drinking only once a week, agree an amount and what type, discourage sexual intercourse and encourage using contraception, etc.;
- if our child starts to self-harm or shows signs of suicidal thoughts, we need to monitor his/her activities and moods without over-reacting. Being sensitive to changes in mood, behaviour or communication is important, while at the same time not treating our child with undue distrust.

Modelling good behaviour

One of the most commonly accepted parenting principles is that children learn most from their parents. One of the most commonly accepted principles about learning is that children learn most from what they witness and experience rather than from what they are told. These principles are particularly true of children's behaviour with regard to alcohol, drugs, sex and self-worth. It is true that children whose parents are drug users are more likely to misuse drugs than children whose parents do not use drugs. It is also true that one of the factors influencing whether a child becomes pregnant as a teenager is whether the child's mother became pregnant as a teenager.

Modelling good behaviour regarding drugs, alcohol, sex and self-worth is one of the most effective ways we can protect our child from these risks. We need to try to:

- serve as our own example of our beliefs and values concerning drugs, alcohol, sex and self-harm. Drink alcohol responsibly, avoid having drugs and alcohol in the house other than for special occasions, avoid having alcohol or drugs at children's events, e.g. birthday parties, engage in mature and responsible sexual relationships and avoid exposing one's children to inappropriate sexual messages, treat one's own body with respect;
- model appropriate coping skills. For example, we should try to show our child how to cope with negative feelings and setbacks by showing what we do when we are stressed – going for a walk, playing a sport, listening to music, talking to others, etc.

Supporting our child

Aside from all of the other strategies we might employ in trying to prevent our child from misusing alcohol or drugs, becoming involved in premature early sexual behaviour or engaging in self-harm, perhaps the most important action we can take is to support our child. When things are going well, this is usually easy to do. It becomes more challenging if our child starts to run into difficulty. Problems involving drugs, alcohol, sex or self-harm often spark strong emotions in us as parents, which can affect our ability to be supportive. We may feel let down by our child or feel powerless to help him/her. What is important to remember is that we know our child best and we are the people best placed to support or help him/her. Therefore, when confronted with such difficulties, we must set aside or control our own emotions and focus on supporting our child. We need to:

- stress that no matter what happens, we are there for our child;
- start by teaching our child strategies to deal with peer and relationship pressures, i.e. teaching him/her how to say no, how to pretend to be using alcohol or drugs to avoid losing friends or having to give in, how to understand, deal with or withdraw from intense feelings;
- be understanding of our child's feelings and not make assumptions. We need to try and find out why our child might feel a particular way and try not to be judgmental;
- react in a supportive way if we find out our child is self-harming. Along with our child, we can try to agree alternative ways to express anger, frustration or annoyance at oneself;
- seek outside help at the appropriate time. If we feel our child's self-harm, alcohol and drug usage, sexual behaviour or suicidal thoughts have become persistent or too embedded for us to change, we need to intervene quickly and seek outside support. While ideally we should try to involve outside supports with the agreement and co-operation of our child, if our child's involvement in these activities is out of their control, he/she will resist any attempts to obtain such support. In these situations we may have to involve others without our child's agreement. These judgments are difficult to make, but ultimately parents need to trust their own instincts, as they are best positioned to make them.

Exploring and clarifying our own attitudes

As with all other risks our children face, their attitudes, decisions and reactions to alcohol and drug usage, sexual behaviour and self-harm are greatly determined by our own beliefs about these activities. Many things influence our personal beliefs on these matters, including our own alcohol and drug-taking history, our sexual history and our history of coping with difficulties.

Many of us may not see the relationship between our beliefs and behaviour and our child's beliefs and behaviours. We may never really adequately assess our attitudes to these behaviours and how these attitudes might have been shaped. Many of us simply do not want to assess them.

However, if we are to adequately protect our children from the risks associated with such behaviours, it is imperative that we think about and clarify our beliefs. While we all have our own individual beliefs, there are some general belief sets that make it difficult for us to keep our child safe from these risks.

1. Kids will be kids

Some of us take a very nonchalant attitude towards alcohol, drugs, sexual behaviour and self-harm. While we are aware of the public discussions and concerns about these issues, we feel the problems are being somewhat exaggerated and that, at the end of the day, 'kids will be kids' – that no matter what we adults do, kids will want to experiment with alcohol, drugs and sex. We believe that even if we wanted to, there is nothing much we could really do to stop them from following this course and that, despite all the negative publicity, plenty of people have engaged in such behaviour and come to no harm. Some of us may even feel that it is good to see our child starting to engage in such behaviours because it shows they are normal and keeping up with their peers.

These types of beliefs tend to arise from a number of different sources. Perhaps we ourselves have used or are using alcohol and drugs and believe that they have not, or are not, doing us any harm. Perhaps we engaged in sexual behaviour at a very young age and felt it taught us a lot and did us no harm. Perhaps we live a very relaxed life and feel sexual experimentation and a variety of sexual experiences are important. We may have had lots of times in our own childhood when we felt depressed and suicidal, when we cut ourselves or took overdoses. We may feel that such episodes are a normal part of childhood. We may still go through such periods as adults and feel that they are a normal part of life.

This way of thinking ultimately reflects our *adult* beliefs, which are based either on an analysis of our own childhoods, which may not be objective or accurate, or on our behaviour as adults. We may not wish to face up to the fact that our childhood was difficult, or that we were lucky not to have been hurt or damaged by our behaviour. We might have been adversely affected by our behaviour in the past, or perhaps are currently being adversely affected by these behaviours, but simply cannot face up to this reality.

It is important for us to accept that we have no right to impose our beliefs on our child, who should be allowed to make his/her own decisions once he/she is mature enough to do so. As we cannot be certain such behaviour will not adversely affect our child and because we know that our child is not mature enough to make a fully informed decision on these activities, it is our job, as parents, to give our child the opportunity and support to be allowed to make his/her own decisions when he/she is ready.

2. Do what I say, not what I do

Some of us are clear about how we want our child to behave, but do not want or are unable to behave like this ourselves. Perhaps we see the damage or difficulties our behaviour causes or has caused us, but are simply unable to stop. Perhaps we do not want to stop, but appreciate that our child has the right to make his/her own choices, or perhaps we feel that it is wrong for a child to engage in such behaviours, but acceptable for an adult to do so. Whatever the reason, these beliefs present us with a dilemma. In order to resolve this dilemma we convince ourselves that how we behave is not relevant to how our child behaves, that it is enough to say the right things and monitor what our child is doing.

Our child will see through this approach very quickly, however. No matter how often or how convincingly we impress upon our child the risks and dangers involved in drug and alcohol misuse, early sexual behaviour or self-harm, it will mean very little if we are engaging in these behaviours ourselves.

This is not to say that all children of parents who abuse alcohol or drugs will in turn abuse these substances, or that all children of parents who engage in promiscuous sexual behaviour will engage in such behaviour. In fact, sometimes such behaviour by parents has the directly opposite effect on children. They see first-hand the effect and difficulties caused by this behaviour and it leads them to totally reject this way of living. Nonetheless, the primary problem created by such beliefs and behaviours is that it normalises these actions and impresses upon children how many people, including the people they love the most, place importance on these things. If the people you love and respect are doing it, then what is so wrong with it? This attitude, combined with other factors, can place great pressure on a child to start engaging in such behaviours.

Resolving this difficulty is not easy. It is not reasonable to suggest that parents, just because they are parents, cannot drink, use drugs, engage in the sexual behaviour they wish to engage in or cope with difficulties in whatever way they feel is appropriate. However, one of the responsibilities that comes with becoming a parent is that our behaviour no longer effects just us and our partner/spouse. Along with the responsibility of protecting and nurturing our child, we have a responsibility to model, as best we can, mature, appropriate behaviour. In this context it is incumbent upon us to work to resolve any difficulties we might have regarding alcohol, drugs, sex or self-harm. Even if we cannot, or will not, resolve these difficulties, it is important for us to at least acknowledge to our child that we have a problem.

3. Fear is the key

Some of us are terrified of alcohol, drugs, sex and self-harm. We cannot think about these activities without becoming anxious or embarrassed and we find it impossible to discuss them. The idea that our child might take alcohol or drugs or might be sexually active or self-harming is simply too much for us to handle.

When the topic comes up, we react by either closing down completely or trying to impress upon our child our fear and terror. Accordingly, discussions about alcohol and drugs become discussions about liver disease and chronic drug addiction; discussions about sexuality become discussions about AIDS and STDs; and discussions about self-harm become discussions about mass suicides. If our child even hints that he/she might be involved in any of these behaviours, we become distraught or aggressive.

This sort of fearfulness about alcohol, drugs, sex and self-harm can have many sources. Perhaps we have had a very bad personal experience of such things in the past, perhaps we find it difficult to handle stress or perhaps we are afraid that we have an innate inability to control our own behaviour, that if we let the reins slacken, we would spiral out of control. Whatever the source of these beliefs, what they serve to do is to make us unavailable to our child. When our child is confronted with peer pressure to take alcohol or drugs, to become sexually active or to engage in self-harm, he/she will not feel able to discuss this with us. Our child will not want to worry, panic or distress us, therefore will not be prepared to take the chance that we will over-react.

Furthermore, fear in itself will not prevent our child from engaging in such activities. He/she will realise very quickly that the fears may be exaggerated and that there are many attractions to engaging in such behaviours. If we have such beliefs, we need to control or resolve them. We need to remember that our child needs and expects us to be mature, reasoned and able to handle such issues.

Learning from our own experiences
While our children will have their own individual way of dealing with the challenges that arise regarding drugs, alcohol, sex and self-harm, it is useful for us to draw from our own experiences of how we dealt with these challenges when we were children.

If we self-abused, ask ourselves why we did this and why we stopped. If we did not self-abuse, we should ask ourselves what prevented us from choosing this option. While we cannot apply our own experiences directly to our child, they do help us remember what it was like to be faced with such challenges as a young person.

Delaying the age of first involvement
The older a child is when he/she first takes an alcoholic drink or drug or first engages in sexual activity, the more likely he/she will be able to make an informed decision about this activity and to understand and deal with the emotional consequences of his/her actions. Therefore, the older a child is when he/she first engages in these activities, the less likely he/she is to develop difficulties in relation to them. For this reason, we need to do everything we can to ensure our child has reached a relatively mature age before first trying these activities.

Where possible, we need to curtail our child's exposure to drugs and alcohol, to sexual messages and self-abuse, including exposure to those role models, such as other children, who are engaging in self-abuse.

SEEING THE RISKS IN PERSPECTIVE

We will never be able to protect our children completely from exposure to drugs, alcohol, sexual messages or emotional difficulties, therefore it is important to see these risks in perspective. We need to be aware of and be vigilant about the risks, but it is equally important to remember that most children will grow up safely and will not be damaged by exposure to drugs, alcohol, sexual behaviour or self-harm. Our primary aim should be to build our child's psychological capability to deal with these challenges, as this is the key to protecting our child. This is best achieved through building healthy families.

Colm's story: Defiance and despair

Colm had always been a poor reader. No matter how hard he tried, he could not remember the words or recognise them. This made him feel 'really stupid' and sometimes the other children in the class would laugh at him when he could not read even simple words. His mother and father were made aware of the problem by the school, which started to give him remedial help. However, his parents thought that, like his father, he was just not academically minded and would go into the family's painting and decorating business when he was old enough.

Any time school or schoolwork was discussed, Colm felt embarrassed and ashamed and his brother delighted in calling him 'thicko'. When he came home from school he often felt like crying and would go to bed until just before his mother came home from work, at 4.00 p.m. He avoided bringing any friends home from school in case they told his brother how terrible his reading was.

During the summer Colm started hanging around the local park with his older brother and his friends. On a Saturday night they would buy cans of beer and drink them in the park. At first, they refused to give him any beer, saying he was too young, but

---

after a while they started giving him a can for the laugh.

When he went into sixth class, Colm started refusing to go to the remedial teacher, saying that he 'hated school anyway and that it was a waste of time'. He told his classmates that he hung around the park each evening and drank alcohol with some of his brother's friends. He told them not to come to the park because he and his brother's friends would beat them up.

By Christmas, Colm's schoolwork and attendance had deteriorated and his parents were called to the school. They had not realised that he had missed so much school because they both worked. They confronted Colm, who said he had been mitching because he hated school and wanted to leave. When they asked him where he went when he was mitching school, he said he just 'hung around'. His mother told her friend, a neighbour, what had happened and she in turn told his mother that Colm was often seen in the local park hanging around with a gang of boys much older than him.

When his mother confronted him about this, Colm denied it. That Saturday night, Colm's father went down to the park at 10.30 p.m. and found him drinking cans of beer, drunk. He brought him home and grounded him. The following night, Colm went out to the park anyway, taking a bottle of vodka from the drinks cabinet.

Later that night he was brought to the hospital in an ambulance, having drunk most of the bottle of vodka. In the hospital the doctors advised Colm's parents that they should seek counselling.

Chapter 9
Keeping Children Mentally Healthy

'**M**ental health' is a term used to describe emotional and psychological well-being. Being mentally healthy is a very important component of our children's welfare. If our children are emotionally and psychologically healthy, they will be happier, more content and better equipped to deal with the challenges that life presents.

When mental health difficulties arise, the effect is twofold: they cause our child to be unhappy, withdrawn or stressed and leave our child vulnerable to other difficulties. If mental health difficulties become too dominant, they can start to impact on a child's ability to function normally. This can result in a child withdrawing from everyday activities or, in more serious cases, being hospitalised for treatment.

In an attempt to resolve mental health problems, a child will sometimes begin to use drugs and alcohol, will become involved in premature early sexualisation or will begin to self-harm. In addition, children with mental health difficulties can be susceptible to abuse by others, who may coerce them into feeling better about themselves for a short period of time. In this context, mental health is an important child welfare issue.

A child's mental health, or emotional and psychological well-being, is determined by a number of factors:

- the type of person a child is;
- the type of experiences a child has;

- the type of supports available to a child;
- a child's ability to understand and resolve emotions.

• The type of person a child is (personality)

Some people are more prone to worrying or becoming sad than others. Even when children are very young, they will have a unique way of dealing with stress and sadness. While we cannot be sure whether children are born with these characteristics or whether they begin to learn them from the moment they are born, what is clear is that every child, as part of his/her personality, has different ways of experiencing and coping with these feelings. It is possible to address and change components of a person's personality, but this can be quite difficult.

• The type of experiences a child has

The amount of stressful, traumatic or sad experiences children have will inevitably impact on how well they cope with these emotions. No matter how good we are at coping with negative emotions, there is only so much we can deal with before these feelings become unmanageable. This is particularly true of children who are still only learning to cope with challenges and intense emotions.

Some people think that the more emotion a person has to deal with, the better he/she becomes at handling this emotion. In fact, the reverse is the reality. The truth is that protecting our children from as many stressful or sad experiences as possible will make them emotionally stronger.

• The type of supports available to a child

Children will cope better with stress and sadness if they have good emotional supports. While support from parents is crucial, the role of siblings, peers and other trusted adults, such as teachers, should not be underestimated.

The key support that a child needs is to feel secure and loved. This alone will be a tremendous help to a child in coping with stress and sadness. Combined with this sense of security, children need to feel confident to speak about and discuss problems and feelings in the knowledge that these feelings will be taken seriously and that their views will be important in deciding how the resulting difficulties are managed.

- **A child's ability to understand and resolve emotions**

Alongside our children's inbuilt ways of experiencing and coping with stress and sadness are the learned ways they cope with emotions. This learning commences as soon as they are born and is influenced by many factors: how they are taught to cope, how they see other people coping and how successful they are in coping.

In this regard, parents have an important role to play in teaching children constructive coping mechanisms. If we, as parents, cannot cope with stress and sadness, then we will find it very hard to teach our children to cope with these feelings. If we are unaware of our children experiencing stress and sadness or do not have the time or energy to help them find ways of coping, then it will be very difficult for them to learn effective coping mechanisms.

Of course, our children can learn how to cope with stress and sadness from many other sources, but the primary emotional educators of children are parents. Our children will value our knowledge and know-how more than that of any other person in their lives.

WHAT MENTAL HEALTH DIFFICULTIES CAN ARISE?

There are a number of different mental health difficulties that can arise for children and understanding them can be challenging. Even those researching and treating these difficulties often do not fully understand all of them, although our understanding and knowledge is continually growing.

While we hear a great deal of discussion about mental health difficulties in adults, we do not hear so much discussion about such difficulties in children. As a result, we sometimes forget that children can, and often are, affected by negative emotions and disturbed ways of thinking.

To help us understand the many mental health problems that can arise for children, it is easiest to divide them into three broad categories: anxiety-based difficulties, depression-based difficulties and difficulties that result in a detachment from reality, often referred to as 'psychotic' difficulties.

Anxiety is best described as extreme, unrealistic worry about everyday life activities. Different terms are used to describe different types of anxiety. Some of the most common include:

- separation anxiety – a term used to describe situations where children have difficulty leaving their parents to attend school or hobbies, to stay at a friend's house or to be alone;
- phobias – a term used to describe unrealistic and excessive fears of certain situations or objects, such as animals, storms, water or heights;
- panic attacks – a term used to describe periods of intense fear accompanied by a pounding heartbeat, sweating, dizziness, nausea or a feeling of imminent death;
- Obsessive Compulsive Disorder (ocd) – a term used to describe a situation where children become trapped in a pattern of repetitive thoughts and behaviours;
- post-traumatic stress – a term used to describe stress that occurs after children experience a very stressful event, the symptoms of which include strong memories and flashbacks.

Depression is best described as a persistent sad and hopeless mood, which interferes with a child's ability to function normally.

Detachment from reality (psychosis) is best described as an illness that prevents people from being able to distinguish between the real world and the imaginary world. Symptoms include hallucinations (seeing or hearing things that aren't really there, or delusions), irrational thoughts and irrational fears. Such difficulties interfere greatly with a person's capacity to meet life's everyday demands. The most common such disorder is schizophrenia.

In order to live life fully, children must experience stress and sadness. They also need to have an imaginary life and to withdraw into themselves for periods of time, particularly if they are facing difficult or demanding situations. However, when these behaviours or emotions start to occur very frequently or begin to occur to the extent that they impede a child's ability to live a normal happy life, then he/she is starting to experience mental health difficulties. Often, the causes of these feelings and behaviours become more difficult to ascertain and our child begins to find it harder and harder to cope with them.

WHAT DO WE KNOW ABOUT MENTAL HEALTH
DIFFICULTIES AMONG CHILDREN?

The *State of the Nation's Children* report (2006) discusses a 2005 study conducted by the Health Services Executive in the south-east of Ireland. The research team screened 3,374 children aged fifteen to eighteen years and found signs of mental health problems in:

* 17 per cent of children aged less than five years;
* 10 per cent of national school children;
* 26 per cent of secondary school children.

The report indicates that in 2005 there were 333 admissions of children to hospital for psychiatric care. The most common reasons for children being admitted were:

* depressive disorders: 26.4 per cent;
* schizophrenia: 9 per cent;
* neuroses (anxiety-based problems): 18.9 per cent;
* personality disorders: 10.8 per cent;
* drug dependence: 9.9 per cent.

The report indicates that the vast majority of the children admitted to hospital for mental health problems were aged between fifteen and seventeen.

The ispcc/Childline service received 5,046 calls relating to depression, sadness, suicide and self-harm in 2006. Of those contacting the Childline online service, 16 per cent were concerned about mental health issues.

In the uk, a report published by the British Medical Association indicates that:

* 20 per cent of children will have mental health problems at some stage in their childhoods and that these problems appear to be on the increase among children;
* one in ten children under the age of sixteen has a clinically diagnosed mental health problem;
* while the majority of children with anxiety or depression will not have mood disorders in adult life, of those with mental health problems at twenty-six years of age, 50 per cent had met the criteria for a disorder at fifteen.

What these statistics indicate is that many children in Ireland experience, or are at risk of experiencing, mental health difficulties. Most worrying is that many of these children may never disclose these difficulties and as a result most will not receive the appropriate support. The statistics from the UK show that mental health difficulties among children are on the increase, suggesting that a similar trend will emerge in Ireland over the coming years.

HOW WOULD I KNOW IF MY CHILD WAS EXPERIENCING MENTAL HEALTH DIFFICULTIES?

One of the main indicators of mental health difficulties is when a child's mood and behaviour start to change for no apparent reason. Of course, mood may change for lots of reasons, but when we find that our child's mood is becoming more agitated or sad and we cannot find an obvious reason to explain this change, then we have to consider the possibility that our child might be experiencing some mental health problems. If their behaviour starts to change, mirroring their mood, then we need to give the possibility even more consideration.

Mood changes and behaviour that might indicate that a child is suffering from anxiety include:

- worrying unduly about academic performance, sporting activities or even about being on time;
- becoming self-conscious, feeling tense and having a strong need for reassurance;
- stomach aches or other discomforts that do not appear to have any physical cause;
- repeated school absences or an inability to finish a day at school;
- excessive 'clinginess';
- unrealistic fear of specific things;
- panic attacks;
- obsessive, compulsive behaviour;
- traumatic flashbacks and memories;
- impaired relations with siblings;
- impaired relations with friends;
- low self-esteem;
- alcohol or other drug use.

Mood changes and behaviour that might indicate that a child is suffering from depression include:

- frequent sadness, tearfulness, or crying;
- feelings of hopelessness;
- withdrawal from friends and activities;
- lack of enthusiasm or motivation;
- decreased energy level;
- major changes in eating or sleeping habits;
- increased irritability, agitation, anger or hostility;
- frequent physical complaints, such as headaches and stomach aches;
- indecision or inability to concentrate;
- feelings of worthlessness or excessive guilt;
- extreme sensitivity to rejection or failure;
- pattern of dark images in drawings or paintings;
- play that involves excessive aggression directed toward themselves or others or involves persistently sad themes;
- recurring thoughts or talk of death, suicide or self-destructive behaviour.

Mood changes and behaviour that might indicate that a child is suffering from a psychosis include:

- sleeping too much or too little or any other major sleep change;
- withdrawing from family, friends and other enjoyed activities;
- difficulty understanding what the person is saying;
- lack of speaking, not having much to say about anything;
- expression of emotions diminishing (acting like a robot instead of a person);
- hoarding objects or rummaging through other's belongings;
- wearing strange clothing or inappropriate combinations of clothes;
- suspiciousness or hostility;
- diminished motivation and lack of any enthusiasm;
- decreased ability to concentrate or focus on anything;
- engaging in strange behaviour that makes no sense;
- thinking that people are after them or trying to kill them;
- hearing voices or seeing things that others cannot see or hear, e.g. believing that the voices are coming from the television or

someone has their home bugged, speaking directly to them;
- having delusions and/or hallucinations;
- engaging in strange, atypical behaviour;
- smelling or tasting things that appear to be real;
- severe paranoia, e.g. believing someone is plotting against them
  and is trying to turn everyone away from them.

It is important to remember that, from time to time, we may become aware of many of these indicators in our children, but it does not necessarily mean that they are experiencing mental health problems. It is only when such indicators become persistent, start to impact on their normal living patterns and have no reasonable explanations that we need to consider the possibility of actual mental health difficulties.

HOW CAN MENTAL HEALTH DIFFICULTIES AFFECT MY CHILD?

Aside from the many symptoms arising from anxiety and depression as outlined above, mental health difficulties, if not resolved, can impact on our child's development and well-being.

For example, children experiencing anxiety may start to miss a great deal of school, complaining of feeling sick, and may become very clingy to parents, not wanting to leave them. Children experiencing anxiety will often start avoiding leisure and social activities and will stop interacting with friends. If unmanaged, anxiety can cause physical problems, such as ulcers, eating difficulties and nausea. In addition, anxiety tends to become more intense and more difficult to handle if it goes untreated for a period of time.

Similarly, depression will cause children to withdraw from friends and family and will often result in them missing or dropping out of school. Sometimes what seems to be bold or lazy behaviour is, in fact, the loss of energy and interest associated with depression. If unmanaged, depression can result in physical problems, such as weight loss, sleep difficulties and constant fatigue. Where depression is unmanaged for a period of time, it can sometimes result in self-harm and suicide attempts.

WHAT DO I DO IF I DISCOVER MY CHILD IS HAVING MENTAL HEALTH DIFFICULTIES?

It is often difficult to distinguish mental health difficulties from the normal mood swings of growing up. Therefore, the first step to take if we become concerned that our child is having such problems is to explore with him/her how he/she is feeling and why, in his/her opinion, he/she feels this way. It must be remembered that being unable to define a specific cause of anxious or depressive feelings is a common feature of mental health difficulties, so our child may not be able to tell us exactly how he/she is feeling or why. Nonetheless, it is very important to give them the opportunity to do so.

DEALING WITH ANXIETY: PRACTICAL TIPS

If we think our child is anxious, we need to:

- recognise that the anxiety is real. As trivial as an anxiety may seem, it feels real to our child and is causing him/her to feel worried and afraid. Being able to talk about anxiety helps because words often take some of the power out of the negative feeling. If we talk about it, it can become less powerful;
- assess whether the source of the anxiety is normal for our child's age. If the answer to this question is yes, it's a good bet that our child's anxieties will be resolved before they become a serious cause for concern. This isn't to say that the anxiety should be discounted or ignored; rather, it should be considered as a factor in their normal development. For example, many children experience age-appropriate fears, such as being afraid of the dark. Most children, with some reassurance and perhaps a practical solution, such as a night-light, will overcome or outgrow this fear. However, if they continue to have trouble or if there is anxiety about other things, the intervention may have to be more intensive;
- we should never belittle the anxiety as a way of forcing our child to overcome it. Telling our child, 'Don't be ridiculous! There are no monsters in your wardrobe!' may get our child to bed, but it won't make the fear go away;
- don't cater to anxieties. If our child doesn't like dogs, don't cross the street deliberately to avoid one. This will just reinforce that dogs should be feared and avoided. We need to provide support and gentle care as we approach the feared object or situation with our child;
- teach our child how to rate worries. If he/she can visualise the

intensity of the worry on a scale of one to ten, with ten being the strongest, they may be able to 'see' the worry as less intense than first imagined. Younger children can think about how 'full of worry' they are, with being full 'up to my knees' as not so worried, 'up to my stomach' as more worried, and 'up to my head' as truly distressed;

- reinforce the security of 'home'. A child can be encouraged to tackle the situation or issue in stages, returning to us for safety before moving to the next stage. The key to resolving fears and anxieties is to overcome them;

- help our child to learn some positive statements, such as 'I can do this' and 'I will be okay,' which he/she can say to him/herself when feeling anxious;

- relaxation techniques are helpful as well, including visualisation (of floating on a cloud or lying on a beach, for example) and deep breathing (imagining that the lungs are balloons and letting them deflate slowly);

- identify what the symptoms of the anxieties are and how they affect our child's personal, social and academic functioning. If symptoms can be identified and considered in light of our child's everyday activities, adjustments can be made to alleviate some of the stress factors. For example, if a child is particularly anxious about lunchtime at school, then we can discuss ways of ensuring he/she meets trusted friends, siblings or is engaged in distracting activities, like sports or helping the teachers.

DEALING WITH DEPRESSION: PRACTICAL TIPS

If we think our child is depressed:

- it is important to keep a positive attitude and focus on the positive aspects of our child's life. It is important to point out the positives for them, but to ensure that these are genuine and real. For example, telling a child he played well in the football match when he did not even kick the ball will not work. We have to find genuine positives in a child's life and remind him/her of these. This can be as simple as saying, 'I really enjoy chatting to you, you are a great listener';

- we need to gently challenge our child's negative thinking, pointing out when this thinking is unduly negative. For example, when a child says, 'I can do nothing right', we need to say, 'That's not true, you are very good at _____';

- we should strive to take away some of the pressure weighing on our child and create opportunities for him/her to find activities he/she enjoys and feels good about doing. For example, even though a girl might be struggling academically in school, if she enjoys dancing and finds it relaxing, it is important that she dances as much as possible;

- we need to encourage our child to be active: going to a movie or playing football is more likely to make him/her feel better than staying home alone doing nothing;

- it is important to help children make friends. Children don't have to be wildly popular to be happy, but they do need at least one good friend. For example, parents often need to step in and organise events with friends. If our child struggles in a group, then we need to organise one-to-one events. If our child needs energy and excitement to put him/her at ease, we need to organise group events;

- the best thing parents can do is to talk to their child. In these conversations we should practise 'active listening': expressing interest in what he/she thinks and validate his/her feelings, rather than minimise them. It's also helpful for parents to share what it was like for them at their child's age, while maintaining their boundaries and not projecting their own issues onto their child;

- if a child makes a remark about wanting to die, we need to talk about it without delay. Talking about suicide does not encourage self-harm acts. It may help clarify what a child meant by the remark or help us determine what might be changed in order to make that feeling go away.

DEALING WITH PSYCHOSIS: PRACTICAL TIPS

If we think that our child might be suffering from a psychosis, we need to:

- pay attention to changes in our child's behaviour and/or abilities;
- trust what we know about our child (we may know him/her better than almost anyone and be in a good position to notice changes);
- don't wait: symptoms of early psychosis are unlikely to go away on their own and early treatment is better. Nowadays, psychosis is

normally treated with low doses of anti-psychotic medication along with education and support for a child and his/her family. Once a child starts treatment, it can take from a few months to one year for a child to get better. Sometimes they will have some leftover symptoms that hang on longer. While they're recovering, they are likely to have a lot less energy to do things, to be a lot quieter, to need a lot more alone time and to prefer not to be in large crowds or noisy places;

- seek support for ourselves in deciding how best to support our child (talk to our doctor, counsellor or other health professionals);
- get the facts: know what is reliable and what is myth;
- face our own fears: don't ignore problems in our child because of any fears we may have about mental illness. It is treatable, non-contagious and dealt with more effectively if it is treated early;
- be around to talk and be positive by giving sincere compliments and gently encouraging our child to do things he/she is good at;
- doing one-on-one things with our child will be better than doing things in crowds;
- children are likely to give themselves a hard time about their illness. We can help by being encouraging and reminding them it's an illness and that they will get better;
- if our child has been diagnosed with a psychotic illness and is receiving treatment, it is useful to remember that for the initial period of treatment we should assume that most of our child's behaviour is due to psychotic symptoms. We need to follow the suggestions we are receiving for managing the psychosis. People with psychosis usually experience negative symptoms, which mimic laziness or depression. Negative symptoms may improve somewhat with treatment, but may not go away completely;
- if our child is diagnosed with a psychosis, it is useful to seek as much information as possible about the early warning signs of this illness. Generally, children will have similar symptoms to when they first became ill. Some initial symptoms are insomnia, restlessness, irritability and anxiety;
- we are the experts in what works for our family and we are most likely to make good decisions. We can, however, seek help to set limits on behavior and teach our child communication and problem-solving skills;
- a child with a psychosis is generally no more dangerous than the

rest of us. A few people when they are acutely ill may become dangerous. Generally, a child is still responsible for his/her behaviour, except when he/she is acutely ill and judgment is impaired. The person's basic personality does not change, but when they are ill, they do act and think differently from their normal behaviour.

Even if a child cannot specifically identify the cause of his/her feelings, we need to listen to what he/she believes might help resolve these feelings. Sometimes a series of life changes that reduce the stressful experiences in our child's life can resolve mental health problems. For example, reducing the number of activities in which our child is involved or moving him/her out of a particular class might make a significant difference. No matter how small a particular issue might seem to us, it could be very important to our child and could be the issue that is making the anxiety or depression unmanageable.

Providing our child with additional supports can help resolve the anxiety or depression he/she is experiencing, and sometimes discussing some coping skills can help him/her manage the difficulties better. For example, teaching a child to think out what is worrying them and seeing how this situation can be resolved can help make their anxiety manageable. Alternatively, teaching him/her to distract him/herself away from negative thoughts can also help.

When these strategies fail to work, it is important to seek additional support, such as counselling or medical advice.

HOW DO I PREVENT MY CHILD FROM EXPERIENCING MENTAL HEALTH PROBLEMS?
In most situations, mental health problems are preventable. It may not be possible to change a child's personality or to protect him/her from all worrying or sad situations, but there are effective ways to prevent worry and sadness developing into anxiety and depression.

1. Self-awareness
The first step in preventing mental health difficulties is to help our child become self-aware enough to recognise when he/she is becoming stressed or sad.

Many people feel that self-awareness develops with age, but this is not necessarily the case. Many older people have poorly developed self-awareness, while many young people have highly developed self-awareness. However, developing self-awareness does involve the ability to self-analyse, a skill children sometimes find difficult.

When self-awareness is characterised in age-appropriate terms, children quickly develop a good knowledge of the type of person they are. For example, saying to a child, 'when you are tired, you get sad' is a way of helping them start to understand the type of person he/she is.

Providing a child with the space and opportunity to explore his/her individual characteristics, emotions and frustrations helps this process. For example, conversations with our child about the difference between him/her, his/her siblings and other children, e.g. 'When you get upset you get quiet, but your sister gets angry and loses her temper', his/her likes and dislikes and reactions to non-threatening emotional situations, like sad or tense films, can all help him/her to develop a good level of self-awareness. Building such conversations into everyday parenting ensures it becomes easier for our child, and for us, to become self-aware and to recognise anxiety or depression if they arise.

2. Self-esteem
Self-esteem is the collection of beliefs or feelings we have about ourselves, i.e. our 'self-perceptions'. Healthy self-esteem is a child's armour against the challenges of the world. Children who feel good about themselves seem to have an easier time handling conflicts and resisting stress or despondency. In contrast, for children who have low self-esteem, challenges can become sources of major anxiety and frustration.

Children who think poorly of themselves have a hard time finding solutions to problems. If they are plagued by self-critical thoughts, such as 'I'm no good' or 'I can't do anything right', they may become passive, withdrawn or depressed. Faced with a new challenge, their immediate response is 'I can't'. In this way, self-esteem is one of the core influences on mental health.

Parents can make a big difference to a child's self-esteem. We can strengthen our child' s self-esteem by:

- **watching what we say:** Children are very sensitive to parents' words. We need to remember to praise our child not only for a job well done, but also for effort. We also need to be truthful and to reward effort and completion instead of only outcome;

- **being a positive role model:** If we are excessively harsh on ourselves, pessimistic or unrealistic about our abilities and limitations, our child may eventually mirror us. We need to nurture our own self-esteem and our child will have a great role model;

- **identifying and changing our child's inaccurate beliefs:** It is important for parents to identify a child's negative self-beliefs, whether they are about perfection, attractiveness, ability or anything else. Helping our child set more accurate standards and be more realistic in evaluating him/herself will help our child develop more healthy self-esteem.

    For example, even a child who is very good at most things will sometimes focus only on those things in which he/she is weak. As a result, the negative self-beliefs take root and start to dominate his/her thinking about him/herself. A child who does very well in school but struggles with maths may say, 'I can't do maths. I'm a bad student.' Not only is this a false generalisation, it's also a belief that will set a child up for failure. Such a child needs to be helped to see the situation in its true light. A helpful response might be: 'You are a good student. You do great in school. Maths is just a subject that you need to spend more time on. We'll work on it together';

- **being spontaneous and affectionate with our child:** Our love goes a long way in boosting our child's self-esteem. Giving our child hugs, telling our child we're proud of him/her, leaving a note in our child's lunch-box that reads, 'I think you're terrific!', giving praise frequently and honestly, but without overdoing it because a child can tell whether something comes from the heart – all of these things bolster a child's sense of his/her self-worth. It is important to show our affection in an age-appropriate way, ensuring he/she is comfortable with it;

- **giving positive, accurate feedback:** When we are giving feedback to our child, it is important to avoid generalisations or 'labelling' statements. A comment such as, 'You are a bold girl' is a generalised labelling statement that can give a child a sense that boldness is in some way part of her personality. It is important to give a child specific feedback on specific issues, for example, 'What you did just now was bold.' This statement, while indicating disapproval, does not give the message that our child is a bold or bad person per se. It does, however, make it clear that his/her behaviour needs to change. Generalised statements are unhealthy because they not only serve to lower self-esteem, but also discourage a child from developing and changing;

- **creating a safe, nurturing environment:** Just as low self-esteem will leave a child vulnerable to risk, creating a safe environment for a child enhances his/her self-esteem. A child who does not feel safe, respected or is being abused will suffer immensely from low self-esteem.

3. Developing emotional intelligence

Linked to self-awareness is emotional intelligence, or the ability to recognise, understand and deal with our own and other people's emotions. Helping our child to develop strong emotional intelligence is important in the prevention of mental health difficulties. If our child has strong emotional intelligence, he/she will recognise anxiety and depression more easily and will be able to find his/her own ways of dealing with these feelings.

Developing strong emotional intelligence, like any other component of development in a child, is primarily dependent on parents. From the time their child is very young, parents can help him/her to develop by expressing emotions in a constructive, appropriate manner and by talking about emotions openly and honestly. We all experience happy and sad emotions. It is important that we show our child that it is good to express and talk about how we feel and that there are appropriate and inappropriate ways of doing this.

For example, parents have an argument and become upset. One breaks down crying, while the other becomes silent and withdrawn. Whether a child witnesses the argument or not, he/she will become aware of the emotion of the parents and will in turn become unhappy or upset. If the parents and the child discuss their feelings in an open, honest manner, then the child, while still perhaps upset that his/her parents are arguing, will be secure in knowing where the emotions have come from and why they have arisen.

If, on the other hand, the emotions are not discussed, the child will become insecure, not knowing why one parent is not speaking and the other is crying. A child in this situation often starts to misconstrue how his/her parents are feeling and where the negative emotions have originated from, perhaps thinking that one parent is angry with him/her and the other is disappointed with him/her.

Sometimes parents feel they must protect their children from negative emotions, but this simply teaches them to hide their emotions. Of course, if we express our emotions in inappropriate ways, such as becoming silent for long periods, using alcohol or being overly sarcastic, critical or aggressive, this will not help our child develop his/her emotional intelligence. Instead, it will make him/her more vulnerable to mental health difficulties.

5. Changing thinking

Mental health difficulties often arise when children begin to develop a certain negative mind-set or belief system, which they begin to use to understand and deal with life experiences. Sometimes this mind-set is part of their make-up, other times it emerges from a particularly stressful or sad situation and sometimes it is modelled on the way his/her parents view life. For example, a child may start to think, 'I am not an interesting, exciting person.' As a result, if somebody talks over him or does not say hello, or the teacher does not pick him to do a message, this viewpoint is reinforced.

To prevent mental health difficulties arising, we need to recognise, support and challenge our child and, if necessary, to change our own way of thinking. In children, negative belief systems sometimes manifest as 'moaning', 'laziness', 'disinterest', 'disrespect', 'rudeness', 'cheek' or 'attention-seeking'. It is important for us to try to help our child recognise and change this thinking pattern as soon as it emerges in order to prevent it from becoming embedded and more difficult to change.

Of course, we all have episodes or incidents of negative thinking, but it is when this starts to become a persistent pattern that our child is at risk of developing mental health difficulties.

5. Changing behaviour

One of the most concrete ways we can help our child to avoid mental health difficulties is to help him/her change his/her behaviour. It is often a child's behaviour that drives him/her to become anxious or depressed, and once he/she starts to feel anxious or depressed, he/she often begins to behave in a particular way.

Changing a child's thinking can sometimes change his/her behaviour. But equally, changing behaviour can sometimes change thinking. For example, to help our child avoid becoming anxious, we need to encourage him/her to build relaxation into his/her life. Most importantly, it is our child, not us, who needs to define what this relaxation is. This is important because often what we regard as relaxing is not so to our children. Watching TV, chilling with friends, chatting with friends on the phone or on the computer or lying on their bed listening to music are the things many children find relaxing. Others like to clean their bedroom or fix their bike. Children will vary greatly in how they choose to relax, so it is important that we allow them the space to make their own decisions. Usually, our child's days are filled with structured activities, which gives him/her no space to unwind and resolve the emotions of the day.

In contrast to this, we sometimes have to structure activities for children and encourage them to participate to avoid them becoming depressed. We may need to work hard to ensure they have frequent contact with friends and are motivated to keep interested in school and other activities. This might involve engaging in more activities jointly with our child to ensure he/she invests energy in the activity and to help us get to know our child better. In this respect, even the simplest activity, such as watching the television together and chatting about the programme we are watching, can help.

CLARIFYING AND RESOLVING OUR OWN ATTITUDES TO MENTAL HEALTH

How we work to prevent our child from experiencing mental health difficulties or how we support our child if he/she begins to experience such difficulties depends largely on our own attitudes and beliefs about mental health. These beliefs can be influenced by many things and by many experiences, as a result of which we all have our own very personal views and beliefs about mental health and illness.

It is not so long ago that attitudes and beliefs in Ireland regarding mental health were extremely negative. While this has improved somewhat over the last twenty years, many people still have gross misconceptions, the most unhelpful of which are the following:

'They should just pull themselves together': Some of us find it very difficult to understand how a person might become so anxious, so depressed or so detached from the real world that they cannot function normally. We may be experiencing many stressful or sad events in our own lives or at times feel like detaching ourselves from what is going on around us, but we force ourselves to cope with the difficulties. We cannot understand how others are unable to do the same. Sometimes it makes us angry when we hear that people 'cannot cope'. While we might not be prepared to say it openly, deep down we feel that people who allow themselves become so stressed, depressed or detached are 'copping out' from their responsibilities.

Some of us have particular difficulty when it comes to children and mental illness. We find it very difficult to accept that anything could be so stressful or so sad for a child that he/she would be completely unable to cope with it. We cannot imagine how a child could become so detached from reality that he/she could not cope. Some of us find that while we have some understanding of how a girl might, at times, find it difficult to cope, we cannot understand how a boy might experience or react like this.

Such beliefs about mental health can stem from a number of different experiences. Perhaps we ourselves have been lucky enough never to have experienced any serious mental health problems and have always had good supports, so we find it hard to relate to mental health problems. Perhaps these beliefs have arisen because we are experiencing a great deal of stress or sadness in our own lives, but are not prepared to acknowledge the problem. We may be finding it difficult to cope, but are afraid or ashamed to seek help. We may not be receiving much support or help and therefore feel a little resentful that others seek and receive such help. We may have been taught or may believe that admitting to mental health difficulties is admitting to a character weakness of some type.

The problem with this type of thinking is that it makes it difficult for us to recognise mental health difficulties in our child and very hard for us to support our child if he/she starts to experience such difficulties.

If we find that we do hold these types of beliefs it is important for us to challenge ourselves. We need to remember not to judge or impose our coping strategies on our child, and try and recognise that the way we cope with mental health difficulties might not be the healthiest and that we want our child to be able to cope better than us.

Most importantly, we need to remember that our child will have his/her own personality, character and coping strategy and we have no right to impose our personality or characteristics on him/her.

How will I live with the shame?: Some of us believe that those who experience mental illness are 'different' or have a type of 'personality' problem. We see anxiety, depression or psychosis as difficulties that define a person for his/her entire life. We associate mental illness with madness, psychiatric hospitals and harsh treatment regimes, such as 'lobotomies', etc. The fact that somebody close to us or somebody in our family might be experiencing mental health difficulties is seen as one of the worst things that could happen to us and something to be ashamed of.

These beliefs can be based on traditional myths about mental illness, which have arisen due to a lack of accurate information. In Ireland, it is only relatively recently that we have begun to assess our attitudes towards such illness and our attitudes towards the treatment of people who have these difficulties.

It is not so long ago that there were very few community-based supports for people experiencing mental health difficulties, such as support groups, counselling, psychological services, relaxation courses, yoga, etc. As a result, those with mental health difficulties usually received no support until such time as the difficulties became so unmanageable that it was necessary to hospitalise the person. As a result, people with such problems were often regarded and treated as 'different'.

These beliefs can also result from our fear of mental illness. Perhaps we have had experience of this sort of illness within our family or among our friends and have seen how others can stereotype people who suffer from such conditions. Perhaps we have experienced or heard stories about disturbing things that people with mental illness have done. Perhaps we are too afraid to explore the actual information about mental illness. Perhaps we ourselves experienced mental health difficulties at times and were made to feel ashamed about it.

As with the other unhelpful beliefs about mental illness, being ashamed makes us unavailable to our child. It will cause us to avoid the issues involved, making it difficult for us to help our child to avoid mental health problems and to support our child if he/she does experience them.

What is important to remember is that many of us experience mental health problems and that the old myths are simply untrue. We need to challenge these myths ourselves and be prepared to challenge them in others. We need to inform ourselves about these illnesses and work to ensure that we are available to our child, having a healthy and constructive attitude towards any difficulties he/she might wish to discuss with us.

It runs in our family, so what can I do about it?: Some of us take a fatalistic approach to mental illness. As a result of such difficulties occurring in our family, we assume or expect that our child will inevitably experience similar problems. We make the assumption that because we, our parents, our partner or one of our other children are experiencing or have experienced difficulties, it is our child's destiny to experience them, too. This belief can be further reinforced by information we hear about mental health difficulties running in families or being hereditary.

Of course, if a family member experiences mental health difficulties, it will have an impact on a child. It will affect that child's understanding about such problems and impact on how he/she might learn to cope. However, having a family member who experiences mental health problems does not make it inevitable that a child will develop these problems. Sometimes a child will learn how to be more aware of and to prevent mental health difficulties by virtue of witnessing a parent or family member who is experiencing, or has experienced, such problems.

If a parent experiences mental health problems, this can impact on the parent–child relationship. A parent encountering and dealing with such difficulties can find it hard to give a child support. If a parent needs to be hospitalised, this will inevitably impact on the time the parent has to spend with a child. In these situations, it is important to remember that if a parent experiencing illness can create as good a relationship with their child as possible and work to support the child as best he/she can, the impact of the mental illness on his/her child will be minimised.

If a parent experiencing mental health problems is open and honest about how he/she is feeling and the difficulties he/she is experiencing, this will help a child to avoid the same types of problems rather than increasing the likelihood of problems developing for that child. If we are experiencing mental health problems, perhaps one of the most important things we can do is to utilise this experience to support our child constructively and help him/her to avoid similar problems.

As with other unhelpful beliefs about mental health, taking a fatalistic attitude towards illness is not conducive to helping our child avoid problems nor to being there to support our child if he/she begins to experience such problems. In addition, fatalistic beliefs can sometimes unconsciously discourage our child from finding his/her own constructive ways of coping with stress, sadness and disappointment. Our own or other family members' ways of coping will not determine our child's ways of coping. We have to work to ensure that we encourage our child to find the most constructive coping strategies possible for him/her.

Resolving unhealthy beliefs about mental illness is an important part of parenting. We need to be influenced by the accurate facts about such illness and to arm our child with these facts. We need to have the courage to challenge any misconceptions, myths or unhelpful attitudes we ourselves hold and to be brave enough to challenge others who harbour the same attitudes.

KEEPING OUR CHILD MENTALLY HEALTHY

Viewing mental health as a child safety issue can be difficult. It reinforces for us the role parents have to play in ensuring, as best we can, that our child is kept mentally healthy. Protecting our child from external threats is difficult enough, but trying to protect them from psychological threats arising within themselves is perhaps more challenging. At times, it can seem very daunting.

We need to remember that many children develop mental health difficulties. Preventing these from arising in our child involves recognising the first signs of problems in our children's thinking, behaviour and emotions, then investing the time and effort necessary to help him/her to change these. As with all other risks to our child, this is best achieved by creating the most positive constructive relationship we can with our child and the most positive family environment possible.

Ann's story: Emotional awareness

Ann was becoming more and more upset with Emily's 'attention-seeking behaviour'. It was bad enough that she and Joe could not even go out for a drink on a Saturday night without Emily making a scene in front of the babysitter, but now her teacher had called them down to the school because Emily was not mixing well with any of the other children. The teacher was very kind and understanding, but seemed to be suggesting that perhaps something happening at home was upsetting Emily.

Ann had discussed Emily's behaviour with her own mother, who felt that she and Joe needed to be firmer with the child. She reminded them that Emily had always been attention-seeking, even as a baby, always pretending to be frightened of the slightest thing and always clingy. To make matters worse, Joe was finding it difficult to cope following the death of his father a year earlier. Joe had been very close to his father and had been shocked by his sudden death.

Ann and Joe decided that they were going to be firmer with Emily from now on, not allowing her make a scene when they were going out and insisting on her making friends. They also decided that they were going to make her return to swimming, which she had given up a few months earlier.

The next weekend Joe and Ann went out, despite Emily crying in her bedroom as they walked out the door. They gave the babysitter strict instructions that she was not to go up to her. When they came home that evening, the babysitter told them that Emily had cried herself to sleep. They did not check her for fear of waking her.

The following morning, when Ann went in to wake Emily, she found her lying on the floor, curled up in a ball, with a picture of Joe in her hand. Around her, she had written lots of notes saying, 'I am sorry Mam and Dad', 'I love you Mam and Dad', 'Don't leave me', etc. Ann was distraught. She woke Emily and asked her why she was on the floor and what all the notes were. Emily said she did not remember writing them.

When Ann told Joe, he became very upset. He said he just could not handle this any more and left the house.

Two weeks later, the family went to their first meeting with the psychologist. During the session, while discussing their worries and fears, Emily said that she worried that her daddy was going to die like her granddad. Joe laughed at this, saying he was very healthy and had no intention of dying.

Chapter 10
Keeping Ourselves Healthy

If we are to be capable of looking after our children's welfare, we need to be able to look after our own parenting welfare. Parenting not only involves a high level of physical and emotional energy, but also many personal sacrifices. Parents who are too stressed, too busy, too emotionally distracted or unable to make the necessary personal investment in their child's life will not be able to meet the everyday demands of parenting. These parents will find it difficult to give the time and energy necessary to ensure their children are safe.

Parenting should be enjoyed, so if we are finding ourselves becoming unduly stressed or fatigued, we are probably doing something wrong. Looking after our parenting welfare or keeping ourselves 'Parenting Healthy' not only involves ensuring we do everything we need to do to keep ourselves physically and emotionally healthy, but also removing any obstacles that prevent us from making the necessary investment in our child's life.

Some parents find being 'Parent Healthy' relatively easy, while others find it extremely difficult. There are many factors which impact on our parent welfare, some of which are outside our control but many of which we can control, to some extent.

Many people confuse parent welfare and personal welfare, believing they are one and the same thing. There is a difference between welfare as a parent and one's personal welfare, although the two are intertwined. Staying physically and emotionally healthy as a parent is aided by being personally healthy, while part of staying healthy as a parent is preventing personal difficulties from impacting on our parenting.

However, being personally, physically and emotionally healthy is not all it takes to be Parent Healthy. Some people can be personally healthy, but still be Parent Unhealthy. Personal welfare issues do not have to impact on our parenting welfare. Many people experiencing personal physical and emotional challenges are able to set these aside when it comes to parenting and as a result are very effective parents.

Ultimately, parenting welfare, staying Parent Healthy, involves maintaining an emotionally and physically healthy attitude and approach to parenting.

WHAT KINDS OF DIFFICULTIES CAN ARISE?

There are a number of different types of difficulty that can impact on our parenting welfare.

Detachment or over-attachment

The type of relationship we have with our children has an important bearing on how we nurture and protect them. While most parents aim to have a loving, secure relationship with their child, for a variety of reasons some parents can become emotionally detached from their children.

Detached parents find it difficult to show or express emotion to their children and hard to relate to how their children might be feeling. While all parents experience times when they want a break from their children or feel they cannot give them emotional or physical attention, detachment arises when this becomes a persistent pattern of parenting.

On the other side of the coin, there can be times when parents find themselves becoming too attached or enmeshed in their child's feelings and welfare. During these times parents find themselves unable to give their child any freedom or personal space and worry about their child constantly. All parents experience times when they can think of nothing else other than their children, but over-attachment arises when this becomes a persistent pattern of parenting.

When difficulties of detachment or over-attachment occur and are not resolved, a child's welfare can be affected, often leading to the child becoming insecure and emotionally and physically vulnerable.

Fear of failure

Having a good relationship with children and being able to care for their welfare and protect them involves making decisions, taking initiatives, having successes and making mistakes. As parents, we understand how important parenting is, but we also understand that there is no such thing as the perfect parent.

Sometimes parents begin to fear parenting and being a parenting failure. This fear can paralyse them emotionally, making everyday parenting decisions and challenges impossible to deal with. Most parents go through phases when the burden of parenting weighs very heavily on them and they feel they can do nothing right, but this is usually balanced by periods of confidence and satisfaction. When a fear of failure becomes the predominant feature of parenting, a parent often becomes ineffective and unable to function as a parent. This will eventually impact on their child's welfare and safety.

Negative views of a child

While loving our children comes naturally, sometimes, for a variety of reasons, parents develop negative views of a child. While there will be times when parents feel negatively about their children, difficulties arise when these negative views begin to dominate their perception of and interactions with their child.

One example of this is parents who have a very challenging child, about whom they find it very hard to identify something positive, thereby characterising him/her solely in terms of his/her challenging behaviour. A persistent and embedded negative view such as this will often impact on a child's self-worth and self-esteem, making him/her physically and emotionally vulnerable.

Inability to cope

Despite having very balanced and positive attitudes to parenting and having self-confidence, some parents find they just cannot cope with the day-to-day challenges of parenting. These parents cannot establish a parenting routine, cannot get all the tasks of parenting completed within the day and often find they do not know what to do in many parenting situations. There are times when all parents feel like this, but when this inability to cope becomes persistent and ingrained, difficulties arise. Children living with parents who cannot cope with their parenting role will become insecure and undisciplined.

WHAT DO WE KNOW ABOUT PARENTING WELFARE AND PARENTING DIFFICULTIES?

It is difficult to ascertain how many parents experience parenting difficulties or find it difficult to parent. Parents who are feeling stressed or unable to cope are reluctant to disclose this and to seek help because there is a general expectation that everybody can parent. Detachment, fear of failure or having negative views of our child are even harder to acknowledge or disclose because of the stigma attached to such admissions.

One measure of how many parents experience these difficulties is the number of cases of parental abuse and neglect coming to the attention of the child protection authorities (see Chapter 2). However, only those parents experiencing the most serious difficulties tend to come to the attention of the authorities.

Research also gives us some insight into the kinds of problems experienced by parents. Again, this does not give us the full picture because most of the studies conducted in this area assess parenting welfare among parents faced with specific challenges, such as children with disabilities. In Ireland, at least, there is little research aimed at assessing general parenting welfare.

One study, entitled *Listening to Parents, Listening to Children*, conducted by Barnardos Ireland in 2007 sought the views of 400 parents and 200 young people on a range of issues affecting childhood. The report found that:

- six out of ten parents surveyed think that parents in Ireland generally do not spend enough time with their children;
- only 36 per cent of parents, where both are working full-time, said that they are very satisfied with the amount of time they spend with their children; this compares with 52 per cent of parents where one parent stays at home;
- 72 per cent of parents think work patterns in Ireland are impacting negatively on children;
- eight out of ten parents think their children are less safe compared to when they themselves were growing up; but the same number think childhood today is better.

Another study, conducted for the Ceifin Centre in 2003 and supported by the Department of Social and Family Affairs, looked at factors that have a bearing on parenting welfare. One of the key findings contained in the subsequent report, *Family Well-Being – What Makes a Difference,* was that there is a significant gap in our knowledge of families in terms of the extent to which children and their parents fall below agreed 'thresholds' or 'benchmarks' of well-being. The report concluded that in order to plan services for families and deliver them in a targeted way, it would be necessary to know the nature and extent of the needs that exist and to evaluate the effectiveness of different ways of addressing those needs.

This research identified that the physical and psychological well-being of parents is shaped primarily and directly by three factors: personality characteristics, family processes and socio-economic environment. The research found that the particular type of family in which one is living has little or no impact on parents' well-being – with the exception of one-parent families, as single mothers tend to have lower levels of psychological well-being than other parents.

The study measured the parent–child relationship in terms of whether the parent felt supported or satisfied with the parental role. It found that the parent–child relationship is influenced by four main factors:

- the psychological well-being of both parents;
- the couple relationship;
- unique to mothers: positive emotionality – the more positive a mother's emotional state, the more positive her relationship with the child;
- unique to fathers: his attitude towards the parenting roles of men and women.

These findings highlight how the parent–child relationship is overwhelmingly influenced by the characteristics of parents and, in two-parent families, by the relationship between the couple. It is also significant that the research found that the parent–child relationship is not influenced directly by circumstances outside the immediate family.

A study conducted in America in 1997 surveying 44,401 households in thirteen selected states found that just over one in five children were living in a stressful family environment. This was defined as the existence of two or more of six stressors, such as the inability to pay bills or obtain food, uncertainty about healthcare, a parent or child in poor health or with a physical, learning or mental health condition. This proportion jumps to one in two children in families with incomes below 100 per cent of the federal poverty level.

The data from this study, entitled *National Survey of America's Families*, suggest that children living in stressful family environments are nearly twice as likely as other children to exhibit low levels of school engagement and four times as likely to have high levels of behavioural and emotional problems. They are also more likely to live with parents who feel highly aggravated and who report symptoms suggesting poor mental health.

The number of parents contacting support services also gives us some indication of the number of parents experiencing difficulties. In Ireland, ParentLine operates a confidential helpline for parents, and it reports that, on average, its services deal with 9,000 contacts from parents per annum. ParentLine in the UK reports that its services dealt with 100,000 contacts regarding parenting problems in 2005. While the problem in Ireland seems small by comparison to the UK, there has been a marked increase in the number of organisations being established to help and support parents in Ireland.

In the last two years there have also been a number of high-profile cases of tragedies occurring as a result of parents experiencing extreme stress. In 2005, in Wexford, a twenty-eight-year-old mother threw herself and her two children into the sea. Just hours before the tragedy, the woman had called to her local Health Centre, seeking support, but none was available. The woman had been estranged from her husband for a number of months. Following her death, it emerged that while this woman had been under tremendous stress, she had received very little support.

In 2007, again in Wexford, two little girls and their mother died at the hands of their father, before he took his own life. In Donegal, a girl who had just made her Holy Communion died at the hands of her mother, before her mother took her own life.

What seems clear is that while the true extent of the numbers of parents who experience parenting difficulties is hard to ascertain, many parents *do* experience significant problems and it is likely that only some of these seek, or receive, the support they need.

WHAT ARE THE CAUSES OF THESE DIFFICULTIES?

Parenting welfare difficulties can arise in response to a specific event or a series of events. If parents are experiencing a very stressful time in work, in their relationship or in their personal lives, this will impact on their parenting welfare. Stressful or traumatic events do not in themselves account for persistent difficulties, however. A combination of factors usually underpin persistent difficulties and a deterioration in parenting welfare.

Feelings of guilt

One of the most common factors underlying parenting welfare difficulties is guilt. Although parenting guilt can have many sources, the most common is that associated with feeling we are not doing enough for our child. Faced with the increasing demands of modern living, many parents now feel that they are not spending enough time with their children, that they are not providing for them as well as other parents are and that they don't know their children as well as they should.

Many parents find it difficult to balance work with parenting and start to blame themselves. They look around and think that every other parent is managing this balance better. They hear some parents talking about all of the wonderful times they are spending with their children and the things they are doing with them, while they do not seem to be able to do any of these things. These growing feelings of guilt can be reinforced by our children, who quickly challenge us for being absent. They might say to us, for example, 'Why do you have to work?' or 'Why do you never pick me up from school?' If a parent is already feeling stressed by guilt, these sorts of comments are given more significance than they might deserve.

Of course, there are other forms of guilt, too: the guilt that arises if we feel we are treating one of our children differently from another, the guilt that arises if we are fighting with our partner or the guilt that arises if we are creating a tense, stressful family atmosphere because of work or personal pressures. Although guilt itself is a negative emotion, it can drive us to realise where we are making mistakes and encourage us to make constructive changes to our lifestyles. Many work–life balance reviews and decisions, although driven by guilt, are resolved by that guilt forcing us to closely and honestly examine our needs and our child's needs.

Nonetheless, as an emotion, guilt can be particularly difficult to resolve and sometimes the necessary life choices it entails can be difficult to make. When parents cannot find constructive ways to resolve their feelings of guilt, they sometimes find unhealthy ways to deal with them, such as detaching from their children because a reduced emotional involvement reduces guilt. Sometimes parents become angry with their children, unconsciously blaming them for their feelings of guilt. Others might completely deny their guilt and see it as their child being too demanding.

Some parents who are experiencing guilt over-compensate and become too enmeshed with their children. They refrain from disciplining their children to avoid trouble, they lavish them with toys and attention and accede to all of their children's demands. This, in turn, creates even more difficulties as their child becomes more demanding and the parents become more and more incapable of meeting the growing demands. This cycle of behaviour serves only to increase the parents' guilt further.

Resolving feelings of guilt is very important to maintaining a positive approach and attitude to parenting. If we are harbouring unresolved feelings of guilt, it is impossible to be Parent Healthy.

Lack of confidence

One of the key factors infringing on parenting welfare is parenting confidence. If we have low confidence in our ability as a parent, then we will find it difficult to maintain an emotionally and physically healthy attitude and approach to parenting. If we have low parenting confidence, we will have an unbalanced reaction to our parenting mistakes and failures.

Parenting confidence is determined by a number of factors. One of these is our self-confidence or self-belief. Strong self-confidence and positive self-belief provide good foundations on which to build healthy parenting confidence. Likewise, we will have more doubts and uncertainties about our ability to parent if we do not have general self-confidence.

Self-confidence and parenting confidence are not one and the same thing, however. Many very confident people will not be confident as parents, while for many people with low self-confidence, their parenting ability and the satisfaction they obtain from parenting may be one of the only sources of reinforcement they are receiving.

Another important influence on our parenting confidence is our experience of and success at parenting. The successes we have with our child reinforce our belief that we are able to parent and are good at it. Failures, or even perceived failures, lower our confidence and present a difficult challenge. If we have other children whom we believe we have parented well, this can help us to be more confident about our parenting of another child. But likewise, if we have had difficulties parenting one child, this will inevitably impact on our confidence in parenting another.

Continuous criticism and second-guessing from our parenting partner, our family or our friends is another factor that can impact heavily on our parenting confidence. Sometimes the various people interacting with our child – the crèche worker, teacher, youth club leader – can have a detrimental effect on our confidence if they are giving us continuous negative feedback. Staying confident about our parenting can be difficult at times, but it is an essential component of staying Parent Healthy.

Our beliefs about our child

Informing and shaping our parenting of our child are deeply ingrained beliefs about children. These beliefs influence every aspect of our parenting, determining how we see and understand our children, the decisions we make about them and how successful we are in communicating with them and supporting them.

The views we hold about our own children and children in general often determine our emotional and physical attitudes and approaches to parenting. These views or beliefs are influenced by a variety of different factors, such as our own experiences of childhood, our experiences of parenting and the views of those whom we value.

Sometimes we do not realise that we hold such beliefs until we start to ask ourselves why we are doing certain things or why we are reacting to our children in certain ways. One example of this is how parents react to a child crying, which is usually determined by their belief systems about children. Some parents see crying as an attention-seeking behaviour to which they should respond, while others see it as an important communication from a child that warrants a response. Whatever our belief about crying, it will usually be underpinned by how our own parents reacted to us when we cried and the beliefs their actions passed on to us about crying.

Similarly, a parent's decision to physically punish their child stems from a belief that without physical punishment, a child will grow up undisciplined and out of control. This way of thinking is usually determined by how our own parents disciplined us and why they chose this method of discipline. If our parents discouraged showing emotion to us as children, we often find it hard to show emotion to our child.

When our general views and beliefs about children are particularly negative, we can start to see our own child in a negative way. For example, if we believe that, left to their own devices, children will behave anti-socially and cause trouble, then we are more likely to interpret our child's tiredness, annoyance or upset as troublesome behaviour. Likewise, not talking or listening to children is often based on negative beliefs about them, such as 'they don't understand', 'they don't know what they want', 'I know what's best' or 'they will do what they are told'.

As parents, we have many ways of masking negative belief systems about children, but acknowledging that we hold such beliefs and ensuring we resolve them can greatly enhance our parenting welfare.

Lack of knowledge and skills

Parenting is the one job we are asked to do for which we do not receive any training. There is an assumption that parenting comes naturally and that the desire to love, care for and protect our children will naturally be accompanied by the knowledge and skills necessary to do this. This is not true: often, we need to learn these skills and acquire this knowledge through experience. This may not be as easy as it sounds, however. Even when we know that we need to learn these skills, we often do not have the time to do so, or we do not know where to go to get the practical information and support we need to enable us to do it.

Of course, one of the best sources of parenting knowledge and skills are our own parents, family, friends and neighbours. However, we need to be able to distinguish between the good and bad of what we learn from these sources. For some of us, these sources are the best sources. For others, while there may be lots of parenting experience and skill being made available, we may not be comfortable with this information or may not feel that this information or parenting approach is best for our particular child.

The first step to building our knowledge and skills is to be clear as to what we want for our child and the type of relationship we want to build with our child. Starting at this point allows us to learn from those around us, but also to learn and develop new ideas and skills that we feel will benefit our child. Being honest and courageous enough to acknowledge that we do not have all the necessary parenting knowledge and skills, or that the knowledge and skills being made available to us are not the best for us, can often be difficult. However, it is important to remember that all parents are, or have been, in a similar position and that to give ourselves the best chance as parents, we must work to resolve this problem.

Lack of supports

No matter how good we are at parenting, it is simply impossible to stay Parent Healthy without support. Most of us have a variety of ways in which we seek and receive support and we are aware that without it, we would most likely find parenting extremely difficult. In the absence of solid support, our parenting welfare will suffer, we will find it difficult to stay Parent Healthy and will lack the necessary confidence to deal with the everyday challenges of parenting.

Ideally, a parent's key support is his/her parenting partner. In a parenting partnership we should be able to reinforce and challenge each other, while all the time ensuring that we never become so stressed, lacking in confidence or hopeless that we become unhealthy as parents. This is of course easier if we have a close personal relationship with our parenting partner, if we live together, etc.

Nonetheless, it is also very possible even if we do not have a strong personal relationship or do not live with our parenting partner. Once parenting partners have a real commitment to their child's welfare, they will overcome any obstacles posed by their personal relationship and will find the will to support each other in their parenting roles. If parenting partners cannot overcome these obstacles, then a key source of support is no longer available to either parent. It is essential that both parenting partners realise this and work together as much as possible.

Another key source of support is family, friends, neighbours and work colleagues. While this support is usually informal in nature, involving having chats, taking our child for periods of time to give us a break, talking over common parenting issues, etc., it is still extremely important. One advantage of these sorts of supports is that they provide us with alternative viewpoints and perspectives. They can help us to see things in a balanced way, to give our partner and ourselves some time together and to reinforce the fact that all parents experience similar problems and stress. A lack of these supports can place great strain on our parenting welfare. Even with a supportive parenting partner, we can lose perspective, can begin to reinforce each other's concerns and stresses and become too inward-looking.

Parents who are experiencing stress or difficulties tend to isolate themselves from their families, communities, friends and work colleagues, worrying that they are the only ones going through these emotions. Therefore, it is often the parents who most need these sorts of informal supports who isolate themselves from them.

Formal sources of support can also be very helpful for parents, such as parenting books, support groups or direct supports, such as home helps, etc. While there is still some stigma attached to seeking or availing of formal parenting supports, many more parents are now beginning to utilise them. Parenting courses have become very popular, for example, as have parenting books. Many parents now opt to pay for or receive additional help within their homes to enable them to make parenting less stressful. Those who cannot afford such measures or feel too embarrassed to utilise them can, in the absence of the other supports, be disadvantaged. Formal parenting supports can help parents stay Parent Healthy, particularly when they find themselves under tremendous stress or isolated from other forms of help.

WHAT IS THE IMPACT OF PARENT WELFARE DIFFICULTIES?
The manner in which parenting welfare difficulties impact on our ability to parent varies greatly and depends on the type of person our child is and the type of person we are. Regardless of the form they take, however, if such difficulties are not resolved, it is most likely that they will impact on the quality of relationship we have with our child.

In particular, parent welfare difficulties will impact on how we communicate with our children, how we discipline them, how we show emotion to them and how we deal with their expressions of emotion. These will, in turn, impact on how we care for and protect our children. Aside from the impact on our parenting, these difficulties will most likely impact on our personal well-being, causing us to become more stressed, unhappy and depressed.

If we are preoccupied with our own parenting stresses and difficulties, it can be difficult to be sensitive to or to respond appropriately to our children's difficulties. This will inevitably impact on our ability to keep our children safe. If, for example, we detach from our children because of parent welfare difficulties, we can leave our children vulnerable to abuse by those who will exploit this detachment by showing them the attention or affection they need and are not receiving from us. Similarly, if parenting welfare difficulties lead us to become overly attached, that imbalance in the parent–child relationship disempowers our child and leaves them vulnerable to exploitation by others who can dominate them.

It is not only our children who are vulnerable in this way. Those with poor Parent Health and problematic parenting welfare are themselves vulnerable to exploitation by others, which can place their children at risk. One of the most common dynamics of child abuse is a parent who is experiencing parenting difficulties being attracted to, or being taken in by, a person whose main attraction is his/her willingness to alleviate these difficulties, e.g. the lone parent who is finding it impossible to cope and meets a new partner who is more than willing to take the lead in parenting and 'take the children off your hands'.

This shows us the importance of striving at all times to being Parent Healthy. It is necessary not only to ensure that we maintain a positive and healthy relationship with our children, but also in helping us to make the right decisions about parenting partners. If we allow ourselves to become Parent Unhealthy, we leave ourselves and our children vulnerable to exploitation.

HOW DO I PREVENT PARENT WELFARE DIFFICULTIES FROM ARISING?

Preventing parenting welfare difficulties involves insight and commitment. It requires us to be open with ourselves about the types of difficulty we might be prone to developing, or have developed, and demands a commitment to controlling or resolving these difficulties. How can we do this?

Self-awareness

Being a healthy parent requires knowing and understanding ourselves as a parent. Without such knowledge and understanding, we cannot hope to understand our child and will find it more difficult to meet the everyday demands of parenting.

What do we need to know about ourselves as parents? It is very helpful if we have some insight into:

- why we decided to become a parent;
- our feelings about being a parent;
- what we expect from ourselves as a parent.

Why we decided to become a parent: One of the keys to understanding ourselves as parents is to have some awareness of why we decided to become a parent in the first place. This is an important question to ask ourselves because often one of the biggest influences on how we view our child and our parenting is why we made the decision to have or adopt a child. One of the cornerstones of being Parent Healthy is an understanding of why we decided to become a parent in the first place.

In some ways, this might seem like an easy question to answer, but in many ways it can, in fact, be quite difficult. There are many different levels at which the question can be considered and the answers we give to it often change as we grow to understand ourselves better as parents. For many of us, the decision to become a parent arises primarily from love of a partner, love of children and a sense that the time is right for us and our partner to start or expand our family. While we might not explicitly contract with our partner to invest jointly in another human being by deciding to have or adopt a child, we implicitly and effectively make such a contract with our partner.

When we consider why we decided to become a parent, it can reinforce for us the special investment we have made with our partner and the special feelings and relationship we have for and with our child. When difficulties arise or when we start feeling stressed and disillusioned, reflecting on why we decided to become a parent can reinvigorate us and can help us to put these negative feelings and stresses into perspective. For example, on those nights when our child is waking every two hours for no apparent reason and all we want to do is sleep, it is often only the thoughts of why we decided to become a parent that keep us going until morning.

Reflecting on why we decided to become a parent also helps us to keep other components of parenting in perspective, such as the inevitable sacrifices involved, the anger we sometimes feel towards our child or the desire we have at times to no longer have to cope with the constant demands of parenting.

For some parents, the reasons we decided to become a parent may be somewhat different, however. Sometimes the primary reason for deciding to become a parent is because we have been pressurised by our partner or by our family. Sometimes we make the decision because we feel we were getting older, that others of our age are all having children, because we worry that there will be nobody to look after us when we are elderly or that there will be nobody to inherit the family business. Sometimes we make a decision to have a second child because we feel our first will benefit from the company.

When considering why we decided to become a parent, we can find that we are presented with answers that we find difficult to accept. In times of difficulty or stress, the reasons we decided to become a parent may serve only to reinforce our feelings of stress, dissatisfaction or disillusionment. For example, if we decided to become a parent because we were being pressurised by our partner, then being woken every two hours by our baby crying makes us angry, either with our baby or with our partner.

Some of us may believe that we did not make a decision to become a parent, that it was an accident or was forced upon us by somebody else. Some of us might believe that while we did create a parenting contract with our partner, we were let down by this partner when the realities of parenting emerged. Such beliefs can make parenting difficulties harder to accept and to resolve.

Our reasons for becoming a parent do not pre-determine our attitudes towards our child or our parenting welfare. When a child arrives, our attitudes, beliefs and behaviours towards that child will change and will be determined primarily by our interaction and relationship with our child. However, in order to enhance our parenting welfare, it is important that we explore the reasons why we decided to become a parent and resolve any negative feelings we might have as a result of unresolved issues regarding this decision. Parenting difficulties will be harder to prevent, tackle and resolve if we have not dealt with any residual negative feelings about our initial decision to become a parent.

Our feelings about being a parent: One of the most important influences on our parenting self-awareness is our feelings about being a parent. These feelings are not only influenced by the reasons we decided to become a parent, but are influenced by a number of other factors, including:

- how good or competent we believe we are as parents;
- how much satisfaction we are getting out of parenting;
- how being a parent fits with the image we have of ourselves.

How good or competent we believe we are as a parent is very important to our parenting welfare, as it will impact on our confidence and on our ability to find our own solutions to parenting difficulties. Some key factors that affect these beliefs are how competent we believe ourselves to be as people and the reinforcement and feedback we receive from our child and from others about our parenting.

What is important to remember is that there are no objective measures of parenting quality. While there are some parenting practices that we know are bad for our child's welfare and other practices that we know will benefit our child, in essence the only people who can really judge how good a parent we are is our child and ourselves. Believing in ourselves as parents and believing that we know how best to parent our child will ensure we parent our child well. In addition, believing in ourselves as parents will enhance our parenting welfare, enabling us to enjoy parenting and deal effectively with the difficulties that arise. If we have doubts about our parenting competency, this will add to our stress and despair.

An important factor determining our feelings about being a parent is the satisfaction we get from parenting. This is strongly linked to our perceived success at parenting and our feelings of competency, but is also related to how much satisfaction we work to obtain from our parenting. Parents often focus on the problems and difficulties of parenting rather than the joy, fun and enjoyment of having a child.

No matter what our parenting circumstances are, parenting should first and foremost be a very enjoyable experience, one that gives us great satisfaction and joy. If we are not deriving happiness and satisfaction from our parenting, we need to ask what we are doing wrong and resolve those issues. Removing our own blocks to enjoying parenting is essential to our parenting welfare.

When we become a parent, it impacts significantly on the image we have of the kind of man or woman we are. We become 'Mummy' or 'Daddy', with new responsibilities and priorities. As a result, our image of ourselves changes radically and irrevocably. We also become aware that other people's image of us has now changed. Our parenting welfare will be affected by how being a parent fits with the image we have of ourselves and how we deal with the image others now have of us.

Many of us embrace the idea of being a parent, easily integrating this role into our self-image. We start to see ourselves as a parent and adapt to the life changes this entails. We enjoy being seen as a parent by others and start to engage and interact more with others who share our parenting interests.

For others of us, however, seeing ourselves, or being seen as, a parent presents us with difficulties. It may be that we define ourselves primarily in terms of our relationships, our career, our hobbies or our friends. It may be that we feel being seen as a parent has negative implications, such as 'we are not focused enough on our career', 'we are getting old', 'we are no longer one of the lads or girls who can party or live it up' or 'we are less attractive than before'. Some of us find it difficult to accept the responsibilities and priorities that parenting involves, so we avoid seeing ourselves as parents. We convince ourselves that although we have a child, nothing has changed and life will go on as before.

Equally as problematic is those parents who, as soon as they become parents, start to define themselves solely as parents, ignoring all the other facets of their lives. For these people, being a parent starts to totally define them as a person and they begin to lose contact with other aspects of their lives.

If we find it difficult to integrate the image of ourselves as a parent into our image of ourselves as a person, or if we begin to define ourselves completely as a parent, then our parenting welfare will be affected. If we find it difficult to see ourselves as a parent or fight against being a parent, this will contribute to our becoming detached from our child and will inevitably contribute to our feelings of guilt. If, on the other hand, we define ourselves solely and only as a parent, this will inevitably lead to over-attachment. It is important that we are comfortable with seeing ourselves as a parent while being confident that this does not define us as a person.

What we expect from ourselves as parents: Our expectations of ourselves as parents have an important influence on our parenting welfare. While we may be comfortable with the reasons we decided to have a child and with our new image of ourselves as a parent, the expectations we place on ourselves as a parent can enhance or decrease our parenting welfare. In other words, having a balanced and reasonable expectation of our abilities and potential achievements is important.

Many of us understand that while we endeavour to do our best for our child, we will do some things right and we will make many mistakes. Understanding that nobody is a perfect parent is important. If we set reasonable expectations for ourselves, we will not get stressed or disillusioned so easily and therefore will not fall into feelings of inadequacy or guilt. If our expectations are too high, we will inevitably fail to live up to them and become disillusioned and downhearted.

That said, it is very important to have expectations of ourselves as parents to ensure that we constantly work to do what is best for our child, to the very best of our ability. Therefore, having too few expectations or having very low expectations can be as damaging as having expectations that are unrealistically high. A lack of expectation can reflect very low self-confidence or a detachment from our child.

It is important that, where possible, the parenting expectations we set for ourselves are our own and not somebody else's, such as our parents', our friends' or our parenting partner's. This is necessary because other people can put us under great pressure to be a particular type of parent or may expect us to be able to balance all of the demands that parenting involves without much difficulty. Such expectations not only add to our sense of stress, but can also prevent us from seeking support.

To stay Parent Healthy, it is necessary for us to challenge what are becoming accepted societal expectations of parents. Mothers, particularly, are expected to be available to their partner, their children, their own family, their friends and to have a good career, a nice house, some hobbies, a number of holidays and state-of-the-art technology. These expectations are promoted by the media and advertising and sometimes by other parents who seem to have achieved all of these things. Attempting to live up to these conflicting expectations will create difficulties and will impact on our parenting welfare. As a parent, the most we can seek to do is to prioritise our child's welfare and safety and build a happy, safe family environment.

While developing parenting self-awareness involves some insight into deeper questions about ourselves as people, and while these questions might be difficult to fully assess, gaining some insight into them does prepare us better for the task of parenting and helps us to develop strong parenting resilience. Most times, the answers to these questions are enough to enable us to approach our parenting with a new vigour and positive outlook, reminding us of the unique joy and love our children have brought to our lives.

At other times, the answers to these questions will be difficult for us to confront, perhaps forcing us to identify that we have never really made an informed decision to have children or to identify negative feelings about parenting. We should not be scared of these thoughts. Being able to confront and identify both the positive and negative responses to these questions is the first step towards developing a positive outlook on parenting.

Developing positive belief systems

While a parent can hold many different types of beliefs about children, positive beliefs are essential to positive parenting. A parent must truly believe that their child, no matter how difficult or challenging, has an unlimited potential to achieve and a tremendous ability to live a happy, healthy life. It is quite natural for parents to go through periods of negativity towards their children when such thoughts seem impossible, but it is when negative belief systems dominate parenting, perceptions and communication with our children that difficulties are created.

Our personal belief systems about children, while continually changing and evolving, are primarily influenced by three factors: our experience of being a child, our experience of being parents and our societal beliefs about children.

Our experiences of being a child: Our own childhood is probably the single most influential factor on how we view and interact with our children. Developing an awareness of the negative and the positive impacts of our childhood on us, and whether we have resolved the emotional legacy of these experiences, is crucial if we are to have a positive view of our own children. For example, if as children we saw ourselves as bold, stupid or unpopular, it will be very difficult for us to see our own children as clever, popular or well-behaved. If we did not believe as children that we were psychologically and socially healthy people with an unlimited potential to achieve, then we will find it extremely difficult to believe this about our own children.

While having negative experiences in childhood does not prevent us from having a positive belief system about our child, ensuring the emotional impact of any negative experiences has been resolved is crucial. Parents must try to ensure that nothing from their own childhood impacts negatively on their views of their child.

Of course, this is a significant challenge for parents. Nobody likes to admit that they might have had negative experiences in their own childhood. It is even more difficult to accept that these experiences may have had a negative impact on us. That is why it takes real courage and commitment to admit that these experiences are having an impact, or could have an impact, on our beliefs about our child or on our parenting. Exploring our personal childhood experiences is not about deciding if our childhood was healthy or not, rather it is a process of accepting that what shaped our childhood was a combination of positive and negative experiences, which in turn have shaped our ideas of what it is to be a child. We need to learn from both the positive and the negative experiences and try to put the things we learn into practice.

Our experiences of being parents: Having more than one child impacts significantly on how we perceive and interact with any one of these children. From the moment of birth, children become a core aspect of our lives, impacting not only on our time but also on our self-worth, emotional well-being and psychological resilience. How we perceive and interact with our second child will be greatly determined by how we have perceived and interacted with our first child.

Of course, our second child will have his/her own unique personality, but we will nonetheless apply the experiences we have gained from parenting the first-born. If our confidence has been reinforced by our experiences with our first child, this will make us more confident in parenting our second. Likewise, bad habits or setbacks experienced with the first child will be hard to overcome with the second.

Societal beliefs about children: We do not parent in a vacuum. All around us there are different ideas and attitudes about children. School, the Church, sports and activity centres, health services and justice systems all have particular beliefs about children which shape the way they are run. Sometimes these beliefs are positive, and sometimes they are not.

Being aware that there are many different types of beliefs about children within all of the organisations and institutions that influence our child's life and our lives is important. We must be able to identify what these beliefs are, to challenge them if we feel they are wrong and to ensure they do not impact negatively on our child.

It is also important to be open to being challenged by the more positive beliefs that exist within these institutions. We cannot ignore the beliefs about children that exist within the society in which we live, but we need to ensure that we work to keep our beliefs positive. We must work with and be influenced by those beliefs within our society that are child-centred.

Working to continually ensure we have positive beliefs about our children, no matter what difficulties or challenges arise, is crucial to preventing parenting welfare difficulties arising and will ensure we enjoy and benefit from our parenting.

Assessing our skills and knowledge

If we are to prevent parenting welfare difficulties from arising, we will need to have the courage to assess our skills and knowledge and to be honest with ourselves about what we do and do not know. As with all activities we engage in, we need to be prepared to acquire the necessary knowledge and skills to give us the best opportunity to succeed at what is a demanding task. Seeking the help and support we need often involves more courage than trying to be self-reliant. It is important that:

- partners support and talk to each other;
- we talk to and get support from other parents we know;
- we use family and friends for support;
- we watch relevant television programmes and read some simple parenting books.

The more skills and knowledge we have, the more confident we become.

Being open to learning and development

Being a healthy parent is not a state of 'being', but rather is a continuous process of analysis and development that poses great challenges to us if we wish to truly create a special relationship with our child.

In this context, maintaining our welfare as a parent involves a commitment to continually assessing and evaluating our parenting thinking and practice and being open to developing this practice so that we can become the best parent we can be.

In this context, we can try to:

- learn how to develop realistic expectations and how to recognise when negative self-talk defeats effective coping, to identify our own self-defeating assumptions and think of alternative messages, to be kind to ourselves and accept ourselves and our child as fallible. Note and use personal strengths and talents;
- use problem-solving, time-management and goal-setting techniques, which are helpful when dealing with stressors associated with raising children and running a household. Assertiveness skills and intimacy skills are important to learn;
- know our limits and be realistic about what we can accomplish. Say no to unreasonable demands;
- replenish energy by ensuring we get sufficient rest, eat well-balanced meals and exercise regularly. Make recreation and relaxation a priority, so that we have some time off during the week;
- learn better coping strategies and use parent support groups to source both skill training and emotional support;
- prioritise play with our child and commit to doing a minimum of one fun thing every single day with him/her.

Parenting can be one of the most enjoyable and most fulfilling activities a person can engage in. It allows us to invest in society in a particularly special way and to fulfil one of the most enriching psychological tasks of our lives. Investing in our welfare as a parent will enrich this experience further for us, encouraging and enabling us to fulfil our full potential as parents.

Rachel's story: The complexity of the parent–child relationship

Rachel was very upset one evening coming home after having a drink after work. One of her younger colleagues had made a comment that had really angered her. Rachel had been telling the girls about her daughter, Ann, and how annoying and attention-seeking she could be at times. Rachel had said that while Ann was her daddy's little pet, she knew how manipulative and clever her daughter could be and was well able for her. Then this colleague had said, 'Rachel, it sounds to me like you are jealous of little Ann.' Rachel was furious. What did she mean? What was she suggesting? She really loved Ann and felt very close to her. She was much closer to her than her own mother had been to her. She simply did not want Ann to grow up spoilt and indulged.

The following day, Rachel mentioned the incident to her husband, who found it funny. Rachel got angry and said that she felt her husband spoilt Ann and let her 'away with murder'. He responded that he felt Rachel was very hard on Ann and never gave her a break.

Rachel reminded her husband that when she was Ann's age she had been expected to make lunches, look after her two younger brothers, vacuum the house and, because her mother was often sick, to make sure her brothers got to school on time and safely. She reminded her husband that Ann never had to do any of these things, and that all Ann seemed to do was her homework and accompany her father to football matches. She reminded her husband that they were both working full-time and that all she wanted was for Ann to help out a little around the house.

Later that day, when Rachel returned from the hairdresser's, Ann had put clothes in the washing machine and filled the dishwasher. As soon as Rachel walked in the door, Ann said she was going out with her dad to a football match. That evening, when they returned home, Rachel was very annoyed with Ann, saying that she had forgotten to separate the clothes and they had all run in the wash.

Conclusion: Creating a Child-centred Society

Parenting does not occur in isolation from the society in which we live and parents are not solely responsible for protecting their children or promoting their children's welfare. Society and societal factors have a significant influence on how well our children are nurtured and protected.

To this end, creating a child-centred society is important to ensure that children's welfare is prioritised and parenting is supported at every level. A child-centred society is one based on a belief that all children are born with an unlimited potential to achieve and with a tremendous capacity to live a psychologically and socially healthy life. A child-centred society is therefore structured and directed at helping children to achieve their potential.

While acknowledging that children are the most vulnerable members of is ranks, a child-centred society will strive to ensure that children are treated as equal citizens and are given the opportunity to participate in society as equals.

In recognition of the essential part parents play in a child's life, a child-centred society will, through its legislation and policies, value and support parenting. Whether, on these measures, Irish society is truly child-centred is a matter of debate. There is no doubt that there are many child-centred policies and laws that do serve to promote the best interests and welfare of children. Equally, however, there are many laws and policies that are not child-centred.

Ireland is committed to implementing children's rights and has signed the UN Convention on the Rights of the Child. We have a National Children's Strategy and over the last number of years have introduced a number of family-friendly laws and policies, increased children's allowance and extended maternity and paternity leave entitlements. Services to help and support families have been developed and better child protection laws and policies have been introduced.

In spite of these advances, there are still many unnecessary obstacles and difficulties created for children and parents within Irish society. Few would disagree that the taxation and social welfare systems do too little to support parents. Children's allowance payments are too low, day-care costs remain too high and taxation benefits to parents are inadequate.

Many of our laws and policies fly in the face of all that we know about children and good child-centred thinking. Our laws still hold ten- and twelve-year-old children criminally responsible, despite the fact that we know that children of this age do not have the intellectual capabilities to make informed decisions about criminal behaviour. Policy-makers are seeking to reduce the age of sexual consent without any real understanding of why or how this will benefit or affect children. Our child protection laws and systems remain inadequate. The support services for vulnerable children and families still operate on a 9.00 a.m.–5.00 p.m., Monday–Friday basis and even during these times they are under-resourced. Vetting and monitoring of those who are a risk to children are not as comprehensive as they should be, and there are many problems with the reporting of child abuse concerns.

More worrying are the types of beliefs about children and parenting currently existing in Irish society, which underpin the lack of urgency visible in responses to these many problems. If we feel it is acceptable to hold children criminally responsible at age ten or twelve, what is this saying about our beliefs about children? If we feel it is acceptable for children to have sexual intercourse at younger ages just because we believe some young people are engaging in this activity, what does this say about our beliefs about children?

Even when it comes to child abuse, there is often a variety of rationalisations informing policy decisions, many of which should be a cause of concern. Some of these rationalisations include: children have always been bullied and will always be bullied; teenage girls have always been susceptible to being assaulted by men if they happen to be in the wrong place at the wrong time; if children dress provocatively, they are looking for trouble; when we were young we all had a few drinks in the park and it did us no harm. Before we can get our social laws and policies right, we need to challenge some of the belief systems that characterise them. Parents have a key part to play in achieving this.

As parents, we need to remember that just as we have to work to ensure we do everything we can to keep our child safe and to protect his/her welfare, we also have to work to ensure that the safety and welfare of all children are protected. The best way for us to do this is to create a child-centred society that values children in every way.

Given that we have so many other priorities, this may seem to be an unreasonable expectation. However, parents are best positioned to identify and to understand the injustices that exist for children within our society. When we look at our own ten-year-old, we know that it is simply unreasonable that he/she would be held criminally accountable for anything. When we look at our sixteen-year-old, we know that he/she should not be placed under the immense pressure of being entitled by law to give informed consent to sexual intercourse. When we struggle every day to balance work, commuting and parenting and still find ourselves financially stretched, we start to understand the unnecessary barriers existing for parents in our society. Assessing the impact of laws and policies on our child and on our parenting abilities will help us to identify what has to change.

More importantly, if parents do not work to create a child-centred society, then who will? Child welfare, child protection and parenting will be prioritised only if parents start to mobilise and demand that they are prioritised. Part of our responsibilities as parents include ensuring we, and all other parents, are adequately supported and that parenting is valued.

So what can we do? We need to hold our policy-makers accountable for creating a safe, child-centred society for all children. We need to insist that the proper value is placed on children and on parenting and that that value is clearly reflected in policy and legislation, which should provide vulnerable children and parents with the supports they need. If we are employers or policy-makers, we should seek to create and implement child-friendly practices, remembering that we have a responsibility to create a child-centred society.

The healthiness of any society is best measured by the way it nurtures and supports its most vulnerable citizens. By virtue of their age and maturity, children are among the most vulnerable citizens within any society. While not all child abuse is preventable, most is. Irish society has a moral obligation to do all it can to promote children's welfare and to do all it can to protect children. As the most important guardians of our children's welfare, parents have a right to be fully supported by the society in which they live.

The future health of Irish society will be determined by how well we fulfil our obligations to our children.

References

1. ABC News Online. 'Internet Schoolgirl Safe, Ex-Marine Arrested'. Abc.net.au, 7/17/2003.
2. American Psychological Association. *Report of the APA Task Force on the Sexualisation of Girls.* (Washington, DC: American Psychological Association, 2007)
3. Anderson, K. and Vandivere, S. *Stressful Family Lives: Child and Parent Well Being.* (National Survey of America's Families. Child Trends, The Urban Institute, 2000)
4. Association of Secondary School Teachers in Ireland. *Bullying in Schools.* (ASTI Survey, 1999)
5. Australian Broadcasting Corporation, Television Programme Transcript. 'Chris Ellison Discusses the Bali Abuse Claims Investigation', *Lateline* 12/4/2005.
6. Australian Research on Harassment in Sport, *A Snapshot in Time: Athlete's Perceptions of Harassment.* (Australian Sports Commission, 2001)
7. Barnardos. *Listening to Parents, Listening to Children.* (National Childhood Poll, 2007)
8. BBC News. 'Babysitters Jailed for Baby Rape.' BBC website, 1/10/2006.
9. Briggs, F. and Hawkins, R. *Child Protection: A Guide for Teachers and Child Care Professionals.* (St Leonard's, NSW: Allen and Unwin, 1997)
10. British Medical Association Board of Science. *Child and Adolescent Mental Health: A Guide for Healthcare Professionals.* (BMA Board of Science, June 2006)
11. Buckley, H. *Child Protection in Early Years Settings.* Paper presented by Dr Helen Buckley, 23 November 2001, Green Isle Hotel, seminar organised by An Cosan, Tallaght.
12. Bybee, D. and Mowbray, C. 'An Analysis of Allegations of Sexual Abuse in a Multi-Victim Day Center Case'. *Child Abuse & Neglect*, 17:767–83. 1993.
13. CNN 'The Au Pair on Trial.' CNN.com. 2000.
14. *Childline Annual Statistics 2006.* (ISPCC annual report, 2006)
15. Children, Youth and Families Children's Bureau. 2005.
16. Clarke, A.M. *Current Issues in the Provision of ICT Technologies and Services for Young Children.* E.T.S.I. White Paper No.2, Young Children and ICT. March 2006.

17. Currie, C., *et al. Young People's Health in Context. Health Behaviour in School Aged Children Study: International Report 2001/2002*. (World Health Organisation, 2004)

18. Department of Health and Children. *Children First – National Guidelines for the Protection and Welfare of Children*. (DOHC, 1999)

19. Department of Health and Children. *Our Duty to Care – The Principles of Good Practice for the Protection of Children and Young People*. (DOHC, 2002)

20. Department of Health and Children. *State of the Nation's Children, Ireland 2006*. (Dublin: Government Publications, 2006)

21. Department of Health and Children. *Strategic Task Force on Alcohol. 2nd Report*. (DOHC, Health Promotion Unit, 2004; interim report, 2002)

22. Department of Health. *Report on the Inquiry into the Operation of Madonna House*. (Dublin: Government Publications, 1996)

23. Dobson, R. and Atwood, J. *Truth about Tweens*. Unpublished paper reported in *The Independent*, August 2006.

24. Findblad, F. and Kaldal, A. 'Sexual Abuse at a Swedish Daycare Centre: Allegations, Confessions and Evaluations'. *Acta Paediatrica* 89 (8), 1001–1009.

25. Finkelhor, D. and Ormrod, R. *Crimes Against Children by Babysitters. Juvenile Justice Bulletin*, US Department of Justice, September 2001.

26. Finkelhor, D. and Williams, L. *Nursery Crimes: Sexual Abuse in Day Care*. (London: Sage Publications, 1988)

27. FOX 10. 'Accused Babysitter Due in Court.' Fox10TV.com. 01/29/2007.

28. Fullerton, D. *Promoting Positive Adolescent Sexual Health and Preventing Teenage Pregnancy – A Review of Recent Effectiveness Research. Crisis Pregnancy Research Report*, No. 2, 2004.

29. Harris Interactive Foundation. *Hostile Hallways: Bullying, Teasing, and Sexual Harassment in School*. (American Association of University Women, 2001)

30. *Have Fun Be Safe*. (ISPCC, 1999)

31. Health Services Executive, National Suicide Prevention Group. *Reach Out: National Strategy for Action on Suicide Prevention 2005–2014*. (Department of Health and Children and HSE, 2005)

32. Health Services Executive, National Office for Suicide Prevention. *Annual Report 2005*.

33. Hibell, *et al. The ESPAD Report, 2003 – Alcohol and Other Drug Use Amongst Students in 35 European Countries*. (Sweden: The Swedish Council for Information on Alcohol and Other Drugs, 2003)

34. Hunt, P. *Report of the Independent Inquiry into Multiple Abuse in Nursery Classes in Newcastle upon Tyne*. (Newcastle-upon-Tyne: Newcastle-upon-Tyne City Council, 1994)

35. Irish National Teachers Organisation. *Adult Bullying and Student Relationships in Primary Schools*. (INTO survey, 1998)

36. Irish Society for the Prevention of Cruelty to Children. *Childline Annual Statistics 2006. ISPCC Annual Report 2006*.

37. Margolin, L. 'Child abuse by babysitters: an ecological interactional interpretation', *Journal of Family Violence*, 5:95–105, 1990.

38. Mayock, P., Kitching, K. and Morgan, M. *Relationships and Sexuality Education in the Context of Social, Personal and Health Education. An Assessment of the Challenges to Full Implementation of the Programme in Post Primary Schools.* (Crisis Pregnancy Agency: Department of Education and Science, 2007)

39. McGee, H., Garavan, R., De Barra, M., Byrne J. and Conroy, R. *The SAVI Report. Sexual Abuse and Violence in Ireland.* (Dublin: The Liffey Press in association with Dublin Rape Crisis Centre, 2002)

40. McKeown, K., Pratschke, J. and Haase, T. *Family Well-being, What Makes a Difference.* (Ceifin Centre, supported by the Department of Social and Family Affairs, 2003)

41. O'Moore, A. and Minton, S. *Tackling Violence in Schools: A Report from Ireland.* Connect UK-001. European Conference, Goldsmiths College, London, UK, 6–8 April 2001.

42. O'Rourke, S. 'Teenage Bullies Hound 12-year-old to Death.' *New Zealand Herald*, Nzherald.co.nz. 11/3/2006.

43. O'Moore, M., Kirkham, C. and Smith, M. 'Bullying in Schools in Ireland: A Nationwide Study', *Irish Educational Studies*, 17, pp.255–71, 1998.

44. ParentLine UK. *Annual Report 2005.*

45. ParentLine website. (2007)

46. Pennsylvania Department of Public Welfare. *Annual Child Abuse Report 2006.*

47. RTÉ *News at One.* '10 Men Could Be Involved in the Alleged Sexual Assault on a 14-year-old.' RTE.ie. February 2007.

48. Robins, S. *Protecting Our Students.* (Ontario, Canada: Ontario Ministry of the Attorney General, 2000)

49. Shakeshaft, C. *Educator Sexual Misconduct: A Synthesis of Existing Literature.* (New York: US Department of Education, Policy and Program Studies Service, 2004)

50. Teachers Union of Ireland. *Survey on Second Level Classroom Disruption.* (TUI: March 2006)

51. Teenage Pregnancy Unit. *Teenage Conception Statistics for England 1998, 2005.* (UK: Department of Health, 2007)

52. Trocme, N., Fallon, B., McLaurin, B., Daciuk, J., Felstiner, C., Black, T., Tonmyr, L., Blackstock, C., Barter, K., Turcotte, D. and Cloutier, R. *Canadian Incidence Study of Reported Child Abuse and Neglect – 2003: Major Findings.* (Canada: Minister of Public Works and Government Services Canada, 2005)

53. Turner, M., McCrory, P. 'Child Protection in Sport'. *British Journal of Sports Medicine* 38, 2004.

54. Unicef. *Child Poverty in Perspective: An Overview of Child Well-being in Rich Countries.* Innocenti Report Card 7. (Florence: Unicef Innocenti Research Centre, 2007)

55. US Department of Health and Human Services, Administration for Children and Families. *Child Maltreatment 2005.*

56. US Department of Health and Human Services, Health Research and Service Administration, Maternal and Child Health Bureau. *Child Health U.S.A.* (Rockville, Maryland: US Department of Health and Social Services 2005.)

57. Wang, C.T. and Daro, D. *Current Trends in Child Abuse Reporting and Fatalities: The Results of the 1997 Annual Fifty State Survey.* (Chicago, IL: National Committee to Prevent Child Abuse, 1998)

58. Webwise. *Survey of Children's Use of the Internet, Investigating Online Risk Behaviour.* www.webwise.com. (2006)

Index

Harris Interactive Foundation, 103
Have Fun Be Safe (ISPCC), 126–7
Health and Children, Department of, 127–8
Health and Human Services, USDepartment of, 29–30
Health Behaviour in School-aged Children Survey, 99
Health Services Executive, 76, 164, 197
  childcare abuse, 77–8, 79
Hofstra University, Huntington, 103
holidays, 122–38
  abusive situations, 130–1
  assessing risk, 126–30
  protection, 131–7
  response to problems, 137–8
  risks, 123–4
hugging, 66

incest, 55
interactions
  child withdrawal, 86
  childcare, 82–3
  school, 109
Internet. *see* technology
Internet Advisory Board, 153
Irish Constitution, 52
Irish National Teachers Union (INTO), 101
ISPCC, 126–7, 141
ISPCC/Childline, 29, 100, 173, 197

'kiddies' clubs', 132
Kilkenny, County, 51

language, 8, 10
lies, 68–9
listening, 7–9, 88–9, 203
Listening to Parents, Listening to Children, 220
local authorities, 84
love, expression of, 5, 207

McCann, Madeleine, 126
McMartin case, 78
Madonna House, 101

malicious allegations, 44–5
manipulation, 65
maturity, 81, 141
mealtimes, 6
mental health problems, 193–216
  categories of, 195–6
  effects of, 200
  within family, 213–14
  incidence of, 197–8
  parental attitudes to, 210–14
  prevention of, 205–10
  protection from, 214
  recognising, 198–200
  response to, 200–5
Microsoft, 152
mobile phones. *see* technology
monitoring
  holidays and sports, 133–4
  preventing self-abuse, 184–5
  technology, 152–5, 161–2
MSN, 152
MySpace, 152

National Children's Strategy, 241
National Committee to Prevent Child Abuse, USA, 80
National Incident-Based Reporting System, FBI, 139
National Office for Suicide Prevention, 176
National Suicide Research Foundation, 177
National Survey of America's Families, 221–2
negative thinking, 209, 219
neglect, 27, 36–7
  babysitters, 140
  in childcare setting, 79
  myths, 47
  by parents, 57
  signs and symptoms, 34–5
New Zealand, 78, 154–5
non-discrimination, 15
Northern Ireland, 100

Obsessive Compulsive Disorder (OCD), 196